KnOCK 'em DEaD
MANAGEMENT

Martin Yate & Peter Sander

Adams Media
Avon, Massachusetts

Published by Adams Media, an F+W Publications Company
57 Littlefield Street, Avon, MA 02322 U.S.A.
www.adamsmedia.com

ISBN: 1-58062-935-0

Printed in the United States of America.

J I H G F E D C B A

Library of Congress Cataloging-in-Publication Data
Yate, Martin John.
Knock 'em dead management / Martin Yate & Peter Sander.
p.   cm.
ISBN 1-58062-935-0
1. Management. 2. Executive ability. 3. Supervision of employees.
I. Title: Knock them dead management. II. Title: Knock 'em dead.
III. Title: Management. IV. Sander, Peter J. V. Title.
HD31.Y335 2003
658--dc21
2003011313

This publication is designed to provide accurate and authoritative information with regard to the subject matter covered. It is sold with the understanding that the publisher is not engaged in rendering legal, accounting, or other professional advice. If legal advice or other expert assistance is required, the services of a qualified professional person should be sought.
　　　　—From a *Declaration of Principles* jointly adopted by a Committee of the American Bar Association and a Committee of Publishers and Associations

Many of the designations used by manufacturers and sellers to distinguish their products are claimed as trademarks. Where those designations appear in this book and Adams Media was aware of a trademark claim, the designations have been printed with initial capital letters.

This book is available at quantity discounts for bulk purchases.
For information, call 1-800-872-5627.

Contents

Part 1   What Is Managing?
1 • So You Want to Be a Manager   3

The Meaning of "Managing" 3

A Brief History of Management 4

Trends in Management Today 5

The New Definition of Management 8

What Makes a Good Manager—Today 10

Management Is about Managing Change 13

Management as a Career Path 13

You're a Manager Even If You're Not a Manager 14

Why Become a Manager? 14

What Does It Take to Become a Manager? 15

Levels of Management 18

What Is a Knock 'em Dead Manager? 21

Summary 24

2 • The Organization Manager—The Many Roles You Play   25

A Visual Model 26

It's Not My Job 28

The Ins and Outs of the Business Environment 29

The External Environment 29

Direct Influences 30

Indirect Influences 31

Internal Environment 33

Moving Ahead 36

The Scope of the Complete Manager 37

Three "All the Time" Management Roles 41

Now, the Five Functions of Managing 44

Keeping Your "Customers" Happy 49

The Biggest Test 51

Summary 52

3 • Getting Started: Stepping into a Management Role 53

Golden Moments 53

Not Too Fast, Not Too Slow 54

Four Steps to Getting Started 55

Remember: Stay Flexible 56

A Dose of Leadership 56

Not Negotiable 57

Making the Most of Your Golden Moments 57

Step 1: Get Organized 57

Step 2: Connect 61

Step 3: Evaluating—"Seeing" the Whys and Hows 63

Step 4: Building—The First Sketches of a Plan 68

Identify Opportunities 68

Make a Clean Handoff: Delegate 70

Summary 73

Part II The Management Challenge

4 • Building Your Staff: Recruitment and Selection 77

A Required Skill. 78

The Cost of Bad Hiring 78

Recruiting Is a 24/7 Business. 79

Job Descriptions in Two Steps. 82

Seven Steps to Defining Realistic Needs. 83

Do You Need the Perfect Candidate? 84

More on Recruiting Resources. 94

Planning the Interview Cycle. 96

Structuring the Interview Process 96

Making the Hire 102

Summary. 103

5 • Coaching and Skill Development 104

What Does Your Company Expect? 104

What Do Your People Need?. 105

Growth, Training, and Development. 105

Why Some Managers Don't Coach. 106

Are You Coach Material? 108

Coaching for Results 113

Company Direction Comes First 114

Building a Development Plan 115

Putting the Coaching Plan into Play 117

Making Coaching Stick 117

Making Time for Time Management 123

A Few More Developmental Tools 124

Remember—Not All Valuable Workers Are Superstars 125

Mentor versus Coach 128

Summary. 130

6 • Performance Appraisal—And Dealing with Problem Employees   131

Evaluating Performance—The Big Picture 131

Standards and Performance Expectations 133

Organizing Performance Review Meetings. 134

The Performance Evaluation Process 137

How Long, and How Much Detail?. 141

The Action Plan 142

Goal versus Task Orientation. 143

Progress Reviews 145

Dealing with Unwanted Behavior 147

From Verbal to Written Discipline 150

Time to Terminate? 154

Carrying Out the Termination 158

Healing the Team 162

When an Employee Resigns 163

Summary. 164

Part III   The Leadership Challenge

7 • What Does It Mean to Lead?   167

What Is Leadership?. 167

Enlightened Self-Interest 169

The Golden Rules of Leadership 170

Elements of Leadership 172

Build a Leadership Style 178

A Recipe for Delegating. 182

Developing a Leadership Style 191

Remember, Leadership Takes Time 193

Summary. 194

8 • Heading the Ship in the Right Direction: Setting and Managing Goals   195

What Are Goals and Strategic Plans? 196

Structured Planning: Goals and Strategies 196

Goals and Strategies: How Many and What? 197

What Makes Structured Planning Work? 199

Planning Elements 200

Organizing Your Planning 203

The Department Plan 204

Solving Specific Problems. 207

What Causes Bad Planning? 210

Summary. 212

9 • Making the Right Decision   214

A Seven-Step Decision-Making Process. 215

Step 1: Define the Situation and Problem 215

Step 2: Identify Knowledge Gaps and Constraints 216

Step 3: Develop Alternatives 217

Step 4: Analyze Alternatives 219

Step 5: Select the Best Alternative and Identify Why. 220

Step 6: Implement the Decision. 221

Step 7: Evaluate the Decision 221

Decision Tools 222

Summary. 226

10 · There Is No "I" in Team—All about Team Building 227

Now, about *Your* Team 228

Team Building in the Real World 229

Building Blocks for Team Building. 231

Effective Communication 234

A Safe and Fair Place to Work 237

Put the Needs of Your Group First 239

Translating Teamwork to Performance 241

R-E-S-P-E-C-T. 243

Sharing "Best" Practices 244

Getting Them *Really* Involved. 245

The Leader Is Servant and Cheerleader to the Team 246

Foster Relationships. 247

Summary. 250

11 · Building Your Managerial Brand 251

What Is a Managerial Brand? 253

Why Develop a Managerial Brand? 253

Build Your Professional Platform 254

Storm Clouds Invariably Follow Sunny Weather 260

Managing Your Employability 262

Archiving Your Job Opportunities 267

Career Transitions: A Final Thought. 268

Achieving Life Balance 269

Summary. 270

Index 271

Introduction

I am not afraid of storms, for I have learned to sail my ship.
—Louisa May Alcott

We suspect that the majority of you reading this book want to be a manager. Some of you probably already *are* managers, and there may be a tiny minority among you who *don't* want to manage but the title and responsibility of "manager" was thrust into your lap anyway. Regardless of how you ended up with this book in your hands, it is our pleasure to indulge you in our "Knock 'em Dead" approach to management.

You are here because you are committed to developing and polishing a set of core competencies and professional skills to use in your career; skills that will take you places; skills that will build and expand your competence, influence, stature, visibility, and your success within your organization. Your sense of fulfillment and accomplishment will expand—along with your *responsibilities* and, we hope, your *rewards.*

As with most other endeavors, business or otherwise, "done right" feels good. In management, it not only feels good to you, but also to your employees and team members. "Done wrong," on the other hand, feels lousy. It keeps you awake at night. You spend more time taking corrective action than getting your job done. Done right means less stress; done wrong means a *lot more* stress. Since you manage a team, and because that team does lots more than you could as an individual, the "feel good" part of "done right" is amplified by the size of the team and impact of the effort. Likewise, the "feel lousy" part of "done wrong" is amplified and can be crushing. For most of us, there is truly no greater satisfaction in the workplace than being the leader of a successful team.

Whether you are the CEO of a large company, the second-shift manager of a fast-food operation, a self-employed book author, or a cubicle-dwelling individual contributor in a large corporation, this book is for you. It will help you do a better job and truly enjoy the tasks of management you confront in your work. The specific skills and tasks required may be different for different jobs, but the basic duties and principles of effective managing are the same across most occasions of business and public life.

Knock 'em Dead Management is divided into three parts. Part I, "What Is Managing?" (Chapters 1–3), describes the deep, broad, multifaceted nature of a management role, how it has evolved, and what it takes to be not simply a good but a "Knock 'em Dead" manager, and how to get started in a management position. Part II, "The Management Challenge" (Chapters 4–6), describes the core functions of hiring, coaching, evaluating, and developing your essential resource—the people on your team. Part III, "The Leadership Challenge" (Chapters 7–11), explores the tenets of leadership, planning, decision-making, and team building to help you move your team successfully from here to achievement. Chapter 11, "Building Your Managerial Brand" describes how to build your influence and expand your personal platform as a manager.

As you read on, you will get a practical, hands-on approach to understanding and applying tested—and occasionally new—principles to your work. We hope this book strengthens your skills and your success as a professional manager.

Part I | What Is Managing?

Discover what today's managers do, what challenges they face, and what it takes to be a manager in today's world.

1 | So You Want to Be a Manager?

Today's manager must be more knowledgeable, ambitious, efficient, resilient, and fast-paced than ever. Do you have what it takes?

The terms "managing" and "management" mean different things to different people—some of it positive, some of it not so savory. Recent corporate scandals have cast aspersions upon many high-level managers. However, stories of brutal, "slave driver" managers, from top to bottom, from CEO to production foreman, are hardly new. Like many things, a few bad apples can tarnish the bunch. As we'll see, "good" management is visibly and recognizably good, and bad management is visibly and recognizably bad. Regardless of your perception of management and managers before reading this book, we hope (and expect) that you will depart with a good feeling about the profession and about yourself as part of it.

The Meaning of "Managing"

Let's get right to it—what does the word "manager" mean? What does it mean to be a manager? From the beginning of time, people have organized themselves into groups in order to accomplish a task or represent a cause. The context and environment have certainly changed since the beginning of time, but the essence of the job has not.

According to the Dictionary

What does it mean to "manage" something? And what is "management"? One might jump to the conclusion that management is easy to define, but as it turns out, even a dictionary definition is difficult, because there are so many elements involved. The *Random House Dictionary of the English Language* offers ten definitions of the word "manage," at least eight of which directly apply to a business or organizational context:

1. To bring about and succeed in accomplishing
2. To take charge or take care of
3. To dominate or influence (a person) by tact, address, or artifice
4. To handle, direct, govern, or control in action or use
5. To contrive to bring about, succeed in accomplishing, etc., usually despite hardship or difficulty
6. To use sparingly or with judgment, as health, money, etc.
7. To conduct business or commercial affairs; to be in charge, etc.
8. To continue to function, progress, or succeed, usually despite hardship or difficulty

From this series of definitions it goes on to define a "manager," not surprisingly, as a "person who manages," and "management" as the "act or manner of managing."

So is the point here to memorize dictionary definitions? Hardly. Rather, it is to illustrate the breadth of meaning of the term "manage." All eight of these relevant definitions describe various aspects of managing and the duty and role of the manager. Managing is nothing if it is not a diverse set of activities. As we'll see throughout this book, a good manager must do many things and must *be good* at many things. The role is more one of breadth than depth. The "depth" stuff is usually best left to the technical experts being managed.

A Brief History of Management

The nature of managing groups—and the burden placed on the manager to do it right—has evolved dramatically. It hardly bears mention that today's commerce and society would not work without management; a "free market" certainly does not equate to commercial anarchy. Efficient economic and social activity depends on someone taking charge, planning, managing scarce resources, communicating, and managing the people involved. An organization, like an advanced organism, cannot function without a head. Over time, the nature and duties of the "head" have evolved.

The Early Days—Position Power

In the distant past, "organizations" were primarily governments, the military, or church-related organizations with appointed (or occasionally, elected, or even inherited) leaders who pretty much did what they wanted, and had consuming authority over their "employees," more accurately known as subjects. More often than not, power was inherent in a leader's position—who the leader was or what the leader did was of little importance. Whether the leader was efficient or effective didn't matter—this sort of position power worked, for there was little to challenge it. Position meant everything; it didn't matter how good you were.

From the Middle Ages to the Industrial Age

As the industrial age unfolded, management evolved from a simple matter of birthright and appointment to something more reflective of what we see today. Management became much more of an economic activity. Scarce resources—raw materials, human resources, and the machinery of production—were all required in managed balance to produce the great products of the day. Managing became more than just being in charge; it entailed actually managing resources of all sorts toward a desired outcome. Human resources were treated as just another input into the production process, valued more for their work than their knowledge. But the seeds of competitive challenge were sown, and management quickly became a matter both of efficiency and effectiveness, a model that persists today. How good you were as a manager started to matter a lot.

Enter the Twenty-First Century

Today, managing still involves organizing a group or team to accomplish a task or represent a cause. The objective of an organization, whether it is a private business or a public entity, in a larger sense, is similar. So what is different today? Many factors have served to make the job of management more complex—and more important. Let's take a closer look.

Trends in Management Today

Without a doubt, the role and function of a manager has changed more rapidly in the past twenty years than in any prior time. The nature of the business environment and the evolution of technology (which in part has driven changes in the business environment) have accelerated the evolution of the management role at a breakneck pace. Here are some of the significant trends and changes.

Streamlining

It is hardly news that companies have worked hard to make their organizations and cost structures more efficient. These measures have reshaped the management role considerably. In the 1970s, it was common for firms to have twelve to fifteen layers of management from top to bottom, with small work groups and very specific responsibilities. Cost pressures, competition, and the need to move faster required organizations to cut the layers to the point where by the late 1990s five to six levels were more common. Result: increased "span of control" (more employees) and a wider scope and variety of duties within the job and within the organization.

Increased Speed of Business

Competition in almost all industries has intensified and become more agile, Markets and products change every day. Faster "time to market" is now required—and achieved—in most industries. Technology, like e-mail, voice mail, tele- and videoconferencing, has made it possible to do in seconds what used to take days or weeks. Managers must fine-tune their inputs and outputs on a daily, even hourly, basis.

Greater Entrepreneurism

In part due to increased responsibilities brought about by streamlining, and in part due to the increased speed of business, managers have greater responsibility and are empowered to do more within their own business unit, department, or location within the corporate geography. Gone in most organizations are the gigantic towers of centralized planning and control.

Greater Complexity and Pressure

Expanded roles, increased responsibility, and faster pace have all exacted their price in making many management jobs into real pressure cookers. More than ever, managers are always on the go, working late hours, retrieving voice mail on vacation, and so forth. No matter what, no matter where you are, you can be found! If you don't keep up, you get left in the dust.

It's More about Knowledge

Advances in technology, and the increasing complexity of things, has evolved management from merely being about units of input to being about knowledge and skills. Compared to 100 years ago, there is a far greater portion of managers who must manage a vast set of information, skills, and tasks toward a complex outcome.

More (and Stronger) Challenges

In the private sector (that is, business) competition makes it imperative to achieve results and use scarce resources—including people—wisely. Marketplace efficiencies and enhanced technology have made it much more difficult to succeed with sloppiness, waste, or fluff in a business.

Rewards Based on Performance

In the past, management responsibility and rewards were based more on seniority or years of service. Today's manager tends to be promoted—and rewarded—more as a result of performance. Result: more pressure and often a more "political," judgmental work environment.

The "Network" Manager

There was a time when all resources supervised by a manager were in plain sight at all times. Today, technology has made it possible (and likely) for work teams to be spread across the country or across the world. Furthermore, streamlining has led to outsourcing, where all but the core functions may be handled by others who are outside of the organization. Today's management role means conducting a lot of "musicians" that you can't see and who may not be part of your immediate "orchestra." This puts today's manager in a more critical and difficult role, and requires special skills not often needed in the past.

Wider Tour of Duty

Yesterday's managers probably moved up through the ranks of a particular organizational function—manufacturing, marketing, finance, customer service, human resources, etc. They went from one position to another—usually the next higher position—until they reached the top. Today's management role requires a broader understanding of the business, and today's organizations want their people to have a wider assortment of experiences and skills to expand flexibility. Result: Most career paths take a manager through multiple organizational functions. Manufacturing engineers become cost accounting supervisors, then marketing product managers before becoming manufacturing managers. Obviously this isn't always the case, but it's certainly more likely than in the past.

The Business Model Describes Everything

The business model has become more prevalent in public and personal life. In the public sector, competition doesn't exist in the same sense as in private business, but increased visibility and scrutiny provide nearly the same need for efficiency and effectiveness. Similarly in our personal lives, we take increasing responsibility for managing our financial affairs amidst a more complex backdrop of financial requirements, tax structures, and so forth. If we don't stay on top of our finances and our relationships, what we value and cherish will vanish in the blink of an eye.

So managing today is much different than it was 500 years ago—or even twenty-five years ago. You didn't need to buy a book to figure that out, right? The main point is, good management achieves results, while bad management doesn't. And unlike five centuries ago, when strength and size were really what mattered, today only the organizations that are nimble, achieve results, and do it consistently, survive. Those that don't tend to fail.

The New Definition of Management

Not only has the role of a manager become more critical, and the difference between good and bad management more apparent, but the role of a manager has expanded *outside* the traditional work "sphere." Today's managers must not only control and direct their organizations, but they must be increasingly aware of and respond to the external environment. They must understand their industries and the competition within their industries, for that is the only way to keep up with the pace of change. Today's managers must be aware of new trends and directions in their customer base. They must be aware of financial performance and the financial environment in which they operate. More than ever, today's managers must be, to use the popular term, *externally focused.*

At the same time, with today's drive for efficiency and available technology, managers must also do more of their own communicating— the days of secretaries and administrative support are gone for most, and endangered for others. Managers have become more responsible for more of their own hands-on work. They must send e-mails, make phone calls, and make their own presentations and presentation materials. Otherwise, they simply couldn't keep up. Today's communications arrive more often, in less formal directives, and in smaller tidbits. Not only does this apply to communications, but also to staffing, measuring, evaluating, and many other "execution" tasks in the organization. It's fair to say the role of today's manager is both broader and deeper than it was years ago. The more specific roles and functions of the manager are described in Chapter 2.

Getting Things Done Through Others

Let's take a moment to return to the definition of management. If we had to offer our own definition of management, one that is broader but perhaps more useful as a working definition than those found in the dictionary, we would say:

Managing is getting things done through others.

No single sentence captures the essence of modern management more clearly. Boiled down, managing is the art and science of effectively organizing and accomplishing tasks through others, even if these "others" don't report to you directly. In almost any business or public affairs exercise, as a manager you are expected to, even *required* to, leverage your own abilities and skills through others to get greater tasks and goals accomplished. In today's business world, just as in the medieval battlefields of yesteryear, you can't get it all done with only your own two bare hands; your ability to get it done through others becomes the standard for accomplishing things worth accomplishing.

Bringing It All Together

The bottom line: You *can* make a difference, and what you do *does* makes a difference. With very few exceptions, you cannot simply land in a management position, take control, and do whatever pleases you that particular day. You must accomplish the five functions of management: planning, organizing, staffing, leading, and controlling. (What do these mean? We'll get to that in Chapter 2.) With few exceptions, you must accomplish *all five* of these functions to some degree, and accomplish them well. Being good at one and ignoring others usually leads to poor results and failure. Being a manager is not only a lot about skills, but also a lot about *balance.* You must be able to do a variety of things well, and as you'll find, often simultaneously.

What Makes a Good Manager—Today

So now you know what roles managers play, what functions a manager must perform, and how the management role has evolved—but what skills are required to be a "good" manager in today's environment? There are many, many specific skills required to be a good manager. To get a basic grip, here are three categories or skill sets: technical, interpersonal, and conceptual.

Technical Skills

Simply put, managers must understand their jobs. They must understand the business, industry, and enterprise in which they perform, and they must understand—to a degree at least—the specific technical competencies and trades employed within their groups and their organizations. They must understand the inputs, the processes, and the outputs of their immediate work group, and the entire business. They don't have to know how to do everything. But they must know enough about how it is done to distinguish productive from unproductive actions—and to plan and make decisions accordingly.

As the management function evolves today, most managers must understand more about their business and external and competitive pressures that might evolve. Likewise, they must stay on top of change and technology, and be aware of the "latest thing" that might change their business, the inputs, the processes, and the outputs of their teams. Managers of yesteryear needed mainly to understand the tasks done by their teams, and were often promoted out of their teams because they mastered the technical skills and evidenced emerging leadership skills. On the other hand, today's managers are more likely to come from outside the organization, and must understand a lot more about the business. They must understand the market position and customer acceptance of the product or service their team produces or supports, and the financial strength and success of the business built around it.

Interpersonal Skills

The need for interpersonal skills has always been part of management. The ability to work with and motivate people, garner their respect, influence their actions and productivity, and so forth, are all integral parts of the job. Managers must have good people skills not only with their employees, but also with "peer" managers and superiors, other employees, and sometimes even customers. The interpersonal role involves much of the popular notion of the manager—developing and working with people, leading them, motivating them, dealing with problems, enhancing morale, and much more. Today's management requires a much more "holistic" view of the individual—their attainment of goals, their development, their career path, and so forth. Today's managers must understand their employees and be able to empathize with them both in and outside the workplace.

Today's managers also take on a much larger and more critical responsibility for *communication.* As the pace of business changes, it is more important to keep employees informed of what's going on in the business, both externally and internally. In performing the informational role, managers are essentially two-way information conduits. Managers must keep employees informed of all things that affect their work, and must provide information to their organizations (and often, outside their organization) about what the work group is doing. They must keep their finger on the pulse, be the spokesperson, and disseminate information strategically in all directions. Keeping themselves, their employees, and their external environment informed of change is a big and growing job. The manager that does this well gets further.

Conceptual Skills

Conceptual skills are hardest to grasp, and are the hardest to learn. Good managers, especially today, must be able to assess what's going on both inside and outside their business, and be ready for action. They must be able to break down problems into solvable chunks, and be able to assimilate small bits of data to "connect the dots" into meaningful issues, problems, and opportunities. They must connect the dots to make decisions. These decisions not only involve routine direction and course change, but also planning, performance assessment, problem resolution, and resource selection.

More and more, today's managers must grasp what is going on in the external environment. They must be able to interpret those signals and make necessary changes in the work. The "internally focused" production line managers of yesteryear still exist, but are becoming rarer. Today's managers need to have an "external focus" on what is going on with the business—how the product or service is performing, how the marketplace is changing, how the business is performing financially. The conceptual skill requires not only seeing the big picture but also being able to take action based upon it.

Skill	Duties
Technical	• Understand the work—the input, processes, and output • Understand the workplace and work environment • Know the product or service, and its role, position, and acceptance in the marketplace
Interpersonal	• Understand employee needs • Lead, motivate, and develop individual employees • Provide employee feedback and corrective action when necessary • Keep the external organization aware of progress and accomplishments • Understand customer needs, maintain effective communication with internal and external customers
Conceptual	• Understand the big picture in business environment, interpret meaning for the work or work group • Collect and assess facts, draw conclusions about business performance • Determine goals and direction, select resources, appraise employee performance, recommend changes inside and outside work group

Figure 1-1. Management Skills

These skills overlap, and more than one of these skills will be used at a time to accomplish something. For instance, hiring an employee draws on all three skill sets—technical, interpersonal, and conceptual. Technical skills are used in determining whether the employee is minimally qualified for the job. Interpersonal skills are used to assess the person's character; how well the person will fit with the team; the person's motivation, morale, needs, and people skills needed for the job. Finally, conceptual skills are used to visualize at a more abstract level whether that person will fit, and whether he is the *best* fit for the job.

You probably guessed—and guessed right—that all r
these hats, and if one hat is missing, it becomes a deficier.
manager. Management jobs that *don't* require doing all of
time are few and far between. This may sound a bit repeti
more than almost anything else you'll do, draws on many

Management Is about Managing Change

If there is one responsibility of today's manager that's different from those of
an earlier era, it is the imperative to manage change—and manage change well.
As mentioned earlier, the speed of business is faster than ever, and the forces of
competition require up-to-the-minute finger-on-the-pulse awareness of what is
going on inside and outside the organization. The successful manager today
juggles many balls—and, if necessary, can change balls instantly without
missing a beat. Managers who stay on top of change and *anticipate* it are more
highly regarded than managers who seem to be consumed by change and are
always playing catch-up. Many top executives regard change awareness and
change management as a number-one skill of a manager.

Management as a Career Path

Go to the career section of any bookstore (maybe you already went there when
you bought *this* book!). Do you see any books specifically about management
as a *career?* No, not really. There are books about different fields—business,
law, medicine, government, and even small business. But there are no books on
management as a career, per se. Why? This might seem like a minor point, but
it really makes a major one: Management occurs in every field and every
profession—it isn't a "field" in and of itself. Whether you manage a
McDonald's, write software alone in a cubicle, or run an assembly line,
some part of your job involves getting things done through others.

You're a Manager Even If You're Not a Manager

We maintain that every job has a "managing" element. As you move up in your organization and acquire more responsibility, your job will be more about managing—getting things done through others—and less about "doing." Can you see that if you're good at getting things done through others in your entry-level position, you will be regarded as a good manager? Those who made that connection get an "A" for this chapter. Indeed, whether you really want to be a manager or not, developing those skills will open doors, get you places, and make you a more valuable player in the organization, even if you choose to stay in your cubicle and write software.

For the software designer, it may be a small part, but somewhere along the way, others will have to be involved in deciding what the software should do, testing it, and getting it out the door. The software engineer will have to manage those people—regardless of whether they report directly to him or her—to get the important inputs to the job and to deliver a finished product. For the production line manager, getting things done through others is probably 80 to 90 percent, maybe 100 percent of the job. For the fast food manager, getting things done through others is a big part, but where have you seen these managers sitting in an office while the hourlies drop fries and sling burgers? They are usually on the first line with their employees (particularly when someone doesn't show for work). So managing—getting things done through others—is a big part, but not the whole job. We will come back to this concept again and again.

Why Become a Manager?

You are probably already a manager, even if you have nobody directly reporting to you. But some of you may be asking why you would want to step up to a work group or organization management role. For some, it is a natural extension of interests and personality. But to be clear, it isn't for everyone. Some of these are obvious, but here are the common reasons to make the leap:

- **Status.** Some people relish the status and importance of the position; it gives them a little more incentive to get up and go to work in the morning. Becoming a manager shows a degree of achievement and recognition from the organization, which can help in other personal and professional endeavors.

- **Financial reward.** With a few exceptions, managerial roles involve more responsibility, so naturally, most managers receive greater rewards—higher salaries and participation in the organization's financial success.

- **Authority.** For some people, the ability to influence others is important. People like to see their ideas come to life, and it is possible to do more when you have a set of "troops" working alongside you to accomplish those goals. The healthy manager likes authority because it enables him or her to achieve greater goals—*not* to control others for control's sake.

- **Commitment to the organization.** Managers have the most influence on an organization's performance or outcome. Managers, more than most people, are driven by success—and the psychic and financial rewards that follow.

- **Desire to drive change.** Managers are people who like to be change agents. They like to influence others toward influencing organizational outcomes and performance.

- **Personal and career growth.** There is little that achieves more for a career and for personal satisfaction than a management role that is done well and is well recognized. When the next hiring manager or recruiter sees "Manager" on your resume, it is almost always a rubber stamp of credibility and achievement.

What Does It Take to Become a Manager?

We wrote earlier of the skills sets required in management—technical, interpersonal and conceptual skills. These skills form a useful template to begin to grasp what it takes to be a manager. As you appraise yourself for the job—whether you're in it or aspire to be in it—here is a list of commonly recognized skills or traits of a manager.

- **Need to achieve.** Achievement motivation is important in all phases of management; the good manager wants to do things better than others and can be competitive. While strong achievement motivation is a plus, achievement motivation at the expense of all else can be problematic.

- **Social skills.** A good manager has a natural ability to work with people in all kinds of situations. This doesn't necessarily require outgoing behavior or extroversion, but it helps. The good manager today must be able to understand the needs and motives of every employee, and be able to actively motivate, develop, and provide responsive feedback. The manager that can't work with people may get along, but strong people skills strengthen chances for success, and—really—make the whole thing easier.

- **Socialized power motivation.** A good manager usually has a "power" motive—defined here as an orientation and ability to influence others. As we've said, the bottom-line definition of management is getting things done through others. Now, why "socialized"? Socialized power refers to power applied for the common good, as opposed to a personal gain. Power used as a stick to control others or for personal ego satisfaction is *not* on the list of positive traits.

- **Communication skills.** A manager must be able—and willing—to communicate up, down, and sideways within an organization, to achieve a number of objectives. We refer to both spoken and written communication. Lack of communication skills will have an adverse effect on even the best manager, as her excellence goes unnoticed and unheeded.

- **Leadership skills.** More on this later, but once again, the manager that gets things done through others is successful. Leadership is the delicate balance of art and science, of words and action that gets people to follow in the direction you want to go.

- **Initiative.** A manager is someone who takes charge, and can move places without being told what to do. If you're a self-starter and can take action without specific direction, you're in the right camp. As you might surmise, management usually entails a certain degree of risk taking. Good managers have the ability to sail through unknown waters—and often seek to do so for the betterment of their organizations.

- **Tolerance for pressure.** Ah, it all comes with a bit of a price. The fast pace, the change, the people issues, the lack of direction, the whims of the "top hats" above all lead to pressure. Management in this era is a "24/7" (twenty-four hours a day, seven days a week) job. Regardless of level, few managers are able to escape the workplace completely during evenings and weekends. Work may "invade" during idle evening hours, while in the shower, or during occasional 3:00 A.M. "work sessions." For some, it's e-mail and voice mail all weekend, with a pager and a cell phone listening for the latest event or disaster.

- **Taste for variety.** If you want to do the same thing day in and day out, don't become a manager. As we will see in Chapter 2, management positions necessarily involve a wide breadth of activities—technical, interpersonal, conceptual—across a wide scope—marketing, financial, and operational. Managers must simultaneously focus on the big picture and on the details. Managers must work *proactively* (look, think, and plan forward) and *reactively* (respond, decide, and adjust). If this sounds like a recipe for variety in the job, you're right. Good managers seek variety.
- **Aptitude for data.** At some level all management positions involve working with data and facts. Whether it's analyzing financial results, calculating inputs (people resources), or planning a department budget, somewhere along the line you'll encounter the numbers stuff. Just as some managers can get by without great people skills, some managers may get along fine without data and perhaps without even touching a PC. But most will do better if they have the aptitude—or at least if they don't panic when they see a bunch of numbers or a chart.

Trait	Description
Need to achieve	Desire to do things well and better than others; competitive
Social skills	Natural ability to work with people in all kinds of situations
Socialized power motivation	Desire and ability to influence others
Communication skills	Ability to listen, speak, and write well in all situations
Leadership skills	Ability to set a direction and get others to follow
Initiative	Ability to take charge and take action without being told what to do
Tolerance for pressure	Deal with fast pace, change, complexity without regard to time of day
Taste for variety and reactive	Broad range of tasks, high level and detail, proactive
Aptitude for data	Ability—and willingness—to work with numbers

Figure 1-2. Personal Traits of Managers

This isn't an all-inclusive list, but gives an idea for the variety of skills and traits required. As you begin to see yourself as a manager (or evaluate yourself if you already are), you should inventory these traits in your self-appraisal. Ask others in your business and personal environment for feedback on these traits. Try to look at yourself as another person would, and as an organization would. Everybody is strong in some traits and has "development opportunities" in others—you don't have to "bat a thousand" to make a trip to the plate. Knowing where you are strong and where you are not is the first step; working on weaker areas is next.

Some people are gifted at management right off the bat; however, most people can develop a reasonably good management skill set—if they choose to. If the traits on the preceding list are unappealing—or even downright scary— then perhaps management in a formal sense isn't your thing. But even if you're an individual contributor or independent entrepreneur, having the skills and traits of a manager, to some degree, will only help you and your business.

Levels of Management

From top to bottom in an organization, there are many levels of management. While the titles, salaries, and benefits vary widely, it's been our experience that the duties and skills required don't change a lot. What changes is the *mix*. If you're a high-level executive in a major corporation, the nature of the job is more conceptual and less technical and interpersonal. The focus is big picture and proactive and requires stronger socialized power, leadership, communication skills, and at least thirty hours a day, eight days a week. But there are aspects of such a job that use all skills and traits mentioned so far. Likewise, if you're a fast food restaurant manager, you will use more of your social and interpersonal skills, and the nature of the tasks will shift more toward detail and reactive decision-making.

As you set forth in your management career, it's good to be mindful of the following four commonly recognized levels of management: top-level manager, mid-level manager, first-line supervisor, and individual contributor.

C Something O

All of us, at one time or another, fantasize about the lives and world of top-level managers: corporate jets, six- and even seven-figure salaries, stock options, special "under the table" bonuses and incentives, knowing what you say goes. To some degree all of these things come with the job, but what a big job it is.

Chief corporate officers or "managing directors" usually represent the top echelon. CEO, or chief executive officer, is number one. The next layer consists of a group of functional chiefs—a chief financial officer (CFO), a chief marketing officer (CMO), a chief operating officer (COO), and nowadays, a chief information officer (CIO). There are usually others included in this list, too. These "chiefs" have ultimate responsibility for their parts of the business. In some organizations, these are known as "functional" managers because they head up a vital "function" in the organization.

These top-level managers usually have large organizations with perhaps five or six layers of management reporting to them. The lower level workers usually tend to details; it is the job of these senior executives to read the outside world, set a vision and a high-level plan or plan framework, and make sure things get done. These are the folks you usually read about in the paper when they're successful, and—lately—also when they fail.

Is a top job for you? It's good to set your sights in that direction, if you're so motivated. Getting there takes a remarkable amount of skill, not only in executing your management duties but also in positioning and marketing *yourself* in the organization. Communication skills are of utmost importance; you must not only do well but be able to demonstrate to others your value and success in the organization in such a way as to appear to be "social power motivated," that is, motivated by the success of the organization. The level of scrutiny is so high that "faking it" probably won't do; you must do well, live and breath the success of the organization, and communicate all of it well. Do it, and the rewards will be there eventually—and so will the pressure.

Sometimes it makes sense to be a big fish in a smaller pond. Manage a small business or store outlet, and you get many of the rewards (though not as much financial reward) as you would in a big organization. There is competition and pressure, but not so intense. Many people are quite satisfied with a goal of managing a smaller organization or business unit.

In the Middle but Not Stuck

Naturally there are far more mid-level management jobs available than top-level or chief officer positions. Mid-level managers usually report to top managers, either directly or through one or two layers, and are responsible for departments or some kind of focused organizational activity. Advertising managers report to marketing managers, staffing managers report to human resource executives, and cost accounting managers report to CFOs. Night shift managers report to fast food chain managers, zone managers report to regional sales managers, and so forth. Middle managers develop and execute plans consistent with company goals and objectives, and are usually responsible for the performance—including financial performance—of the department. Mid-level management provides a comfortable living and a substantial sense of achievement, and is a viable career objective for most management aspirants.

On the First Line

First-line managers, or supervisors, manage a work group or work unit that produces a specific output for the organization. There are production line managers who manage production workers, first-line information technology supervisors who manage computer programmers, and financial reporting supervisors who manage financial analysts. Job titles and duties vary greatly. These managers usually manage anywhere from one to perhaps twenty or twenty-five workers and are directly responsible for their hiring and performance.

In today's flatter organizations, often a single manager will perform duties resembling mid-level and first-line supervisor. An advertising manager may be responsible for the function and simultaneously manage "production workers" (perhaps copy editors), other managers (the graphic design department), and a host of outside parties (the TV/radio placement agency, market researchers, recording studios, and the like). Meanwhile, first-line supervisors may manage outsourced partners and play a greater role in organizational planning and decision-making. Did we say "variety" earlier? Yes. The role of the first-line supervisor is richer, more involved, more forward looking, and more rewarding than in yesterday's world, although many "traditional" loading dock supervisors and the like still exist. Nearly every top- and mid-level manager starts out as a line supervisor, so, regardless of your training and background, it is usually good experience—and good organizational politics—to spend some time in this role.

A One-Person Band?

Increasingly, in the modern business world, a manager may be called such without any direct "reports," that is, employees. Organizations have come to pay increasingly high regard (and reward) to project managers, product managers, and program managers. These positions may be a single box on an organization chart but possess a wide range of duties, and require skills of at least a first-line supervisor, and often a mid-level manager or higher. These types of managers create strategies and plans for an important part of the business—a project, a product, or a program (which is a synthesis of the two)—and take responsibility for its performance. Often this requires stronger management talents because these individuals manage people who don't directly report to them. They manage entire outcomes of organizations—for example, the information technology piece—and usually have responsibility for a product's or function's financial performance.

Many of these positions are "one-person bands" because they work within the organization and also manage resources outside the organization—marketing agencies, contract programmers, and the like. Individual contributors must be highly resourceful and creative, in addition to having the typical management traits mentioned earlier. Even though these managers don't manage people directly, social or people skills are an important component of their job. These skills are even *more* critical, because these managers have to motivate and lead others over whom they have no direct or formal authority. Individual-contributor managers are highly sought after by organizations, and the position provides a rewarding career path for any management aspirant.

What Is a Knock 'em Dead Manager?

It's a fair question to ask at this point. You bought this book, and you've read through a few dimensions of the job of management (and are about to read through more). As you begin to grasp what a manager is, we'll show you the traits of a manager really pointed in the direction of success. Knock 'em Dead managers make stronger impressions on an organization (or on customers, suppliers, etc., if an entrepreneur). The basics of management will provide sustenance and security, but becoming a Knock 'em Dead manager improves your chances to succeed beyond the rest, and good things will come your way. Simply put, Knock 'em Dead managers do the basics, but also go an extra step beyond to deliver greater value to their organizations. The traits you employ as a manager all become part of your *management style,* which will be discussed throughout the book. Persons whose Knock 'em Dead style is clearly identifiable usually go further with greater ease. Here are seven traits of a Knock 'em Dead manager.

Think Outside the Box

The Knock 'em Dead managers constantly think outside the realm and constraints of their immediate job function. They look at the big picture and are proactive no matter what their level of responsibility and tasks are. This doesn't mean that you dismiss the task at hand to think outside the box—quite the contrary (and this is where many aspirants make a mistake). You have to do the job assigned for the organization, but if you look at it from outside the box, and recommend ways to make the job or the organization better, sooner or later you will be rewarded. *Innovation counts.* Sooner or later you deliver greater value to the organization, and it shows the organization you're ready to do bigger and better things. "Think globally, act locally" is a rough 1970s translation of this ethic—you get the idea.

Know the Big Picture

Good managers keep close tabs on what is happening with their business or industry outside their own organization—in the marketplace, financially, among the competition, in the supply chain, and so forth. That is, they know what's happening in the marketplace, with customers, with financial analysts and shareholders, with the trade press, and with the local newspaper. A good manager must be externally focused! If your work group makes good widgets, that reflects well on you. But if you understand how well the widgets are doing in the marketplace and financially, that will shed light on how to make *better* widgets. It will also qualify you for jobs in different functions, which in turn makes you more useful and employable. Companies are always looking for people who can lead their organizations to make better widgets—and who are more employable.

Add Value Everywhere You Go

This goes hand in hand with the first two principles we've discussed—good managers add insight and energy to their business. Doing more things, in new ways, for more people, more cost effectively, and more quickly adds value. Take on new projects or new tasks, and serve on strategic decision-making committees and planning sessions. The First Law of Physics for a Knock 'em Dead manager: Give more energy to an organization than you take away. You've seen the "one person bureaucracy" managers who just seem to get in the way, to add inertia to any job or process. They must check off and "approve" everything, and anything that wasn't their idea gets close scrutiny and (usually) resistance. They draw energy off of their organizations and slow things down. Don't be one of these managers.

Create a Success Environment

It is often stated that the Number One job of the manager is to create an environment where employees (or team members) can be successful. We couldn't agree more. Make things good for yourself, and you can succeed. Make things good for your employees, and everyone will be successful, thus multiplying your success by however many people involved. That means providing resources, clearing hurdles, communicating expectations, balancing workloads, and soliciting employee feedback—all the things that you would want if you were an employee or team member.

Make Your People Better

Time invested on improving employee skills, motivation, and judgment will always pay off. The Knock 'em Dead manager realizes that developed, motivated people need *less* control. Make sure they have the skills, know the boundaries, and have the motivation and *support* from you. Think *trust* and *empowerment.* And remember two wise old adages: Treat people like children and they act like children. Give a person a fish and he eats for a day; teach a person how to fish and he eats for a lifetime.

Be Proactive

We've offered that any management role has proactive and reactive components, some more than others. Our observation: The more proactive you are, the better you will do. Not that you ignore the reactive part of management (if the French fryer breaks you must do something about it), but if you have vision into how to prevent the "break" in the first place—and particularly how to serve your customers better during the downtime—you will differentiate yourself from those who fail to do these things.

Train Your Successor

Knock 'em Dead managers invest time in training and developing their successor. Any good manager does this. Why? Once considered, the reasons are obvious. First, you get a competent individual (or individuals) to whom you can delegate critical tasks, relieving some of your day-to-day burdens. Secondly, once you have a successor, it becomes easier for your organization to promote you or give you additional responsibility. Out of insecurity, many managers—especially new ones—fail to recognize this. They like being "top dog" and want to keep it that way. Don't fall into this trap.

Trait	Description
Think outside the box	Don't let boundaries prevent you from adding greater value to your organization.
Know the big picture	Know the *business*, not just your department's function. Understand your company's marketplace, finances, and supply chain.
Add value every-where you go	Add energy to your business—don't deplete it.
Create a success environment	Create a working environment where your people can succeed.
Make your people better	Focus on making your people successful, and you will be successful. Develop and empower your team.
Be proactive	Look ahead and be prepared at all times.
Train your successor	Managers who "clone" themselves deliver more value and can move up in the organization.

Figure 1-3. The "Knock 'em Dead" Manager

Summary

Managing in the twenty-first century is far more a "fine art" than it was years ago, when most managers attained their positions through appointment or seniority. Today's manager must manage more, manage faster, and be true stewards of the business or enterprise for which they work. They must look to the outside—to the satisfaction of their customers and the performance of the business—not just the workaday accomplishments of their subordinates. Increased information content and globalization of most commerce serve to make the task even more complex. There is more information to keep track of, and it changes faster. More than ever, today's manager must have a keen sense of the business, know how to get things done through others, and have not only a tolerance but an appetite for change.

2 | The Organization Manager—The Many Roles You Play

Effective managers add value to their organizations in many ways—probably some you've never thought of.

Managers bring value to their organizations in a variety of obvious and not-so-obvious ways. True, as described in Chapter 1, they get things done through others. But it hardly stops there, for that begs the question: *what* things? Getting things done through others is where the rubber meets the road for a manager, but the true scope of most management positions is much larger. Today's organization manager must be a versatile, informed *steward* of the business.

In a nutshell, managers must read and interpret the needs of the business to provide direction for their work group, and often for the organization. Once that is done, they must make sure the organization gets there and that the work group does its part. Reading and assessing the business requires good business skill, intuition, an open mind, and strong conceptual and technical skills as described in Chapter 1. Providing the direction and making sure the organization "gets there" requires (again) a lot of technical skill, and incorporates people skills to get things done through others to achieve the goal. Finally, getting there requires good conceptual skill to appraise performance and take corrective, constructive actions to keep things on course.

To say the job of management is multifaceted, dynamic, and varied, requiring a broad, balanced set of skills would be repeating the message of Chapter 1. We don't want to repeat that message, but rather add to it. In this chapter, we take the message apart to further explore what managers do and the environment in which they operate. You've heard of "The Organization Man"? We'll dedicate this chapter to "The Organization Manager."

A Visual Model

It seems that everything in business—and in business books—is described by models. What is a model? A model, like a scale model of an airplane or train, is a simpler, smaller-scale representation of the real thing. Management is not only big but also very conceptual, so it is useful to try to build a model that not only simplifies but lends itself to being put on paper. The following figure shows a model of the typical management position.

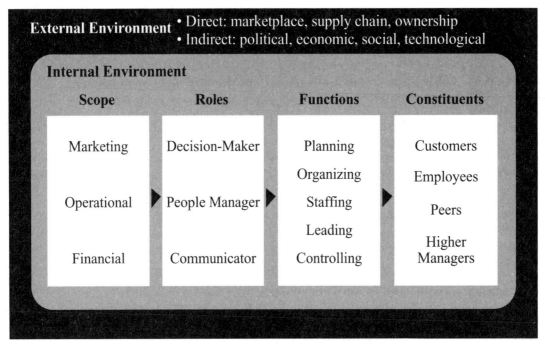

Figure 2-1. A Managerial Model

While not particularly artistic, this model serves to designate and connect the various elements of a typical manager's job. The large boxes represent the internal and external environments in which the manager operates. These environments shape what needs to be done. The internal environment, in particular, determines what *can* be done and how it *should* be done.

Within these environments, the scope of a management job *at minimum* includes the three primary elements of business: marketing, operations, and finance. These elements all influence the work process and work climate, whether they are product specifications, time-to-market requirements, required quality, or cost constraints. The manager must be aware of these elements and how they affect the work. It's a two-way street; they also must be aware of how their work affects the business. As physicists say, "every action has a corresponding reaction." That applies as well to today's manager. It is a marketing manager's responsibility to understand how his decisions affect the company's operations and finances; a production supervisor's responsibility to understand how his decisions and actions affect marketing and finances; and a financial manager's responsibility to understand how his financial decisions affect the company as a whole—you get the picture. Managers don't manage in a vacuum.

Once the big-picture influences are taken into account, the manager puts on the "role" hats of decision-maker, people manager, and communicator to get things done. Decisions are made affecting all aspects of the work, from selecting resources to producing output, to making key changes, to doing things better. People management, as described in Chapter 1, enters every step of the way, whether employees, suppliers, customers, or even bosses are being managed (influenced) to get to the goal. Finally, neither decision-making nor people management works unless there is communication; communication is the grease that keeps the organizational wheels turning.

The Big Picture

The term "big picture" is used frequently in business and especially in management, and refers to the business as a whole, or large segments of the business. As a manager, you need to make decisions in the context of the big picture, so as not to "micromanage," that is, pay excessive attention to minor details at the expense of the whole. Looking at the big picture of a business often means looking at the business or business component the way an outsider would.

What managers do can be grouped into the five functions: planning, organizing, staffing, leading, and controlling. These activities are the subject of much of the rest of this book, for they must *all* be done well and in balance.

Finally, managers should recognize that they have far more "stakeholders" than just the employees or team members who work directly for them. Managers must think about customers, whether "real" external customers to the business, or (more likely for most managers) internal customers in the organization. For example, a fast food manager has "real" customers standing at the counter, but also external customers such as district managers, franchise owners, and even a state health official or two to contend with. There are direct and indirect customers, too. A production line supervisor has a direct customer in whoever handles the next part of the line. The marketing manager, who needs widgets to deliver to the "end" customer, is an indirect customer to the production line supervisor, and so is the finance manager who must keep track of costs. Managers also have peer customers—other managers or members of the greater team who depend on them from time to time for insight, help, and in some cases, the actual output of the work group.

It's Not My Job

The Knock 'em Dead manager takes stewardship responsibility for the success of the business. "It's not my job" is not part of the vocabulary of a successful manager. The reality is that a good manager acts in the best interest of the whole organization, whether or not a particular issue or task concerns her immediate work group. If the manager can't solve a problem or doesn't "own" the resources to do so, it is still the manager's duty to find a home for the issue, and do what she can to facilitate the resolution. A good manager is like a small business owner, who sees what needs to be done, and either does it or makes sure it gets taken care of. So management not only involves a breadth of duties, but also a responsibility and a sense of ownership for the organization's success. As you can see, the phrase "it's not my job" rarely applies to the typical management position.

> **Stewardship**
> Loosely defined, "stewardship" means taking care of something as though you were the owner. In the business management context, you may "own" only a certain department or function of the business, but as a good manager, you accept stewardship—that is, a responsibility—for the greater whole and the greater good of the enterprise.

Are we trying to scare you by making the management role look complex and all inclusive? No, not at all, but if you're a little apprehensive, we understand. There is a lot to learn and experience in a management job, and nobody is going to get everything right the first day on the job. You will get good at all facets of the job over time, and there will always be some areas in which you are better than others. That said, the more we can prepare you for the job (or strengthen your position if you're already in it) the better.

It's best to think of the "vastness" of the position as an *opportunity,* not a problem; that is, an opportunity to succeed in the unknown and undefined, and bring back more for your organization as a result. Throughout the history of business (and the history of the world, for that matter), the leaders most recognized for their success dealt with the complex and unknown and were good at many, many things, both internal and external to their jobs. Want an example? Try Lewis and Clark, for one. Do you think they looked at their early nineteenth-century expedition as scary? Or as an opportunity?

The Ins and Outs of the Business Environment

As we've already suggested, the manager who labors oblivious to the internal and especially the external business environment is headed for trouble. Good Knock 'em Dead managers spend time understanding both environments and how they affect the work and the work group. Again, balance is in order. A manager completely focused on the internal environment will miss external cues; the manager focused completely on the external environment will have trouble getting things done within the organization.

The External Environment

As time goes on, the external environment takes on greater and greater importance to a business work unit. The fast pace of change and the demands of competition make it critical to stay on top of what's going on. The manager must keep up with the business and its marketing, operational, and financial elements that are observable outside the window. The true Knock 'em Dead manager becomes an expert on his business. The Knock 'em Dead manager can describe what is happening to the business—to a complete stranger—without special preparation. That manager knows it, breathes it, and lives it.

One can divide the external environment into two segments, or spheres of influence, each having its own effect on the business and management role. Direct influences usually come from factors connected directly to the business, and have immediate and often measurable impact. Indirect influences, on the other hand, represent trends and changes in business conditions or constraints.

The effect of indirect influences is more abstract and conceptual, and subject to interpretation. A good manager keeps the "finger on the pulse" of both types of environmental factors, and does a good job of interpreting and proactively managing the potential effects.

Direct Influences

External factors directly influence the business—and a manager's job—in a variety of ways. At first blush, some of them may seem to be distant, or someone else's job, and indeed, a narrowly focused or internally focused manager may get away with that for a while. But as the following examples show, sooner or later direct external influences will catch up with you, and the proactive manager will be in much better shape to respond and do a good job. The reactive, internally focused manager will always be surprised—with negative effect—by these influences.

Checking Out the Marketplace

There are many influences in the marketplace; the easiest to grasp is probably competition. If a competitor introduces a new product or changes the price or delivery of an existing product, your business must at least assess the change—and most likely react to it. The reaction takes many forms, and even if your role doesn't directly include managing the response, the change is likely to affect you sooner or later anyway.

Suppose you're managing a fast food outlet and the neighboring competitor comes out with a new product, reduces price, and hits the market with a big ad campaign. Rest assured that (1) your volume will drop, at least temporarily, and (2) eventually, from somewhere will come the imperative for you to do something in response. Do these things influence your decisions as a manager? You bet. You may need to reschedule or cut staff. You may need to order less food. Then you will have to turn around and gear up when the response campaign comes down from above.

Links in the Supply Chain

Your supply chain is the system of suppliers that provide all of the resources and inputs for your business. Narrowly defined, "supply chain" refers to material supplies, such as food, paper napkins, straws, and ketchup, if you're managing the fast food restaurant. The "chain" includes the suppliers themselves, and the information linkages used to manage these suppliers, place orders, and so on. More broadly defined, "supply chain" includes labor, third-party suppliers, and suppliers of services to your business. It isn't hard to see how problems in the supply chain can affect your business—material shortages, price changes, late deliveries, labor difficulties, and so forth. And if supply is the direct province" of some other manager, fine; but sooner or later, the impact will come your way. Obviously the good manager must be aware of the supply chain as part of the external environment.

What Is the Supply Chain?

"Supply chain" refers to the network of suppliers and processes that furnish the raw material, services, or intellectual property you need to run your business. A golf club manufacturer would consider the businesses that supply club grips, shafts, and heads part of the immediate supply chain, as well as the foundry that casts the head and even the safety testers who ascertain club safety under rigorous test conditions. Book authors consider their network of research contacts as part of the supply chain.

Indirect Influences

Indirect influences are broad, sweeping changes in the global environment in which the business operates. Usually they are distant and long-term in nature—trends in business cycles or human behavior that take a long time to "gel" before specific business actions become necessary. Indirect influences include political, economic, social, and technological influences. Occasionally, as in the case of new laws and regulations, indirect influences may have immediate and direct impact on the business. In addition, certain changes in weather can be an influence if, say, you're in the food processing business that relies on farm products as a resource input. Think broadly.

Inside and Outside the Beltway: Political Influences

New laws and court decisions have obvious influence. Less obvious, but still to consider, are the influences of political climate—who is in charge, which party is in charge. And we don't just mean the federal government; state and even local political climates can have more effect on business than Washington. Read the paper (or the Web) and watch the news.

Size of the Pie: Economic Influences

Clearly the performance of the economy as a whole is worth keeping track of. A stagnant or declining economy sends one signal to the proactive manager, while a growing or expanding economy sends another. There could be an entire book written on the meaning of different economic indicators—we won't attempt it here.

Don't forget to watch what's going on within your industry, or within other industries that your business deals with. If you're working for an auto parts supplier, it pays to keep track of what's going on in the auto industry. If you're in the health care field, you must keep track of the latest trends in managed care and the HMO industry. Again, read the paper. You might take it a step further and read the trade press—journals and magazines covering the particular business you're in. These are often free to qualified subscribers, meaning *you,* if you're in the industry. Or watch the "business wire"—Reuters, Dow Jones, and so forth. Get in the habit of reading a general business magazine such as *BusinessWeek* or a newspaper such as *The Wall Street Journal,* or even take a daily trip through an Internet finance portal such as *http://finance.yahoo.com.*

The Pride of Ownership

Arguably, ownership could be considered an indirect, or even internal influence. How direct this influence is depends on how the business is owned. If you work in a small business owned by individuals, what's going on in the minds of those owners will have a direct and sizable impact on your business! Owners will invariably want more or want something different, and the alert manager will see these things coming a mile away and adapt accordingly. If you work for a large corporation, the ownership chain is more diluted (with millions of shareholders, little common voice) but it is still there. Poor performance leads to shareholder discontent which leads to management changes; the chain is far less direct but still worth staying aware of. As a manager, you should at least stay aware of how the business is performing and how the owners or Wall Street, if a large corporation, appraise that performance.

Important Social Influences

Social influences tend to be even more abstract. How are people's tastes and values changing? The 1970s saw an intensive environmental movement that profoundly affected the conscience and buying behavior of many people (not to mention changes in the political and legal environment). That fervor has cooled somewhat, but "green" is still an important movement and likely to affect you if you work in certain industries. Today the movement is toward family values and, in the aftermath of 9/11, as the airlines have so painfully found out, staying home. There are underlying demographic trends, such as shifts in average population age (aging baby boomers) and shifts to later retirement (better health, less wealth in old age) that are worth tracking. These trends must be watched carefully by marketers, but will influence you no matter where you are.

Automate, Automate—The Influence of Technology

If you're in the technology industry, the influence of technological change is obvious and probably direct. If you are in another industry, managing effectively means keeping track of technology and how it can be harnessed to improve your business. You might be managing an auto service operation using paper work orders. Suppose an automated system is available and your competitors are using it. Whether or not you decide to adopt it is a conscious management decision, but you must at least be aware of it and what it can do. Otherwise, you end up "behind the curve" and get left behind by competitive offerings and high costs, making implementation at a later date that much harder. Bottom line: You must keep up with technology. The *Knock 'em Dead* manager becomes the organization's expert on what's happening with technology and how it might have an impact on the business.

Internal Environment

The internal environment refers to those factors found inside the organization—the structure, the culture, the modus operandi (MO) of day-to-day corporate life. Businesses do different things, but they also have different *ways* of doing things. These different ways of doing things can result from a formal and conscious establishment of process, or they can also evolve from tradition, the personality of leaders, and even the external environment in which businesses operate. The Disney Corporation operates with a much different internal environment than a top-secret defense contractor. You get the picture.

There are many factors influencing the organizational environment including organizational structure, rules and policies, philosophy, and culture. A peculiar nature of organizational life is that sometimes it is easier to understand the external environment than the internal one, particularly for a new manager. Many aspects of the internal environment are tangible and spelled out in writing, but many more are intangible.

Internal environment is largely driven by company history and leader personality, and since you weren't there in the beginning, and can never be one of the original influencing leaders, many features of the internal environment are hard to pick up. They don't appear in the employee development manual; they often must be learned from experience. Translation: Many of them are learned from mistakes! The point is, pick up as much as you can by keenly observing, talking to others with experience, finding mentors, and above all, learning from your mistakes.

Organization Structure

The formal structure of your organization naturally has a lot of influence on your job. Where you sit, and where the others around you sit, and what they do, should be internalized. You need to figure out what people and functions will influence you the most—the shipping supervisor if you're responsible for monthly shipments, the financial reporting manager to get your financial statements and prepare budgets, and so forth. Building personal relationships, and understanding how what others do is connected to what you do is critical.

Beyond the formal organization structure is most likely an informal one. Different players emerge as "experts" or informal leads on different subjects. Certain managers have more influence than others in decision-making and in meetings. There is no informal organization chart, but being aware of who's who, who's respected, and who's the expert will only help you in your role.

Rules and Policies

This one's obvious. Every organization has its policies on different matters, and they usually come straight from the employee manual. It's also a good idea to learn the operating rules of other departments. If accounting needs its numbers on the fifth working day to close monthly books, you need to know that. Some organizations run with a lot of formal rules and guidelines; others have a fairly slim rule book, and allow a lot to run on general principle, decision, and precedent, or plain old common sense. If yours is the latter, you may have to spend some time "tuning in" to get comfortable with the way things are done.

Philosophy: Mission, Values, Goals, Business Model

Now it starts to get more conceptual. Organizations adopt "mission statements," and occasionally "value statements" to try to capture who they are and what role they play in the marketplace. Corporations and top-level managers have conceptions about the market, about the product, product quality, customers, customer service, employees, the look of the buildings, and so forth. Dell Computer approaches a tough market with the goal of being a price leader and easy to do business with. Its mission and philosophy is to have the simplest product offering, most streamlined processes, build-to-order products, and the leanest cost structure in the industry. Southwest Airlines likewise wants to be a price leader with very reliable service. As a result, it flies only one kind of airplane and uses the Internet extensively to deal directly with passengers. These marketing goals and practices blend with operational philosophies to become the business model for these organizations. The business model will affect what you do as a manager at all times.

Culture and Climate

Some organizations take a militaristic approach to managing, while others have a more laid-back, laissez-faire climate. The words "culture" and "climate" are often used interchangeably, but there are subtle differences, and at the end of the day, climate is really a subset of culture. Climate refers to the tone of the workplace environment and the nature of human relationships within it. Climate is often a function of leadership personality and style—a style that fosters innovation may create a laid-back, spontaneous, achievement-oriented environment. A style that is control focused will be more intense and structured; more "militaristic" with fewer freedoms and more demands on employees. You may have guessed that leadership style is driven in part by the organization's goals and philosophy, and in part by the nature of leadership in the company's history.

Culture is really a blend of climate with other values and features of an organization's existence. Many high-tech companies have an innovation culture—a strong emphasis and reward system based on innovation and product leadership and an organizational climate that fosters these aims. The historical Hewlett-Packard and the modern-day Apple Computer, Cisco Systems, and Sun Microsystems are examples of such cultures. Other high-tech companies have a pedal-to-the-medal culture that rewards consistency and the ability to meet this quarter's shipment goals—Dell and Intel could be put in that box. You probably have a pretty good idea of your organization's culture already, but taking inventory and stepping outside (figuratively and literally) to look at it as others would is often advisable. If you manage by culture A in an organization with culture B, you are flirting with failure.

Company Politics

"Politics" is a term you'll hear often in informal business talk. "Politics" loosely refers to the maneuvering for power or influence in an organization to get support for one's ideas, to get resources, career opportunities, and so forth. How this maneuvering is done, how much there is, and how effective it is are all part of an organization's climate. Some organizations tolerate little of it—your role is your role, power comes from the top, and that's that. Other organizations take a more Darwinistic survival approach, and a highly politically charged work environment can result. The political climate will ultimately influence your management role and style.

Resources

Resources have more tangible effects. Working for a "deep pockets," cash-rich, profitable organization is different from working for a cash-strapped, "tight" organization. (If the organization has the resources but doesn't make them available, that's more of a "culture" issue). Some organizations have generous financial and intellectual resources (as in staffs of technical experts); some don't—either way, it will affect your actions as manager.

The discussion of environment will pop up again in several places in this book. For now, it's sufficient to say that environment—internal and external—has a lot to do with what you experience and what you do as a manager. No manager can be complete without understanding the environment to some extent; the *complete* and *effective* manager understands it *well*. It's part of the job.

Moving Ahead

From this point on, we switch gears from environment to examining what a manager *does*. Referring to Figure 2.1, dimensions of the managerial job include scope, roles, functions, and constituents. Scope is really the bridge between environment and specific duties of the manager; managers must wear marketing, operational, and financial "hats" to properly and completely interpret the external environment into actionable plans for the work group. Roles are things managers do in a higher-level sense, and include decision-making, managing people, and communicating. Functions are more specific task areas managers must do—and do in balance—to effect results in the workplace. Finally, constituents are the recipients of much of a manager's action—and are key inputs to the process as well.

The Scope of the Complete Manager

As we said, good managers wear marketing, operational, and financial hats. That doesn't mean that, in wearing your marketing hat, you work in the marketing department. Rather, it means that you are aware of what marketing does and how it impacts your business. You also are aware of what goes on in the marketplace itself, and how that impacts the business. You are also aware of how the output of your work group influences—and is accepted—in the marketplace.

Oh, and one other thing—the marketplace we're talking about isn't necessarily the external marketplace. As a manager, you have internal customers too—other work groups, other managers, even your employees. You must capture the needs of these constituents, and make sure your "product" meets their needs. Likewise, you need to be aware of the financial performance of the business and how you affect it; you must also be aware of how your actions and decisions affect the financial success of the department next door.

As you move higher in the organization, your scope will get larger and larger. You will have to consider the big picture more and more. We offer that the more you understand the big picture and its marketing, operational, and financial elements, the higher you will go. Let's explore a little about the marketing "you," the operational "you," and the financial "you."

You, as Marketer

The marketplace constantly sends signals that even the most detached manager should see. New products, product prices, customer demand, customer response to your products all, sooner or later, shape your product and ultimately your job. Your job as marketer is to see these signals and understand how they affect your part of the business.

The true Knock 'em Dead manager makes a special effort to see how the company's products are doing in the marketplace. For example, a manager in the PC printer business would check out store displays and talk to store clerks as well as customers and friends to get feedback. Not only does this help the manager see what lies ahead, but it may give her an idea or two that she can turn into rewardable innovation within the organization. At the very least, it will give her credibility and knowledge to more strongly influence the next organizational decision.

The Hewlett-Packard Company made the phrase "managing by wandering around" (MBWA) popular in the 1940s and 1950s. Then, it referred primarily to the workplace; that is, to see what was being done by your work group as well as other teams and to collect feedback firsthand. Nowadays it refers not only to wandering within the company but within the marketplace as well—the stores, the press, cyberspace, and other places where customers and your products appear. Yes, you could walk a lot of miles in those shoes.

Marketers think in terms of strategic and tactical marketing (see Chapter 8 for more detail on this subject). Making a very long story short, strategic marketers figure out what product will sell to what market. They think about how the product is positioned; that is, how it compares to the competitive offering (better, cheaper, easier to get, better supported, and so forth). They figure out how to sell it to that market—directly, through retailers, on the Web, and so forth. They also determine price and what features, accessories, and add-ons will sell more or better. They figure out how to build awareness in that market through branding and promotion. The list of variables goes on and on.

The Four Ps of Marketing

Marketing, as a business discipline, is a highly integrated set of activities that, taken all together, work to bring a product or service to market. The four Ps are a handy mnemonic—that is, a memory tool—to remember these activities. They are:

- **Product.** The definition, features, colors, functions, options, package, and services that go with the core product or service itself. For example, the box of detergent as it sits on the shelf and the 800-number customer hotline that goes with it.
- **Price.** The price charged for the product, but also quantity discounts and things like maintenance fees or costs of related products (for instance, the cost of razor blades, if you manufacture razors).
- **Promotion.** The visible form of marketing—advertising, publicity, special events, sales, coupons, and affiliations with other products and brands.
- **Place.** Where the product is sold and how it is delivered.

A fifth P might be positioning; that is, the strategic competitive placement of your product or service. For example, compared to your competitors, your four Ps might be a better product, a lower price, promotion to a target audience or niche, or placed with better retailers.

Tactical marketers determine the best ways to execute the marketing strategy—what kind of advertisements, promotions, offers, publicity, affiliations, loyalty incentives, and so forth—to move the product according to plan. The complete manager keeps up with the marketing strategy and also puts the tactical plans in place to execute that strategy.

What Is "Share of Customer"?

"Share of customer" is a contemporary marketing concept referring to the "mindshare" or "share of mind" your products, services, brands, and even your company gets from the customer. If the customer automatically thinks of your company and product when in the market, and is likely to "repeat purchase" without special incentive or new marketing promotions, you have high "share of customer." Given the high cost and relative ineffectiveness of much of today's mass marketing techniques, building share of customer is becoming an increasingly important marketing strategy. Companies such as Starbucks, Mercedes Benz, and Tiffany's use this strategy very successfully.

The Operational "You"

MBWA helps you to understand the operational components of the job or work group you manage. A walk on the production floor, in the shipping department, or through the customer lobby will always help. But just as it works in marketing, MBWA should take you outside to look at how others do similar jobs, what new tools and processes are available, and what third-party services might be available at what cost. Even if you manage the third-shift janitorial operation, you should know what new cleaning products and methods are out there, what the cost of labor is, how your supply chain works, and what can be outsourced. It will affect your job and your employees sooner or later, so if you are proactive, you'll do a better job and be recognized for it.

What Is Outsourcing?

Outsourcing is the acquisition of goods and services from outside organizations, in contrast to making or developing them yourself. Subcontracting is a form of outsourcing. Many companies—particularly large ones—choose to define, assemble, and market a product, but don't produce the components that make up the product. Companies avoid the detail, overhead, and distraction involved in hiring lower-level unskilled and skilled workers to produce the actual nuts and bolts, and outsource that part of production instead. The reason: to reduce cost and stay flexible in order to respond to changes in the marketplace and business climate. You'd be surprised what firms outsource these days: customer service representatives, sales force, even research and development, and human resources activities. As a manager, you will almost certainly have to manage some outsourced inputs into the business.

As . . .	Duties

Marketing manager	• Keen observer of marketplace
	   • Customer acceptance
	   • Competition
	• Strategic marketing
	   • Product, price, promotion, place
	   • Campaigns, loyalty, "share of customer"
	• Inside and outside organization

Operations manager	• Technical "expert": production, service delivery methods • Product delivery and product support • Supply chain
Financial manager	• Financial performance of business • Financial performance of department or work unit • Cost and profit drivers for the work unit and the business

Figure 2-2. The Scope of a Manager

The Financial "You"

The days when finance was completely left to the accountants and bookkeepers is gone. While they still have a strong role and do a lot of the "heavy lifting" in terms of keeping the financial house in order, you as manager need to be aware of your external (and internal) financial environment. How much money do your competitors make producing similar products or services? What are the costs? What are the profit margins? What kind of equipment do they have and how much does it cost? Are these companies financially successful? Are their stock prices rising or falling? At what volumes does the business operate efficiently? Financial savvy supports better decision-making; those managers without financial savvy tend to make poorer decisions and, moreover, have less credibility with their organizations.

To become a more complete, Knock 'em Dead manager, you should discover and learn all of these disciplines and how they are applied in the business. Your first job as manager is to accomplish the specific objective and output assigned to you by the organization (or by the customer, if self-employed). But beyond that, as a complete manager, you'll be involved with the marketing, operational, and financial success of the organization, and will see greater rewards if you bring complete understanding of the business to the table.

Let's move on to further uncover what the manager actually does in the workplace. We start with the roles that a manager plays—as decision-maker, people manager, and communicator, then move on to examine how a manager plays those roles in their functions as planner, organizer, staffer, leader, and controller.

Three "All the Time" Management Roles

If this starts to get confusing, we sympathize. Arguably, one could say a complete Knock 'em Dead manager plays the roles of marketer, operations manager, and financial manager, which we defined as the scope of a manager. Now, it's important to "get down to brass tacks" and describe the specific things a manager does in the job. The roles we identify next is decision-maker, people manager, and communicator. You play these roles simultaneously while executing the functions of management: planning, organizing, staffing, leading, and controlling. And you play these roles all the while you are marketer, operations manager, and financier.

Still not clear? Let's try an example. As a parent (for those of you who aren't parents, try to imagine!) you play the role of decision-maker at all times (unless your child is thirteen or older—we won't get into that). You play that role as you execute a function as a family—perhaps eating dinner, going on vacation, or whatever. You play that role inside the scope of your duties—as father or mother figure, as teacher, as coach, as explainer and interpreter of the outside world, and as role model or example. You are decision-maker. For that matter, you are people manager and communicator, too, at all times, in all situations, in your family, as parent. Are we getting somewhere now?

As Decision-Maker

Decision-makers, naturally, make decisions. Through decisions, large and small, they guide their work group and the larger organization through arrays of choices. How well—and how quickly—they do this is a defining quality of an effective manager.

We'll examine the art and science of decision-making in a later chapter. For now, it's worth pointing out the duties of a manager as decision-maker include identifying alternatives, evaluating the alternatives, making assumptions, making choices, communicating and validating choices with the organization, and measuring and evaluating the downstream effects. These decisions can be large or small, short- or long-term, or strategic. They can cover the gamut from major strategic planning choices down to solving today's problems on the production line or with the French fryer. They can be about people, places, or things. Managers are paid to make decisions, help the organization with bigger strategic decisions, and make sure the decisions *work.*

As People Manager

The role of people manager is the first thing that jumps to mind when you mention the word "management" to most people. As a people manager, you must interact with individuals inside and outside the group to deliver results. This is where the "getting things done through others" definition of management hits the ground running. In managing people, a manager must understand those people—their motives, their needs, their histories, their personalities. Then the manager makes decisions about what those people can and should do, and what they should *know.*

The effective manager plans, motivates, and provides feedback to the people within her group. A manager positions her needs and accomplishments outside the group. A manager develops teamwork within the team and outside the team. Finally, a manager evaluates performance, provides feedback, solves problems, and coaches and develops people. Along the way, the good manager is positive, friendly, accessible, and easy to communicate with—all things we refer to as "people skills." As the rest of this book unfolds, we'll highlight many of the other things that make a good people manager.

As Communicator

W. Somerset Maugham once said that "money is like a sixth sense, without which you cannot make as effective use of the others." In a similar way, communication is perhaps the "sixth sense" of management, because without it, you can't use the other skills as effectively. We can't exaggerate the importance of communication in business and in management. Why? Because, nine times out of ten, whatever else you do while wearing a manager's hat bears less consequence if not communicated well.

Communicating in this context means communicating with your people and with your team as a unit. Communication is spoken, written, electronic, and, yes, nonverbal. It is regular, formal communication and irregular, informal, "hallway" conversations. It goes two ways—outbound "talking" and inbound "listening."

Every manager has a communication style. While style does vary among managers, it must serve the multiple purposes of (1) allowing critical input and feedback and (2) conveying your messages effectively to ensure being listened to and heard by others. Communication sent but not received or understood is noise; communication received that is stifled or made difficult is valuable information lost.

Communication happens within your team but also with others in your organization, and often with others outside your organization (partners, customers, and so on). As manager, you must be able not only to communicate results, but also to "be heard" as a vital element in the organization's success. Today's managers must publicize—must *market*—their accomplishments to establish credibility and influence their organization. As organizations get larger and business moves more quickly, it is more important to be *heard.* Those who aren't heard are more vulnerable to the next downsizing, the next strategy shift, the next outsourcing campaign.

It is simply not enough to get the job done; you must build credibility and influence in your organization to maintain the chance for long-term success. Even if we were not the authors of *Knock 'em Dead Business Presentations* (Adams Media, 2002), we would still be saying this. That book saves us from having to explore the details of business communications in this book, but where appropriate we do make reference to the why, when, and how, of business communication.

Let's review the three roles of a manager and the associated duties in Figure 2.3.

Roles	Duties
Decision-maker	• Identify and evaluate alternatives • Establish assumptions • Make choices; decide • Communicate choices; delegate • Follow up and measure effect of choices; take corrective action • Solve problems
People manager	• Understand needs and motives • Interact • Provide direction, advice, coaching • Solve problems • Evaluate performance, provide feedback, develop skills, foster growth
Communicator	• Listen • Keep team members informed; two-way information conduit • Keep others outside organization informed

Figure 2-3. Three Roles of a Manager

Now, the Five Functions of Managing

Management scholars and scientists have written about the functions of management for years, and while each version is slightly different, all have, more or less, the same list of management functions: planning, organizing, staffing, leading, and controlling.

All managers at all levels of any organization—including individual contributor managers—perform these five functions at some level. The amount of effort spent on each one may vary greatly with the type of position and level within the organization. For example, the fast food store manager will spend more time staffing and controlling, while a chief marketing officer might spend more time planning and leading. Unlike the roles, which are played at all times, managers spend time on one function, then another, according to the situation. But all managers in all organizations, large or small, public or private, technical or people oriented, experience all five functions in their jobs, to some degree. Here is a deeper look at the five functions of management.

Planning

"Planning" means developing a plan to get from here to there. Planning involves identifying the "there"; that is, the goal, what the team or group of individuals wants to achieve, in specific terms. Planning also identifies the "how to get there"; that is, the structured set of strategies and resources required to get to the goal. An organization or team without a plan is unlikely to accomplish anything. It is the manager's imperative to create a plan, get "buy in" within the organization and externally, manage team activities according to it, and adjust it when necessary. Neglect in any of these areas can endanger success or cause failure.

It may seem that planning is a stand-alone activity, and that one chapter devoted specifically to planning would suffice. Not so—some degree of planning is required for all functions and aspects of management. Nearly every managing job requires a certain amount of formal planning; that is, a formalized effort to document and implement plans for an organization. Formal planning, which includes a structured goal, a strategy, and delegation, is covered in Chapter 8.

Organizing

The next step, once a plan is in place (or at least started) is to get organized. Organizing means grouping and deploying resources—human and otherwise—in the best way possible to achieve the plan. Creating teams, assigning leadership and responsibility, and delegating tasks are all part of organizing.

Organizing usually happens during the beginning of a management assignment or execution of a business plan. Organizing is more art than science, requiring subjective judgment on which resources should be allocated to which tasks. When the resources are people, this becomes a matter of instinct and interpretation of past performance as much as anything else. Organizing comes up in Chapter 3 and again throughout Part III where we discuss building teams and handling people.

Staffing

If you were to read "old" management texts and articles, the staffing function might not appear. "Staffing" refers to the acquisition and building of a work team. It includes finding people and resources to do the job, but also includes the less obvious area of deciding what kinds of resources are needed in the first place. Times have changed to the point where "throwing people at problems" is *not* the right course in most cases; now managers have more resource choices at their disposal. *Whether* or not to outsource, *what* to outsource, *when* to outsource all become part of the staffing function in its expanded sense. As may be obvious already, the functions of "organizing" and "staffing" work hand in hand.

In many organizations, most of the responsibility of obtaining staff have shifted from the personnel or human resources (HR) department to the manager who will actually manage the resources. The role of HR has become more administrative; today HR is more often a function taken on by the manager to find the right candidates, particularly lower- or middle-level staff. Managers are required to network, be it in their community organizations or their industry, to find the right people to get the job done. Arguably, this is the best course, because the manager responsible for getting the job done has more control over the resources. This illustrates the expanding role of managers already discussed.

And does staffing stop with the hiring decision? Unequivocally, no. Once you hire someone, you can't just give that person a desk, a phone, or a French-fry machine, and expect stellar results. Good training is part of effective staffing; it is your responsibility to make your employees and other resources more productive. In today's more complex environment, that usually means more than "getting the knack of" shoveling coal or bolting wheels on a car. Even a fryer cook must occasionally step in to run the register or handle a customer complaint. Good training means getting your staff off to a good start and cross-training and developing them so that they can do a more complete job. The elements of staffing are covered in Chapter 4.

Leading

Leading is probably the most challenging function of a manager, and arguably the most differentiating characteristic of a *good* manager. Many individuals can plan, organize, staff, and communicate, but only a select few can truly lead an organization. Leading means not only making decisions and directing the course of action; it also means motivating people to do a good job through effective planning, communication, and, last but not least, rewards for accomplishment. It requires getting people to think in alignment with you and the organization, not simply go through the motions. Motion without motivation works for a while but has its limits for producing sustainable results.

Leadership also implies managing change. Leaders typically take their organizations to new places. In some cases—as the 1914 South Pole explorer Ernest Shackleton would brilliantly exemplify—it takes exceptional leadership just to prevent disaster. Shackleton, who risked his life to save his crew, is an extreme example, but there are Lee Iacocca, who resurrected Chrysler, and others serving as examples on a smaller scale.

Leadership is a rare blend of people and process skills including listening, decision-making, communicating, evaluating results, and taking corrective actions. However, there is no formula for leadership; it requires a certain personality, and a blending of personality with organization that we call a leadership style. There are many ways to lead, and many good styles of leadership. The style you learn and choose will be a function of your personality and your company's environment; it is generally not something that can be learned from a book. We'll focus on the nuances and importance of leadership in Chapter 7, and as they occur throughout the book.

Controlling

A manager's job is not complete without a continuous and robust assessment of results against goals. Controlling means making sure things are done within the confines of operational rules and planned goals, and taking corrective action where deviations exist. Managers who can plan but can't keep track of execution or apply corrective action, are less likely to succeed. Controlling includes the assessment of individual performance and coaching and development of that individual, which is covered in detail in Chapter 5. Performance measurement and managing progress toward goals are taken up in Chapter 8.

Figure 2.4 reviews the five functions of a manager and the duties that go along with each function.

What is the difference between a manager and a leader?
Managers work inside the structure, define the structure, and run the structure. They are responsible for policies, procedures, schedules, process, incentives, and administration. They keep the structure running, keep it on course, and keep it productive.

Leaders move the structure in new directions, and may work *beyond* the structure. They have vision, face new challenges, manage change, seek innovation, and sometimes take risks. As people managers, leaders strive for congruence in thought, not just action.

Function	Duties
Planning	• Converting external business environment into meaningful team goals • Structuring strategies and resources to get to the goals • Articulating the plan inside and outside the team
Organizing	• Defining and creating teams; informal and formal organization structures • Assigning the right responsibility to the right team members • Communicating responsibility to team members and outside the team
Staffing	• Determining what resources are required • Obtaining those resources
Leading	• Listening • Motivating • Providing direction as needed
Controlling	• Rewarding accomplishments • Monitoring results • Problem resolution; taking corrective action • Performance appraisal and coaching

Figure 2-4. Five Functions of the Manager

Keeping Your "Customers" Happy

As a manager, you must satisfy many "customers," or constituents affected by you and the outcome of your work. When you take inventory of all the people within and outside your organization affected or influenced by you and your work, you're likely to find a staggeringly long list. Some are obviously more affected than others—you will have your "A" list of critical customers, then a list of others who may have some interest but aren't critically affected. You get the point—there are lots of people and even whole organizations affected by your work. A good Knock 'em Dead manager understands these relationships and what these various constituents need—and consistently tries to meet those needs.

Customers

Anybody in business has customers. Whether they are "real" customers on the other side of the cash register, or internal customers in your organization, they are customers and they need to be taken care of.

The fast food outlet manager will focus mainly on "real" customers. The production line manager should keep "real" customers in mind, because ultimately the customers will benefit from the product. But more than likely there are several intermediary customers—the next production line; the shipping department; the marketer or salesperson selling the product. And don't forget the sales channel as an intermediary customer. If you are building a packaged product, for instance, the quality and effect of the package are very important, as are such things as on-time delivery and traditional product quality.

Every manager should size up the needs of the customer base, whether internal or external, and continuously track how well the company is meeting these needs.

Employees

It almost goes without saying that employees are a key management constituent. Yet, with poor managers, employees often fall somewhere toward the bottom of the list of critical customers. If you don't have employees (or team members) somewhere close to the top of your list, and if they aren't garnering a sizable chunk of your attention, something is probably wrong. How much attention employees receive usually depends on the nature of the job. If you're managing a union shop, employees will be on the top of your mind. If you're managing a small, well trained, and experienced work force, these employees will typically require less direct attention—but don't forget, they have needs, too.

Like customers, you want to understand employee needs, and go a step further to understand their motives and work history, and how the world looks through their eyes. Effective managers get the job done while satisfying employee needs. Did we say "while?" Often, it is *through* satisfying employee needs. Remember, Job No. 1 for the effective manager is to create an environment for employees to succeed.

Peers

Peer managers can be some of the most difficult and elusive constituents. Depending on the organization, the relationship between peers is often poorly defined. Moreover, there may be a natural conflict or competition between peers. For example, performance measures and organizational imperatives may pit two production line managers against each other, rewarding the one who produces the most. Likewise, for the fast food manager, the manager of the next outlet across town is a peer, and the relationship may be competitive.

Similarly, the nature of job functions may create tension or conflict between peers. Typically, marketing and operations people don't always see the world the same way. Marketing wants to sell whatever the customer wants—a product with a completely customized set of features delivered yesterday. Production, of course, can't do that, and wants to produce the same thing for everybody. Marketing wants to spend money. Finance wants to save money. Production wants to invest in equipment. Finance wants to see the return on investment (ROI) before the check is even cut.

Peers may get in the way at times, but more often than not, they can help you. In the case of competitive peers, they see the world through the same eyes as you do. It helps to build a good relationship because somewhere down the line, they will help *you* out. For example, if you're in marketing, it's good to build a positive relationship with the production manager, because then he will be more likely to help you out when you need help. The key is to understand your peers, what their motives and issues are, and to build a positive and productive relationship with them. The golden rule applies: Do unto others as they would do unto you.

Higher Managers

Ah—the Boss, the Big Cheese, the Top Hat, the Big Kahuna. That your boss is a constituent goes without question. Obviously, what you accomplish on the job must please the boss. But it goes further—the effective manager knows how to *manage* the boss.

There are numerous examples of managers who are very effective at managing their work groups or teams, but fall apart in their relationship with their boss. Like an employee, that boss can have many needs, motives, and a unique style. But the boss also has something that makes your relationship with him unique—the boss has "position power," which is authority granted by virtue of the position itself.

That boss may consume far more time and energy than really necessary, or may stay detached, only to show up when least expected demanding something be done yesterday. The key for the manager is to understand the needs of the boss and then develop (and maybe agree on) an effective work style that works for both. Too many managers don't own up to this responsibility. They assume the boss is the boss, and they must passively respond to whatever goes. Not true. Good managers are proactive with their boss in every way. They try to anticipate needs, and deliver results or information before it is needed. They establish the work "rules," or protocol, at the outset. Just as a manager should make it easy for employees to do their jobs, they should also make it easier for the higher manager to do his job.

The Biggest Test

Every management position has its challenges, from the CEO to the middle manager to the first-line supervisor to the individual contributor or network manager. The challenges will be different, and will occur in different proportions, but each position has its "biggest test."

CEOs have bottom-line responsibility for everything, and must deal with complex conceptual issues quickly and with little room for error. They have a lot of position power, but must look after a great many people and things—all at once.

Middle managers probably have the most diverse set of tasks and responsibilities, driving vision and strategy, managing people, leading, problem solving, and so on. They have position power, but the unique nature of the position between top and bottom means that they must deal with a lot of pressure from both directions—above and below. Middle managers must carry a lot of personal power (the ability to influence) into the position. First-line supervisors must exhibit strong people skills, problem solving skills, and an enduring nose-to-the-grindstone focus on results.

Finally, we get to the individual contributors—the project, product, or program managers with no direct reports. These network managers often carry one of the greatest management challenges, which is to get complex tasks done with *little to no* position power whatsoever. Everything these individuals accomplish comes about through sheer personal influence. They must obtain support from other teams throughout the organization. They must beg, borrow, steal, and wire together solutions however they can. They must communicate like crazy. They must exhibit true leadership to the hilt, to get others to follow with mind and body without any sort of formal authority. Our hats go off to this unique and talented organizational species—this book is for *you,* too.

Summary

There are many dimensions to the management job. As a new (or existing) manager, you should take the time to think about these dimensions. Look at your job, and think about the internal and external environment, the marketing, operational, and financial aspects of not only the job but also the business. Then try to internalize your roles—as decision-maker, people manager, and communicator. Understand the functions you deliver to the organization (the "how" of delivering those functions comes up in the following chapters). Last but not least, think of your constituents. Remember that the effective manager manages well up, down, and sideways in the organization. Also remember that in managing, as in life, the golden rule always applies.

3 | Getting Started: Stepping into a Management Role

The first few days, weeks, and months of a new management role are critical—learn how to capitalize on your "golden moment."

The management "torch" now rests in your hands. How you got it doesn't really matter. The torch may have been passed on for you to manage an existing team or organization. Or you may be charged with building an entirely new staff or program. Perhaps you're already in charge, but have been given "marching orders" to reorganize and restructure a department. Regardless of the specific situation, every manager faces a "Day One"; most seasoned managers face Day One over and over again during their careers as they take on new teams and new responsibilities.

Understandably there may be a few butterflies in your stomach. Very well—that is perfectly normal. Frankly, if you didn't have the willies, we might diagnose you as a bit overconfident or cocky. From the time you accept the new assignment to the time you take charge may be quite long or ridiculously short. ("Can you take charge of this project team and prepare a senior management update by Friday?" is a mandate often heard in today's fleet-footed business world.) In either case, it is a time to ponder carefully and get your act in order. Why? Because the first few days can be *the* most critical period of your entire management assignment. During this time, "golden moments" emerge, during which you and your ideas can really connect with the organization. Do it right, and you pave the way to a smooth assignment. Do it wrong, and you may face bumps and ruts for the duration.

Golden Moments

In this chapter, you may notice that we talk about starting out in a management role, even before explaining the philosophy and processes of management. Is it out of sequence? Should we be learning the facts and principles, and *only then* how to apply them? Well, that "orthodox" approach might work here, too, but we've found from experience that most managers don't have time to read a whole book before starting, and their golden moments disappear quickly.

What is a golden moment? It is that magical period when, right away, you *learn* the most and *influence* the most. Your team, your customers, your peers, and your managers are excited by your new presence and expect you to do and say important things—things important *to them.* They want to find out about you just as you want to find out about them. They want to learn your style and what works with you, just as you want to learn the same of them. They want to see you in action, and are naturally curious about what you bring to the table. It is like the golden moment for a public speaker—that hushed anxiety at the beginning of the speaker's presentation when the audience is riveted and excitement looms in the air. Most golden moments for a speaker occur at the beginning but they also occur during highlights and transitions throughout the speech.

Golden moments in management occur throughout your assignment, too, and as with a speech, many occur at the beginning and can be most critical for your long-term success. In the beginning, people are "all ears" to find out more about you, help you, establish a good rapport with you, and become your "best buddy" in the workplace. Naturally it's important not to squander these golden moments.

Not Too Fast, Not Too Slow

The first few weeks or months can make or break you as a manager. Why? Because during that period of time you will build the basis for sustained relationships with your team, as well as other individuals, managers, and divisions outside your immediate group. You can quickly assess what is going on, and add a dose of outside experience and perspective, that others inside the team don't have. You will bring new ideas and "aha's" to the table about the work, and your organization will expect you to do that. You will probably make changes, and the organization will expect that, too. But guess what? You walk a fine line; if you come on too hard and too fast, and try to make unwanted changes that are unfounded or too hasty, the organizational "antibodies" will rise up and resist you every step of the way. So approaching a new management position is not unlike guiding a space capsule toward re-entry into the Earth's atmosphere. Enter too fast, and the dense resistance of Earth's air will cause you to flame out and crash to Earth as a burnt cinder. Enter too slowly, and you'll bounce off and head forever into outer space. You will have no impact, and the organization will go on as it did before; as if you weren't there. But unlike the job facing the astronauts, which today is an exact science of mathematical calculations, finding the right angle of entry into a management position is as much art as science. In any case, it is of utmost importance.

Four Steps to Getting Started

The rest of this chapter guides you through the key steps involved in starting out in a new management role: getting organized, connecting, evaluating, and building.

1. **Getting organized** is the first part of "getting started." Getting organized means getting your act together—yes—mainly in a housekeeping sense. This is your chance, for once you start actively managing, you never get a chance to return to this preparatory step.
2. **Connecting** involves getting to know your team and the organization, establishing lines of communication, observing, listening, and generally weaving yourself into the organization's fabric.
3. **Evaluating** is the art and science of assessing strengths and weaknesses of your group and organization, and the individuals in it. Your evaluation should also identify the most important opportunities to address first. As you evaluate, you begin to map out a vision and a plan for what needs to be done, and what you want to accomplish.
4. **Building** is part of your planning process; you build communication paths, networks, and protocol for getting things done. Along the way, you line up key resources to get the job done, and set expectations with your team, your peers, and the more senior managers who'll be watching.

As we explore these steps in more detail, you may notice that they appear to overlap. For example, as you get organized, you will begin the process of connecting with individuals in the organization—maybe with the information technology (IT) folks who set up your e-mail. As you connect, you will begin to evaluate the people, the departments they are in, and the job they do. As you evaluate, you will begin to plan. ("Mary over here is really the expert and 'star' of this group—wonder how I can deploy her to get that 'new new thing' done.") As you plan you begin to build—in your mind, anyway—*how* you will accomplish what you want to accomplish.

Remember: Stay Flexible

As is true with most management processes, the "getting started" process is not like a recipe out of a cookbook You don't start with Step 1, end with Step 4, brush the dust off your hands, and move on to the next set of tasks. Becoming a manager is rather more organic than that. In evaluating and building you may realize that you must connect with another team to get the work done or accomplish the objective. Your initial planning may make perfect sense and be accepted "right off the bat"—but more likely, you will adapt and adjust to valid inputs you pick up along the way. It is particularly important to be flexible as you launch yourself into a management position. Otherwise, you will both alienate the teams you work with and miss important cues to steer your launch in the right direction.

A Dose of Leadership

But don't be *too* flexible in the opening stages. If team members and peers sense they can "play the experience card" and talk you out of everything, your golden moment for influencing your team will vanish. After all, you are assigned or hired to influence the organization and its outcomes—in other words, to get your way. At this early stage elements of leadership enter the picture. You must get your team to see some things the way you do very early in the game. Forcing your will or coercing others doesn't work over the long term, and can lead to some pretty gnarly beginnings, particularly for new managers.

The right approach is to defer to the team's experience and judgment at times, while sticking up for your own at others. Your people want to be involved in your Day-One exercise, too; they want their chance to shape the initial outcome of your tenure. While you exercise your influence, it is good to let them exercise theirs, so they feel some degree of importance and self-determination in their roles. A good adage to remember: People who create tend to support. That is, people involved in the process of creating something—a product, an organization, a new beginning—tend to support its development and outcome. You can envision what happens when people are denied the opportunity to participate.

Not Negotiable

You need to remember that managing a team is not a matter of negotiation. "I'll do Task No. 1 and No. 2 your way, if you'll do Task No. 3 and Program No. 4 my way" usually doesn't work. Time and energy tend to get wasted on arriving at these negotiated solutions, and, as competitive urges start to surface, everybody on the team starts thinking in terms of "winning." You don't want to negotiate with your team, nor do you want to set up a situation where they judge their success on how much goes their way. Again, leadership is the key— getting people to see things your way while allowing them some freedom to do things their way to achieve your way.

Making the Most of Your Golden Moments

So why do we provide this "getting started" guide here in Chapter 3, not at the end of the book? To help you get through the first days of your assignment, take advantage of golden moments, and to get things off on the right foot. You can read the rest later to improve and refine your technique. If you're in the middle of an assignment you may find this helpful to recover lost ground and prepare for your next assignment.

Step 1: Get Organized

Getting organized may sound like a menial task, something administrative, obvious, basic, and wished upon you more often by your mother than anyone else as you were growing up. True, it does resemble cleaning up your room in some ways, but it goes further than that. The main idea is to prepare yourself for the avalanche—yes, *avalanche*—of information and activity that inevitably follows.

Is getting organized important? In a word, yes. To underscore the importance, let's take a look at the frustration of dealing with a manager who *isn't* organized. Everyone has had one of those, right? He can't remember your appointment. Everything gets rescheduled. Phone calls aren't returned, e-mail boxes are full, and worst of all, he can't remember what *you* said nor what *he* said yesterday. So much wasted communication, so much backtracking and reworking, so much confusion on who is doing what, what's been done, and what needs to be done. You can't find him, you can't communicate effectively with him, and everything seems to take twice as much effort to get done.

Yes, getting organized is designed to remedy this, and the single best time to get organized is at the beginning. You're not likely to get another chance. Not only will you not have enough time, but once others perceive you as disorganized, that impression sticks. Being organized isn't just common sense—it's part of your personal public relations plan. So, organize yourself. Set up your desk, get project and employee files, set up e-mail and voice mail and so forth. Sounds basic, but many managers eager to hit the ground running without having the basics in place can find the initial going frustrating—or worse.

We won't go into so much detail as to recommend a certain size or model of calendar, specific voice-mail greetings, or specific staff meeting formats. Some books do this, down to the point of evaluating the differences between 8½-by-11-inch daily calendars and 5-by-8-inch weekly calendars. Everyone is different and every situation is different. But we do have a few recommendations.

Get a Calendar

We're not too picky about what kind of calendar, whether it hangs on a wall, sits on a desk, or arrives electronically through your laptop or PDA (personal digital assistant). The point is, you'll need to keep track of meetings and key due dates somehow. We like the following features in a calendar:

- **Immediate access.** You will need to check your calendar frequently, both to manage your own time and allocate time to others. "Can you attend a meeting at 2:30 next Monday" is a request you'll need to respond to immediately. So don't set up your only calendar on a laptop you access infrequently. Don't set up calendars on your wall or on your desk blotter if you spend even small amounts of time away from the office. Calendars that aren't immediately accessible don't get used, and calendars that aren't used have no value.
- **Space for simple phrases and lists.** A calendar should have enough space to write a descriptive phrase or two for important time milestones. The phrase "decide project launch date" is more effective than just "meeting." Better yet, leave space to write ideas and to do's of your own. A good calendar depicts not only important time commitments but

also your important to do's for a particular time block. That way, all the day's important tasks—whether inner directed or outer directed—can be found in one place.

- **Easily accessed by others.** More and more, people need to access your calendar, and guess what? You'll be unavailable to tell them what time you *are* available, because you're already in a meeting or traveling. For those in "wired" offices, technology offers solutions—the networked Microsoft Outlook calendar. If you have an administrative assistant, give him or her a copy. You can also set up someone in your group as a dedicated calendar keeper to maintain everyone's calendar. In some work environments, the "in" and "out" board works, and should be considered if it helps everyone make the most efficient use of their time.

To PDA or Not to PDA?

Modern technology, among other things, provides some wonderful solutions geared toward boosting office (and manager) efficiency. The PDA, or personal digital assistant, is a prime example. With a PDA at your fingertips, you can control your calendar; keep track of important facts, figures, lists, and phone numbers; and, with the right connections, even keep up with e-mail. Palm and the HP/Compaq IPAQ are the major brands. Should you get one? The rule of thumb for these devices (and all others) is, they are good options *if you get more out of them than you put into them.* If it takes more time to input lists, calendar items, and phone numbers than it saves to retrieve them, these devices don't make sense. And don't forget time spent learning how to use them (and effort expended recovering data when the batteries fail). In short, you must get really good at *using* these devices to get the promised payback. We don't think these devices are completely "there" yet, unless you have a technology bent or they provide some "killer app," such as real-time calculations, that you might need. Check back with us when PDAs include a cell phone.

Files, Files, Files

Again, a long drawn-out treatise on filing and organizing a desk is well outside our scope. Having said that, it is important to get your hands on important information left by your predecessors—employee files, old department and project plans, and so forth. You will want to devote a lot of time in the beginning to perusing these files, particularly if you're very new to the organization or team. Most new managers do this at night or away from the office—just try to allocate the time to do it and do it well. You'll pick up important facts and reasoning for why things are the way they are. If nothing else, you'll figure out where everything is for future reference. And like all else in this section, if you don't do it in the beginning, you'll likely not get time to do it later, and many tasks will result either in frantic file searches or reinvention of something that was done before.

In today's world, "files" means not only physical, paper-based files, but also stored computer files, including files of data, old presentations, project plans, employee evaluations, and so forth. Depending on the situation, you may get access to some, all, or none of this, but make sure to inquire about information stored electronically.

It may be too early to set up and organize new files. You don't know yet what you will need to file, nor a file's relative importance. Still, it's a good idea to set up physical (and/or electronic) locations for at least a few things— employee files, department plans and strategies, suppliers, vendors, customers, and whatever other categories are key success drivers. The "desktop pile" filing method seldom works for long.

"You Have Reached the Voice Mail Box Of . . ."

Setting up clear communication channels is obviously important. Anything that impedes communication will cause trouble sooner or later. Make sure your voice mail is set up correctly and has appropriate greetings. Get yourself set up on e-mail and make sure it works. If you travel a lot, make sure you get proper phone and e-mail connections so that you aren't "dark" while gone. Get a phone card or account so that you can call back to the office, or a cell phone if your organization permits. Also, set up lines of communication and authority to handle tasks while you're gone, particularly those not requiring your full attention. The rule of thumb: Think through what others might experience as they try to contact you when you're not available. Is it what you would want to experience? Is it effective? Or is valuable information and action likely to be lost.

Internet E-mail

You may not have a laptop, or you may have security layers that are too hard to crack to make remote e-mail worthwhile. How do you stay connected to e-mail? Set up your own Internet e-mail account and share the address with key individuals. Such accounts can be set up on Yahoo! (*www.yahoo.com*) or MSN/Hotmail (*www.hotmail.com*) for free. You can access these accounts from anywhere, any time.

Step 2: Connect

As you settle into your new management assignment, one of the first and most important steps you should take is to establish communications—to introduce yourself—to your team and others outside. This is the "look and listen" stage, where you get to know your people and what's going on with their work. The initial golden moments of your management assignment are filled with precious openings to start relationships on the right foot. Try to do it later, and you're asking for trouble. Establishing open dialogue and clear communication early on makes the going easier later; barriers created at the outset are hard to get rid of. Developing relationships, dialogue, and discovery are the main objectives of this stage.

Formal and Informal

The look-and-listen process has both formal and informal elements. You will want to set up specific times to meet and talk to your employees, peers, team members, and outside managers. Be sure to set an agenda and desired outcome for each of these meetings. You will use these meetings to establish relationships, find out important facts, and form impressions, both about the people and the work. Never underestimate the importance of these get-togethers.

Tour the Plant, and Go Outside

By necessity there will be a lot of informal "wandering around" when you are in the process of connecting with a new organization. You will want to "tour the plant" to learn where everything is and how everything fits together to deliver your organization's product. You will learn where your team's "product" fits in to the whole. But you will also pick up little signals about people's work styles, attitudes, what's important, and what's not. Every new manager should tour the plant.

Beyond that, every new manager should tour what's outside the immediate plant: suppliers, customers, and other work teams upstream or downstream from yours. Talk to your suppliers; look at their Web sites. Ditto for customers. Even better, if you have a customer service or call center, set yourself up to listen in on some phone calls to learn about your customers, their issues, your business, and how your company handles customer problems. If you sell to customers in person or through a retail channel, spend some time observing customers making their purchases. If there are other physical locations in your business, set up a time to visit them and introduce yourself to the people working there.

Get to Know Your Staff

This one seems obvious, but it is amazing how often it gets pushed further and further down the to-do list, as a new manager gets immersed in myriad duties. Guess what happens then? It *never* happens!

A new manager should set up a one-on-one meeting with each employee. These are usually short, perhaps one- or two-hour affairs. They can be in the office, at lunch, or someplace outside. It is important to keep these meetings interruption- and distraction-free in order to get undivided attention and honest comments—employees may act differently or not tell as much if others are present.

The one-on-one should cover both job-related and personal subjects. You want to know the individual as a person—interests, background, and motivations. You also want to know what the employee has done and can do for the organization. You want to get his impressions of how well things are going, and the plusses and minuses of the work environment. You want to get a sense for how well he understands the business and fits into it. You want to discover his successes and failures. You want to find out what he believes he is good at, and not so good at—and why. If he has ideas for how to make things better, listen in.

If he has something to say about his own skills and performance, listen, but don't let it become a gripe session. And make sure you tap him for an impression of the previous manager, which can tell you *a lot* about what you face in the new role. Finally, it is important that these discussions are as candid as possible, and that the employee feels no threat for sharing important information.

Remember, employees are as interested in finding out about you as you are in finding out about them. Make sure to allocate time to discuss your background, experiences, previous jobs, interests, strengths, weaknesses (yes, weaknesses), and motivation. Employees who see you communicate openly will do likewise. But for heaven's sake, don't take up all the time talking about you! Think about what kind of impression *that* would leave.

Don't neglect the golden moment to get to know your employees. Not only will you establish valuable lines of communication, but it makes the next step—evaluation—much easier. You will be able to use your knowledge and solid impressions of the employees to evaluate who fits where; to find the right jobs for the right people; and to build the most effective and efficient task alignment.

The Cake Test

One senior vice president of a major U.S. technology company took a management metaphor from her mother's kitchen: the cake test. By simply looking at the outside you can't know for sure if a cake is completely cooked, but you can stick a toothpick in it to see if any batter sticks. If the toothpick comes out clean, that indicates that it's probably done. Good managers apply that metaphor to examining their business. You can't know everything or have all the information you may need at any given time; however, as you wander around, you can use the cake test. For example, ask an employee on the production line to explain what she's doing and how well it's going. Ask a similar question of the administrative personnel. Another employee here, a manager there, maybe a customer and a supplier, heck, maybe the guy in the mailroom. The bottom line: It pays to poke around. It shows people that you take your job seriously. These cake tests will also give you great insights without investing the overwhelming effort to understand everything everywhere. You can use the same tactic later on to evaluate results.

Step 3: Evaluating—"Seeing" the Whys and Hows

The opening phases and golden moments of your management assignment are all about your powers of observation. Not simply looking and watching, but *seeing* and *observing*. There's a difference. The keen observer not only watches and "sees" activity, but strives to understand that activity and the "why" behind that activity. Why is the department organized the way it is? Why is a particular stack of papers kept by the receiving door? Why is there a Monday morning war-room meeting to discuss customer service issues? Why did Mary Sue just get reassigned from finance to production?

You can see that some of these observations are driven by sight, but many others come from understanding events and occurrences. So don't just stand there and look—ask questions. Learn the history of your staff, your department, and your organization. Not just *what* happened, as if you were studying in high school history class, but *why* it happened.

This also goes a step further. Perceptive observation not only delves into the "why," but also the "how" of the workplace. As manager, you need a clean, clear sense of how things really work in the organization. How do decisions really get made? How does delegation work best? Does your team work independently? Do tasks have to be spelled out, or can your staff think on its feet? How much structure does your staff require? Are good results rewarded, and bad results corrected? To know all of this you must ask a lot of questions—of team members, peers, and upper managers. You may have been brought in to create some change, but you will be better off if you don't knock heads with the current way of doing things.

Cake testing is a good tactic here—ask a lot of "what if" questions and try a few experiments. Ask a peer manager, "What would happen if I tried to delegate the monthly report to Brian?" or "What if I asked Emily to lock up the storeroom every day?" Or, you can try making new assignments or creating some new rewards, and see how people respond. Most groups are responsive to, even enthusiastic about, change and new ideas, so long as it feels like evolution and not revolution. People are generally uncomfortable with change for the sake of change. As you perform this in-depth causal and behavioral observation, you may think you're already in the next step—evaluating. That impression is valid, because these steps blend together, and if you aren't evaluating as you're observing, you're probably not really observing.

Once you've made your connections and begun to absorb what is going on in your organization, it's time to make some assessments. Eventually, you will have to allocate resources—human and otherwise—to most efficiently achieve goals and results. In this phase, you collect inputs, put them together, and start to take inventory of what you have and what you need to be successful. Observation is an analysis phase. You will spend time alone in your office, alone in Starbucks, or alone in the shower going through what you've got in your mind.

Your Staff: Strengths and Weaknesses

Do you do a full-blown performance evaluation of each of your team members? Not at this stage. But from what you observe, pick up, or hear directly, you can start to figure out who fits in well and who doesn't, who is assigned to the right tasks and who isn't. You may also see some functions or responsibilities that could be done outside the group or even outside the business (as in outsourced). Make a mental note of these.

Peers and Stakeholders

You will want to evaluate your own team, but also go outside the boundaries to understand the strengths, weaknesses, and motives of those around you. Direct contact, plus outside research, can help determine whether the supervisor or manager in the next department is an asset or a liability to your cause.

You will find that others in your organization have a stake in what your group accomplishes. The results you and your team achieve will influence *their* results. Perhaps your product or service passes through them on the way to the customer. Or the numbers you generate are important toward a "whole" that they manage. We dislike the jargony term "stakeholder," but there are usually dozens—even hundreds—of stakeholder relationships around the organization. Stakeholders are like customers: They expect certain things and will make life uncomfortable if you don't deliver them. You should go out of your way to understand your stakeholders—who they are and what they want.

Informal and Formal Organization

Every organization has an informal and formal structure. The formal structure is what is printed on the organizational chart—who reports to whom and is responsible for what. Some new managers will spend hours, even *days,* memorizing this chart to learn who reports to whom. This may be overkill, but understanding the structure and *why* certain organizational units exist, and *how* they relate to you is usually a good idea. It never hurts to have a senior manager, a peer, or a mentor sit down and explain the organizational chart.

Find Your Mentor

What is a mentor? A mentor relationship is an informal relationship with someone in the organization, usually at a higher level. This person provides advice and coaching, and acts as a sounding board for your issues and concerns. Mentors may also offer career advice and help you get jobs. They will often help you get started and learn the informal "scoop" in your new job. You may enter a job with an existing mentor from a previous job. If you don't have one or have one that is too distant from your new role, you will usually find someone in your new organization who will "show you the ropes." Occasionally a mentor will seek you out—perhaps the mentor believes she can get the job done better having you on her side; maybe the mentor went to the same school you did or has some other common experience; or maybe the mentor just plain *likes* you. A mentor may be a "peer" manager—a manager of another close-by function. Or, often, you will need to look around for someone whom you respect and would like to emulate, and perhaps with whom you have some common experience, and build the relationship upon that. Know that you may not always succeed in initiating the relationship if the potential mentor doesn't see the relationship the same as you do or just doesn't have time. Whatever the case, it's good to establish a connection with a mentor and use it a lot. But beware of political agendas. Be careful of the mentor who expects you to be an ally on key issues in return for his help.

Are We There Yet?

As you wander around and evaluate your organization, you should receive an impression of the maturity, or evolution, of the work team and the organization. Generally a work team goes through the same maturity cycle as a business. The phases of this cycle are: start-up, rapid growth, maturity, and decline. In the start-up and rapid-growth phases, there is experimentation and change, more tolerance for risk and ambiguity, less structure, and a stronger need for pure leadership. In the mature and declining phases, there is more structure, less change, and a greater need to manage scarce resources efficiently. In the declining phase, your task may actually be to bring change to restart the organization. As a new manager, you should form an impression of where your team and business is on this scale of start-up to decline. Exploring new territory requires a different management style from the style used to maintain and perfect a status quo.

By the end of the evaluation stage, you should have a pretty good idea of your team's strengths and weaknesses, the nature of your team and its links to other teams, and the overall environment. Most of what you've found out are initial impressions to be confirmed or amended as you go forward. You will continue to connect and evaluate throughout your management assignment, but now it's time to begin building a management process that works.

Sultans of SWOT

SWOT, or "strengths, weaknesses, opportunities, threats" analysis, is one of the most useful and popular tools for evaluating business, or even situations in your personal life. SWOT analysis involves setting up and filling in a four-part grid (just like the expensive management consultants do!) as shown in Figure 3.1.

Strengths	**O**pportunities
Weaknesses	**T**hreats

Figure 3-1. The SWOT grid

The definitions of the four parts are fairly straightforward, but deciding where to place different aspects of your business can be an interesting judgment call. You may choose to start with a detailed approach, or more of a high-level approach and work in the details later.

- **Strengths.** Naturally these are areas of your business that are doing well or are ahead of plan, or at least there is a plan in place (better than no plan).
- **Weaknesses.** These are, of course, the opposite of the strengths—areas where you have trouble or are behind where you should be.
- **Opportunities.** If there are identifiable opportunities in your business in the external environment, identify them.
- **Threats.** Working against the business plan are any of the various threats to be overcome: loss of market acceptance, increased cost, labor shortages or problems, competitive challenges.

From a good SWOT analysis, you can identify the most important issues in your business and build actionable goals around them.

In the observation stage you will begin to define and lay out your intentions, process, and style as a manager. Very early on, your team will want some direction as to where to go, and they will want a process for working with you. Just as construction workers need a set of plans, your employees need a framework in which to operate. So the "build" phase includes the first steps of planning, organizing, and setting up department protocol for things like meetings and regular communication.

Step 4: Building—The First Sketches of a Plan

Planning is a function done throughout your management life. The planning process is thorough, detailed, and has several purposes and outcomes. It forces you to think about your business from the inside out. It creates a structure which your team can operate within. It forms goals, and the means to achieve those goals, so you know if you've done a good job and if you have contributed to your organization. Planning is not just an "up-front" exercise—it is maintained, reviewed, and refreshed throughout your tenure, and always adaptable to change and new business requirements.

You can't possibly know enough or have enough time during your first days as a team manager to assemble a thorough, structurally robust plan (that process will be covered in more detail in Chapter 8). But it helps to put together a sketch early on in the process. It enables your team to know "where you're coming from" and where you want to go. And it forms a basis to come back to later and build a *better* plan. An initial plan is like an architect's sketch of a building—it needs to be good enough to get the general idea across, get the go-ahead to proceed, and build out a formally drafted rendering later on.

Identify Opportunities

As you wander around, you'll build a composite sketch in your own mind of what the big opportunities are. You capture impressions of the workplace, understand past performance, "read" what people tell you, and digest what your superiors and peers expect of you. Your brain processes it all, consciously and subconsciously. Pretty soon, you'll be able to identify a list of opportunities best positioned for success, problems to solve, and opportunities to move forward quickly and effectively. Keep track of these opportunities. For some, it helps to write them down, because seldom do they all become apparent at once.

Decide How Much Formal Planning Is Necessary

How much and what kind of planning does your team need? It depends on several factors. Is there already a plan in place? Are goals clearly outlined? Are tasks dependent on other functions for completion? Is the team in a start-up or rapid-expansion phase, where a clear plan is necessary to keep things moving toward a goal? Is the team centralized or geographically dispersed? A dispersed team will need a more formalized plan because you aren't there to guide them directly. Do your employees feel the need for a complete and structured plan, or can they do okay thinking on their feet and dealing with what comes along? Depending on how you answered the above questions, you may need a more formal and elaborate plan, or you may get by with a few simple items and task assignments.

Assign Roles

Formal organization evolves over time, but via the first impressions of your team, you need to assign roles to individual team members. The first step is to figure out what the roles are, how much responsibility they involve, and what skill sets and time commitments are required. There is no set formula for doing this, but your experience and the prior experience of your work team, your organization, and peer managers can help. Draw an organizational chart with each role included. Add a short definition of each role, and a "gut" estimate of how much of a person's full-time work is needed to accomplish it. You might also jot down what specific skills and tasks are required to do each position. Don't expect to get it completely right the first time; reorganizations are part of business life. But to properly assign duties and carry out a plan, you'll need to establish at least some organizational structure. If you are managing managers of other teams, the organizational structure is more complex, but is also already defined by your subordinate managers.

Assign Tasks

That you need to assign tasks to those most qualified to perform them is obvious. But you also need to think about things like balancing workload (giving everything to your top performer is not likely to work) and sharing some tasks where the combined input of two or more individuals produces a better outcome than what might be achieved by a single individual.

Just as in defining the organizational structure, you may want to involve others in this process. Naturally, your team members would like to contribute, and would probably feel better if consulted before you assign roles. You can't fit everyone into a perfect position, but if you try, you will probably get a better buy-in.

Make a Clean Handoff: Delegate

Once you have established a structure, and the roles of individuals within that structure, you now need to more formally assign or delegate tasks to those individuals. The art and science of delegation is one of the more important things you will do as a manager. Obviously, if you don't delegate, nothing will get off your desk, and you'll wind up doing everything and accomplishing nothing. Failing to delegate effectively is one of the most common pitfalls for a new manager. New managers feel they have to do it all themselves to get it right, and they don't know how to get others to do it for them. Delegation requires task clarity and communication clarity:

Task clarity means breaking down the task into meaningful, achievable bits. "Make our fourth quarter number" is not an effective task to delegate, but one that can be delegated is: "Learn about our customer returns, how many are there, how much money is involved, and the top three reasons why customers make returns, and report to me no later than five days after the end of the quarter." It is specific in both the objective and the nature of the duties required, with a specific outcome (the report) and a specific time frame (five days after the end of the quarter).

Communication clarity is more obvious. A well-defined task is obviously easier to communicate, and thus to delegate. Delegation is best done as a two-way conversation (in person or by phone) where the task is explained, the receiver listens and acknowledges, and finally, a record of the delegation is made, so that there is no confusion later on. As a manager, you should keep a log of delegated tasks, so you can come back to them at a later date to review performance. It will also help you in balancing workloads.

Many new managers start with an excellent base of technical knowledge and people skills, but fail because they can't delegate effectively. Their people don't know what to do, and the manager retains too much task responsibility to stay focused on managing. Particularly if a manager has moved up through the ranks in his team, that manager may feel squeamish about telling others, who are former peers, what to do. This notion must be overcome right away. As a new manager, you must establish your authority at the onset to let former peers know who is the boss and gain the respect you deserve. It will be more difficult to do it later.

Delegating Authority

Task delegation is fairly simple and straightforward, once you understand the tasks and get the hang of it. Somewhat more complex and abstract is the idea of delegating your authority to make decisions in lieu of making them yourself. This is where many managers—particularly new managers—get really uncomfortable. They want to maintain control, and fear that someone else may make a bad decision, which in turn reflects badly on them. This is an understandable instinct, but the sooner you get past it, the better off you will be.

Delegating authority brings us to the important concept of *empowerment.* Empowerment is the transfer of "power" or decision-making authority to subordinates. With empowerment comes not only decision-making authority, but also a degree of responsibility for those decisions. In essence, you are letting the employee be the manager for a small but important component of the business.

Delegating authority does three things: First, it keeps you off the firing line and away from having to make every decision. Second, it places decision-making authority in the hands of other, often more experienced, members of your team who are closer to the customer or the first line. Ever talk to a call center agent who is empowered to do nothing, and thus comes off as sounding inflexible and unhelpful, and has to get the boss involved for the slightest issue? Does that satisfy your needs or get things done efficiently? Hardly. Empowering your people leads to fast, effective, customer-focused decisions leading to greater rapport with customers and more efficiency in your own group. Of course, there needs to be some boundaries on the authority, and some occasional cake tests to make sure it is carried out properly.

Finally, delegating authority is a powerful employee-satisfaction tool. Employees empowered to use their judgment and ability, without your constant intervention, are usually happier. They feel like adults, not children. They feel as though what they do and what they think matters, and they can grow through effective use of their empowerment.

Delegating authority, like delegating tasks, must be communicated clearly. Delegatees must be completely aware of what they are empowered to do and when. They must know the boundaries of their empowerment, and know what to do after reaching those boundaries. It's not a bad idea, particularly with a new delegatee, to ask the person to keep a log of the decisions he makes, so that you can review them and provide constructive feedback later. For all forms of delegation, you need a control mechanism to make sure the task or authority delegated is carried out and carried out correctly. Delegation is covered in greater depth in Chapter 7.

Assign Responsibility and Accountability

As you organize your team and delegate tasks and authority, you must also create a system of accountability. All team members must know how their performance will be evaluated. They must understand what yardstick they are being measured by. They must also understand the goals of their position and how that fits into the organization at large. They must understand when they need to report back to you and in what form. If you have a system to collect performance information, they should be privy to that system, so they can monitor their performance and not be surprised by your feedback long after they have ability to control their destiny. The art and science of performance evaluation is covered in more depth in Chapter 6. Suffice it to say that organizing and delegating tasks work much better if people know what they are being held accountable for.

Establish Protocol

Finally, we get to a more concrete maintenance item—communication and meeting protocol. Here, you set up the MO (modus operandi) for your organization. What kind of staff meetings will you have? What other communication forums and sessions will you have? What information do you want your employees to report back to you, and when and how should they do so?

In our view, all organizations should have some kind of regular staff meeting. How frequent, how long, whether in person or by phone, are all variables to consider in context of the environment. During staff meetings, managers should provide the latest news or information about the organization or the business. They should review accomplishments versus goals. Time should be allotted to discussing changes or adjustments to plan. Finally, each employee should be given a chance to give a synopsis of what she has done or observed since the last meeting. How long or detailed these discussions are doesn't matter, so long as a forum is provided.

Many organizations, particularly when under time pressure or are vastly decentralized (for example, when everyone is traveling), tend to cast staff meetings aside. This creates difficulties, particularly for new managers, as their finger slips off the pulse of their department, learning opportunities are squandered, and respect and control are harder to gain.

Many managers, particularly new managers, will ask their employees to summarize their accomplishments and challenges in writing, perhaps weekly, biweekly, or monthly. This is an effective tool, not only to provide discipline to the employee, but also learning for the manager. It provides more complete closure—"here's what I said I would do, and here's what I did"—and makes the formal performance review process easier. This tactic is recommended for new managers, and particularly for managers of professional or salaried employees.

Summary

As a new manager, you can't do everything starting Day One. But a methodical approach to getting started will get you off on the right foot, and minimize painful restarts later on. New managers should get organized and prepare for the immense amount of activity that follows. You need to connect with your team, your peers, your customers, and your suppliers. There is no one formula for how to do this—each group and situation are different. But new managers who follow these ideas are more likely to succeed, and seasoned managers will find the going easier if they keep these concepts in mind.

Part II | The Management Challenge

Learn how to build
your organization
and business team,
and how to shape it
to meet the organi-
zation's goals.

4 | Building Your Staff: Recruitment and Selection

Managing means getting things done through others. Thus, selecting the "others" becomes critically important. Learn how to identify employment needs and find the people to meet them.

The first tenet of management is to get work done through others, which means developing your people to do the job as well, or *better than,* you can do it yourself. Developing people is obviously a major role of a manager, but it's important to select the right people in the first place. How well you do this will determine your success as a manager.

In the natural turn of events staff will get promoted, retire, leave for new opportunities, and sometimes get their sorry selves terminated. The quality of the team you develop over time will very much depend on your making good hires; replacing and adding to your existing staff roster is an important aspect of your job. So, if the raison d'être of your existence as a manager is to manage the human capital of the company productively, it stands to reason that you must hire selectively if you are to manage effectively.

All managers have made bad hires. However, a company sees a manager who consistently makes inappropriate hires as someone obviously ill suited to getting work done through others—sadly, a manager who cannot manage. No one knows how many managers have stalled or truncated their careers this way; we just don't want you to swell their ranks. To succeed as a manager over the long haul of your career, you must become a competent recruiter and interviewer.

The foundation of getting work done through others is effective recruitment and selection. While many larger companies do have management training programs in place, you may not work for one of those companies or be chosen for such training. No one cares about your career as much as you do, so practically speaking, you have to educate yourself in this area.

A Required Skill

In the majority of companies, you are expected to be able to select employees and staff effectively. In fact, your ability to recruit and select employees is a skill likely to be examined at interviews for any management position. Explaining at a job interview that "it's a gut feeling that comes with experience," and that "you know 'em when you see 'em," is not going to land you on that next rung up the ladder. Selection and interviewing is considered a core management skill. You will develop it over time by experience. Here we will provide some of the principles and thought processes involved.

The Cost of Bad Hiring

It goes without saying that your life as a manager will be easier if you hire good employees. Ineffective, or high-maintenance individuals will drain energy, not only from you but from the rest of the team and organization. If you're building a house, use good materials; if you're building a department, use good employees. Sounds simple? Yes. Simple in practice? We'll see.

Beyond your own expenditures in time and energy, note that poor hiring also costs your organization in real dollars as well as productivity. A Labor Department study shows that 50 percent of new hires last only six months in the position for which they are hired. Now common sense tells us that some were superstars and were rapidly promoted to other positions while others either quit or were fired.

Those bad hires have a verifiable cost attached to them. This is referred to in human resources vocabulary as cost per hire (CPH). CPH is calculated by taking the total costs for the recruitment of all hires in a given period (usually a month or a quarter) and dividing by the number of hires. On average, hires from advertising cost about $1,500 each, hires made from employee referrals only $500, while employees hired through headhunters run about $12,000 and can be much higher.

Another way companies estimate the cost of bad hires is to estimate replacement costs. Typically these costs include the CPH, as well as the cost for severance pay, lost money spent on benefits (including retirement), plus the costs of training the new hire. The estimates here are even more substantial: $5,000 or more for a clerk, and upwards of $30,000 for a professional/ technical/middle-management employee. This ignores the hidden costs of time and money spent in trying to make a poor hire viable. Ouch!

Recruiting Is a 24/7 Business

While you may not be actively seeking employees every day, you will be responsible for leading the charge when it does come up. Further, even when not actively recruiting employees, Knock 'em Dead managers always have their eyes open for people who might be a good fit. Human resources are like other hidden natural resources. You are best served to always keep your eyes open even if you're not actively exploring for them, because you never know when you might need them. A variation of Murphy's famous law could be "good employees are always available except when you need them."

Your job is to make good hires, and to help those hires become successful on the job. It is much more effective to learn from the mistakes of others than to make them at your own expense. So take note of the various reasons for most poor hires:

- Poor analysis of real-world job functions, responsibilities, and core skill sets required for successful execution of the job
- Inappropriate job description developed for recruitment purposes
- Inadequate screening of potential candidates
- Inadequate interviewing and questioning techniques
- Poor use of second opinions
- Job, career, and earnings potential oversold
- References not checked

In this chapter we will look at these issues, outline the recruitment procedures a company will likely engage on your behalf, and the angles of attack you can implement for yourself.

A Lasting Legacy

If you're still not clear on the importance of hiring and staffing, remember that your hiring decisions not only affect your performance as manager, they also serve to shape your legacy. Your hiring leaves a lasting "DNA" imprint on the organization—the organization and its outcomes will "bear your genes" for many years to come. Any good manager wants not only to be successful on the job, but also to leave a lasting positive influence on the organization, visible for many years thereafter. The benefits to you and your career, as well as your own sense of satisfaction, are obvious. Remember to consider both the short-term and lasting effects of your hiring practice.

Know What You Are Looking For

Years ago, when Martin (coauthor of this book) was an international head-hunter, he or a colleague would be weeks into a search, present a short list of candidates, and schedule first round interviews with the hiring managers only to get feedback like "couldn't do the job, nothing like what I need!" Or "She looked all right on paper, but she really lacks the experience I want." Any headhunter can tell you the same story. This is the way it always worked out: After a number of interviews the *client would redefine the position requirements.*

What was the problem here? There are a finite number of job titles in any company, and over time job descriptions get developed for all of them. Likewise, help-wanted ads and electronic postings are deployed on the Internet. Now while the world of work changes, and with it the skills required to execute every single job in the workplace, the existing job descriptions and help-wanted ads are not always updated to reflect the real requirements of the job. All too often managers don't recognize the anomaly at all—or they realize it only after wasting considerable time and energy in the wrong direction. A little careful analysis can keep you on the right track.

Evaluate the Position Before You Recruit

Given the rapidity with which job titles and their functions are changing, there are two essential questions you should evaluate as soon as a position becomes open:

- **Is the job necessary as it is defined?** When a job opens up you need to identify if the job has changed, and if so, *how* it has changed. Don't simply rely on the predetermined position title and set of functions and responsibilities that were written up for the last position holder. Has the job changed drastically enough (increasing or decreasing in complexity) to warrant a different title and pay scale?
- **How frequent is the turnover in this position?** If turnover is frequent you need to address *why.* Perhaps because the job description doesn't match the real-world requirements of the job. Perhaps because the job is really more than one person can handle, and needs to be split into two or more separate functions. Perhaps you don't have a good grasp of the skills or background *really* required.

Get answers to these questions beforehand, and you may well reduce the confusion and costly turnover of hiring someone to do an impossible job, or getting a candidate whose skills don't match the practical requirements of the position. Making the job "recruitable" in the first place goes a long way toward selecting employees successfully. A job that is poorly conceived will be hard to fill, just as a poorly designed house is hard to build.

Give Your Whole Group a Once-Over

Making a job recruitable starts with giving your department a functional checkup. You need to identify who is doing what in the department, the skills they are using in the process, and then match your findings against the extant job descriptions and the role your department is expected to play in meeting company goals. In the process you may discover that the makeup of the department is out of sync with company objectives, or that turnover in a particular position is because people are required to do tasks for which they lack the experience and the training. The anomalies you might find are endless, but the point is this: Someone held that job before you, and you don't want to inherit that person's headaches for want of a little intelligent thought. If you continue to use the same old job descriptions (and the same tired old hiring process), the odds are that you will continue to give birth to the same old problem down the road. To avoid this, give your group that all-important once-over and ask yourself some questions to help you define the real needs of the job, before you start the recruitment process:

- Is the department living up to your and the company's expectations? If not, where is it falling short?
- Has the company made any recent directional changes that should affect the manpower and skill set makeup of your team?
- What positions are needed to successfully meet your department's goals?
- Could you perhaps save money and increase productivity by providing existing staff some other resource, such as another admin assistant?
- What specific skills are needed to execute each job or position?
- What level of experience is required? Should you hire three junior account managers, or would a seasoned pro recruited from the competition really fit the requirements better?
- Who can you talk to in HR to mentor you in this evaluative process?

Try to visualize the skills, attributes, and personality of the perfect employee in the position. Granted, perfect employees don't exist. But when you don't know exactly what you are looking for, the chances will be that you either won't recruit the right candidate or won't recognize the right one when he does come along. And be careful about "leaving well enough alone" if change is truly mandated.

Even if your company has written job descriptions, you should be cautious about relying on them as recruitment and selection tools for two reasons. First, they are probably too vague for your needs. Especially in big companies, job descriptions are written to cover a broad range of positions and skill sets. Second, they are purposely written this way in order to protect the company in the event of employee lawsuits. As you give your group the required checkup, you can create your own supplemental job description with details on the specific duties, measures, and skill sets required.

Job Descriptions in Two Steps

Following is a simple yet effective two-question review process that will enable you to write accurate job descriptions. It will give you an understanding of what you have and where room exists for growth with existing staff. It will also provide you with sound information with which to write effective job descriptions for recruitment purposes.

1. **Have your staff develop their own job descriptions** to reflect the work they are doing day to day; and have them identify areas where they would like to improve skills. Make sure they are specific about desired results, responsibilities, and tasks. You will notice when reviewing the paperwork where the strengths and weaknesses lie. This will give you an insight into possible training programs to enhance staff competencies and also alert you to key criteria for successful new hires.

2. **List the five or ten major functional responsibilities of each position** based on how the person in each position actually spends his time. Compile everyone's input, and combine the firsthand knowledge of the people doing that job with your management objectivity and view of the larger picture. Once you have made the list, prioritize the functions. Once your list is complete and weighted appropriately, go back to each function and identify the skill sets or special knowledge required to execute that function successfully.

Seven Steps to Defining Realistic Needs

A recruitable job description is one that is specifically relevant to the current functions of the job, rather than a description that has been inherited from your forebears. If you have an HR department in your company, you will find colleagues ready and willing to help you in each of these steps.

1. **Write down the job title.** You may or may not have much leeway in this. Just be aware that we are a title-conscious society and that every employee at Citibank, and many other companies, is a VP of something, even before she has conquered adolescent acne. If the job title is genuinely out of step with those used at other companies for the same function, it may make the recruitment process more difficult. You may want to oversell a job a bit with a fancy title, but be careful not to end up with someone who is taking the job just because of the title. Also, realize that fancy titles can turn into arrogance. Job titles can be funny things. If your job title is out of sync with the rest of the business world, talk to your boss and HR about possible solutions.

2. **List the major functional responsibilities and the skills required for the position.** What will the employee do? How will the employee's results be measured? What skills will be required to do it and do it well?

3. **Determine educational requirements.** Be practical about educational requirements. Is a bachelor's degree a mandatory requirement for being able to execute the job, or is it merely nice to have? The technology industry is an interesting case in point. A profession where degrees are largely the norm for entry is one with a preponderance of company founders who dropped out of college to start their own companies. On a practical basis, don't put too much into credentials unless they are mandatory, and your company has a policy of credential verification. As many as three out of every ten resumes carry embellishments in the area of educational attainment. Relying on educational attainment as a tiebreaker between candidates can frequently be an exercise in self-delusion. Remember, unless you check employment history, there is a 30 percent chance you will be making decisions based on faulty assumptions.

4. **Identify the depth and quality of experience required.** Identify a range of experience, but be open-minded enough to look at people from outside that range. A sharp young pro who has four years of

progressively diverse experience, can often be a better bet than the ten-year seasoned pro, who has in reality merely repeated one year of experience ten times. Also, consider *what kind* of experience the candidate has. Solid internal experience is good for certain jobs and responsibilities, but experience and leadership from an outside perspective are sometimes more important.

5. **Determine the requirement for stability.** A candidate's job stability is increasingly hard to assess given the climate of layoffs and downsizing that have plagued the American worker. Best not to rule people out because of apparent job-hopping before you determine the real reason for the frequent job changes. This is something that can quickly be determined over the telephone, and reinforced with reference checks. By the same token, while you might dream of hiring someone with an Ivy League education and twelve years on the current job, you could end up with an educated layabout who is afraid of change and real effort. So it's a good idea not to rely on employment history to initially rule candidates in or out; use it instead as an opening to a line of investigation.

6. **Consider the position's interaction with other people, levels, departments, and customers.** What kind of communication skills and customer skills are required in the position? Do they add any additional experience or skill requirements to the job description?

7. **Future role for person and position.** Good managers train their successors, thus enabling future promotions, not only for employees, but eventually for you. If your current position is secure and you hope for further promotion, you must bring succession planning into consideration. Is this open position a key stepping-stone into your role, or to other important company roles?

Do You Need the Perfect Candidate?

In the early days of their success, the Marx Brothers went to Chasen's restaurant in Los Angeles where Harpo apparently looked down the long French menu, then up at the waiter, and reportedly said, "Yes please, and a cup of coffee." Moral of the story: You *can* have too much of a good thing.

If you find a candidate who has everything you are looking for, chances are you will have to hire that person at the very top of the authorized salary range for the position. Ask yourself how you will keep the new employee motivated over the long haul when there is no room for raises without a promotion into a higher classification. Additionally, if someone has all the skills for the job and can essentially do it in her sleep, how will you keep her motivated if she isn't learning and growing? Overqualified candidates become dissatisfied, are constantly looking for the next challenge, and can be difficult to manage. Not to mention, they are hard to find and expensive.

Go through the functional requirements of the job again and separate the "must haves" from the "nice to haves." Often the best choice for the job is someone who can do the essentials of the job, but will need to grow professionally and personally. Someone like this will be motivated to put a great deal of effort into the new opportunity. You will land the person lower in the approved salary range and be able to give your employee good raises, as well as provide plenty of professional growth opportunities to keep the employee loyal to you longer.

Start the Recruitment Process by Looking Within

In my (Martin's) years working as a headhunter and consultant to the headhunting industry around the world, I was often amused, confused, and sometimes astounded at the way company A would spend a fortune to steal candidates from company B. At the same time, company B would spend a similar amount of hard cash raiding employees from company A. Like the fisherman who knows that fish are always near that far bank of the river, in business we are often blind to the great catches within our own ranks.

Your first action should be to look within your own department for someone to promote. Look at it this way: You are dealing with a proven track record when you deal with someone you know. It also sends an important message to the rest of your staff that hard work and talent are rewarded. In addition to these benefits is one other that won't be lost on your superiors—you made an inexpensive and effective hire.

Depending on the structure and reporting relationships within your company you should also look for candidates from other departments. Beware, however, of "Greeks bearing gifts." News that a department manager is looking for an internal hire could get an unscrupulous colleague to unload a problem employee on you. Look throughout the company, but stand firm in your right to hire only someone you believe would be right for the job. Rigorously interview internal candidates just as you would a total stranger from outside the company. Being coerced into hiring someone else's headache will only make you look bad later in the year.

Note also that sometimes getting "fresh blood"—an outside candidate with the perspective to see and do things in new ways—is often required. Internal candidates, whether from your team or outside the department, often mean more of the same old thing.

Personal Referrals

Your next logical step in the recruitment process is to canvas employees, coworkers, and professional colleagues for leads. However, if there is one source to avoid it is your immediate circle of family and friends, because you invariably end up in a no-win situation. You will have a miserable Thanksgiving if you don't hire your nephew as a favor to your sister, and a lousy Christmas if you do and then have to fire him, not to mention your loss of credibility in your organization for making a bum hire. You have to take a much wider view of recruitment than your circle of family and friends.

Active Networking

The hunt for good people will be an ongoing part of your professional life, in your current job and in the next one. Good employees are the lifeblood of any company, and they are also the lifesavers of every manager. Recruitment is not a "once in awhile" event, but an integral part of your everyday life as a manager.

Make a promise to yourself that you will take responsibility for becoming connected to the people in your profession: those you work with, those for whom you work, and those who will work for you. They can all help you in ongoing recruitment efforts, and this expanded circle of personal influence can also be tapped for your own career moves.

If you have read the Knock 'em Dead career management series over the years you will be aware of the importance of staying connected professionally because it gives you an inside edge on new opportunities. By being connected to the movers and shakers in your profession (and in your geography) you will not only benefit from increased career exposure for yourself, but will have a far bigger pool of personal contacts from which to recruit. The bigger your pool of applicants, the wider your choice for hires; and the better your hires, the more successful you become as a manager.

Building such a pool and being able to dip into it at will requires two consistent activities on your part:

- **You must become connected to your profession.** Take membership in professional associations and participate in their activities. There are countless organizations for every profession that will give you a wider sphere of personal influence and a professional edge. Once you have joined, one of the first things you should get is the membership directory, complete with names, titles, and contact information. When the time comes for recruiting for a key position you have a greatly expanded network of peers from whom you can source directly. They will likely help you due to the collegial relationship engendered by your membership in the same association.
- **You must be active in your professional life outside the company.** Belonging to and taking an active role in your professional associations will have their own reward in skill development, and probably in getting to know the more senior members of your own company who are also members. Belonging to Toastmasters International is an example—and you get a chance to work on your speaking and meeting skills as a fringe benefit. You should make the effort to learn a little bit about the responsibilities of everyone you meet, and get a business card so that you can establish contact at some future date.

Treat all referrals as nothing more than an interesting lead. Interview and evaluate candidates exclusively on their own merits. Remember, the referral you get from a well-respected president of another company could turn out to be a problem employee he has been waiting to get rid of.

Your Professional Contacts Archive

It's important to keep track of who's who in your professional world. When you create a personal, private, perhaps electronic database, it will stand you in good stead over the long haul of a management career. Not only will the information from business cards go in there, but also the resumes sent for your review via HR and e-mail. Executive recruiters keep files with all sorts of tidbits on people—not only resumes and business cards, but also announcements, publications, newspaper articles, and articles from company literature. Much of the information you collect will not be relevant for your needs of the moment, but will be valuable six months from now, or in your next job, or as something to offer as goodwill to another manager looking for referrals. An ever-growing resource like this can be an invaluable asset; you never know when you'll need it down the road.

Take responsibility for your own long-term success and build an archive or database of professional contacts. As you gather referrals and collect resumes, try to get electronic documents, for example, resumes, when you can, because this makes it much simpler to build your all-important personal database. It will start with just one resume, but over a relatively short time will evolve into a viable management (and career management) tool.

A nice touch after asking for referrals from peers in your company or in other companies, is to offer them a quid pro quo: A person that isn't a match for your department may be another manager's perfect candidate. It helps to have the rest of the world recruiting on your behalf.

Don't Forget HR

Recruiting, selecting, processing, and terminating employees comprises an area of expertise all its own. Regardless of whether your outfit is a *Fortune* 500 company or a small factory, when it comes to processing new employees, you are trampling around in someone else's area of responsibility and expertise. Learn the rules and play by them. The HR department typically bears overall responsibility for recruitment in your company. If your outfit is too small to have an HR department, the office manager will frequently oversee employment processing matters. All managers play a role in selection and recruiting, but in a small company you will need to carry much more of the associated workload. If your company does have an HR department, remember that managing is getting things done through others, so let your HR department do what it's there for. You will play a simultaneous role of "customer" for HR service and a role in assisting HR find candidates, construct interviews, and so forth.

No only does HR have to generate and manage an ongoing flow of applicants in many different areas, it is also required to administer and track the selection process. It is HR's responsibility to contain costs, protect the company legally in the delicate area of equality and workplace rights, and maintain the company's public image.

Being sensitive to this will enable you to have a more fruitful relationship with HR. While other professional peers can have conflicting agendas, when it comes to HR, if you don't look good, HR doesn't look good, and vice versa. HR almost always has the responsibility and final say on the allocation of money and resources for employee recruitment and advertising. Let's explore some of the traditional recruiting tools employed by HR.

Help-Wanted Advertising

Once you and HR have a position authorized for filling, and have exhausted existing files and the personal referral network, the next step involves more costly recruitment methods. The least expensive of these is help-wanted advertising, in the local and national press, and in specialist publications, although not necessarily in that order.

Obviously hiring local talent is cheaper than relocating a new employee from across the country, so we tend to logically start with the local newspaper. However, the professional associations addressed earlier have local chapter newsletters in addition to their national publications. While overall readership is likely to be small in comparison to your local newspaper, the readership is obviously more targeted.

Before making recommendations of your own to HR about specialty advertising as a recruitment vehicle, you might want to ascertain what success has been achieved with advertising this type of position in the local newspaper. If local newspaper advertising has provided inadequate responses, and you think some other publication, such as a professional association news magazine, might be effective, do your homework first. Look in past issues to see if companies use the publication on an ongoing basis. Call some of the advertisers to see what kind of success they have had, and gather helpful contact information and advertising rates to pass on to your HR contact.

To begin with, you might want to consider keeping your ads "specifically vague"; that is, specific enough to whet a lot of readers' appetites, but vague enough that they don't wrongly rule themselves out. If the response is overwhelming and inappropriate for your needs you can narrow your parameters. When advertising for a single position, you can be more specific than when you are trying to add a half dozen employees.

You may have some input in writing the ad, but you do not want to stick yourself with overall responsibility. Let the pros in HR, who do this on a daily basis, take care of it and make your effort one of being supportive and helpful whenever you can.

Temporary Help Agencies

Temporary help companies are typically used for handling critical work overloads and outsourcing of certain functions. They exist for all levels of expertise in all professions, providing companies with staff from a fill-in-for-the-week junior assistant's assistant all the way to an interim CEO. They can put a body in the seat while you look for a permanent hire, but are typically used only when not doing so would impact delivery dates, commitments, and deadlines; they can also help you if your work is truly cyclical, seasonal, or otherwise irregular. But remember, you will pay more per unit of work with an agency.

Job hunters, who have lost their jobs unexpectedly, will sometimes use "temp" agencies as an interim measure while job hunting. If you play your cards right this can be a good resource for permanent hires, where you get to "try before you buy." If budgeting will allow for it, having a number of temps coming through on short-term assignment gives you the opportunity to see a number of different personalities and skill sets in action, without a long-term commitment. Talk to HR about this option and how it might help you in your recruitment efforts. Be sure to understand the contract and policies of the temp agency—you don't want to get yourself nor the employee into legal trouble. It's a good idea to have HR involved in contracting with these firms.

The Headhunter Option

Employment agencies and contingency search or retained search firms can be a great resource for high-quality candidates. However, these agencies tend to be expensive. The going rate for these types of services ranges from 10 percent to 35 percent of a candidate's projected salary. As a rule of thumb, the higher the salary levels, the higher the fee percentage. Additionally, the candidate hired is most often guaranteed for only thirty or ninety days, except for the highest level positions.

The recruitment industry is a billion-dollar industry, and like any big industry has its share of charlatans. Your company may have very specific and strict guidelines on when and how to deal with outside agencies. You must learn these guidelines, and strictly adhere to them. You must also understand how the recruiting process works for both retained search and contingency search firms. Retained search firms are essentially consultants who are paid whether they are successful in finding a candidate or not. They may or may not help out in the job definition and final selection of a candidate. Contingency firms are paid only if they place someone. Result: They throw as many people at you as possible, hoping someone sticks, particularly if you are less than clear in the beginning about what you want. (For more information, refer to *Kennedy's Pocket Guide to Working with Executive Recruiters,* Kennedy Information, 2003.)

Headhunters can be of real help with a particularly tough-to-fill position. With a good relationship they can also be instrumental in your climb up the professional ladder (that good relationship you build may help you find a great opportunity someday, too!) The best way to develop a productive relationship is first to be well prepared, straightforward, and honest with your recruiter.

- Have clear objectives and job descriptions. This is critical for working with a recruiter, because he can't know what you're looking for otherwise.
- Give the recruiter enough department and company background so he can evaluate how well candidates fit.
- Be available to answer questions and take calls, or return them quickly. The recruiter may ask you unusual questions but the end result may be a better understanding of the profile for your ideal candidate. The timeliness issue is important in all business relationships but especially so when someone is working on your behalf on a contingency basis. Contingency recruiters will naturally invest more time and effort in clients who are most responsive.
- Be honest in your dealings at all times, and in all circumstances, and you can develop a highly symbiotic relationship.

You are likely to be inundated with calls from people in the employment services industry on an ongoing basis, and you can't work with all of them. Ask HR and senior managers who and how many at a time they recommend you to work with. Personal recommendations can be real time savers. The firm you work with is only as good as the headhunter working on your account; choose individual headhunters as carefully as you would your accountant or divorce lawyer. Ask potential headhunters questions that will give you insight into their potential capabilities.

Job Fairs

When your company is involved in a major expansion, it may seek out candidates through job fairs. Professional job fair companies set up most of these events, but a consortium of local companies, or the local Chamber of Commerce, can also sponsor them.

When your company is involved in a job fair, you might consider volunteering to "work the booth." This means attending the fair and standing at the booth all day, smiling and talking to every passerby you can get into conversation. This is hard work, so the people in HR might just consider your offer in a favorable light. But if this is hard work why should you do it?

Primarily because no one can recruit for, or sell, your openings better than you can. But there are also two other reasons:

- To widen your expertise and sphere of influence within the company
- To widen your sphere of influence outside the company with other management-level professionals

In the event you do become involved with your company's job fair activities, you will be working as a team member under a different management team. Make every effort to do your job as a committed member of that temporary group.

Online Recruitment

Electronic job hunting has been one of the few proven successes of the Internet. Job hunters love the ease of electronic job hunting, which means that electronic recruitment could be effective for you. It is not, however, a guaranteed cure for all your recruitment challenges. You should not use it as your only approach to recruitment, but as an integral part of any individual campaign. With the advent of the Internet, help-wanted advertising has simply moved online. As a result there has been a boom in sites that offer job postings from employers. Keep in mind that you don't want to take over the writing and recruitment process from HR for whom this is the daily grind. But you don't want to abrogate the responsibility entirely, either. Ask to see the online posting, ask questions about the wording, and if you have suggestions of your own, make them diplomatically.

Electronic job postings differ from traditional help-wanted ads in one very important aspect. In print, space is at a premium, so help-wanted ads tend to focus on the "must haves" of the job—job title, skills required, educational requirements, location, and contact information. Space considerations mean that other selling points also get omitted from print advertising. But space considerations don't apply online, so you can post these "nice to have" points which increase response:

- Career development possibilities
- Location
- Company selling points
- Training
- Work environment
- Benefits and other considerations

You need to understand the importance of "keywords" in online recruiting. Unlike the local newspaper, online job sites list millions of openings, so hunters don't read through them to find something suitable. Instead they punch in a few keywords and let the database search for files (read job postings) that contain such words, and then return a list of the matching entries to the job hunter. Often, ambitious and technically savvy candidates set up search "bots" (short for "robot," a program that runs automatically) to alert them of openings with specific keywords. Those postings with the most matching keywords are prioritized. This means that for your postings to get read by human eyes it must contain appropriate keywords. If you're searching for a market research expert with experience in customer surveys, put those keywords in your posting.

In searching databases the job hunter is typically given certain options. She is asked to pick a category of job: management, technical, professional and executive, sales and marketing, engineering, administration, manufacturing, and so on. Many job sites also offer the option of choosing multiple industries. Here again, if you have the option of more than one choice you should take it, because many jobs in the modern world of work can easily cross industry lines. If your job opening isn't registered in the right category, your posting will never be seen. Fortunately, most sites allow you to register your ad in multiple categories; you should take full advantage of this option whenever it is offered.

Online postings always have space for a company profile and your company probably has a template already developed. Nevertheless, this is an opportunity for you to include some enticing information about your department. Keep in mind that most people change companies for the same job in a better environment and with enhanced possibilities—better daily work environment, greater appreciation of effort, good boss and communication with boss, opportunities for professional growth, and, last but not least, money. With this in mind you can craft an enticing paragraph or two about the work experience in your department.

An electronic posting invariably includes a salary range, unless the range for the position is not competitive and might therefore reduce the number of responses. You should be aware that by omitting a salary range you are immediately reducing the response rate, because money is a major consideration of any job hunter. If you want comparative information about your salary range you can visit *www.wageweb.com,* where you will find comprehensive information on a wide range of jobs and salary issues.

Remember that job hunters are time sensitive and will always look first at the most recently posted openings. You should keep track of how long those hard-to-fill positions are posted, and occasionally repost the openings to keep them fresh in the databases.

Surfing for Resumes

When your company advertises on Web sites it also gains access to each site's resume bank. So you can readily take an active role in online recruiting by spending some time checking the resume banks yourself. Online recruitment is a wide and complex field, especially due to the wide array of recruitment sites. To learn more about online recruiting, take a look at any of the Web employment portals: Monster (*www.monster.com*), HotJobs (*www.hotjobs.com*), and Careerbuilder (*www.careerbuilder.com*) are currently the largest and best known.

And of course, don't forget that most companies with their own Web sites have job posting boards within their sites. Find out who manages this part of your company site (probably HR) and work with them.

More on Recruiting Resources

As a recruitment program ramps up, you have to start evaluating the applicants. While interviewing potential candidates is a very important part of your job, it is also enormously time consuming, so you'll want to organize your selection process to minimize both the number and duration of the interviews you have to conduct.

How many interviews does it take to make a good hire? It depends on how comprehensive those interviews are. It has become customary to conduct second and third interviews with job candidates, and in some cases many more. After initial interviews the norm is to ask subordinates to meet with potential candidates and also to ask other managers to "have a look and tell me what you think."

Read this next sentence slowly, then read it again: When you ask someone to "have a look and tell me what you think," you are invariably wasting everyone's time. When there are multiple interviews for an opening, the interviewee invariably gets asked the same question multiple times; just think of your own experience in job interviews, and you'll recognize this for the surprisingly self-evident truth that it is.

Remember the number of job interviews you had for the company you work for today? Then you'll also recall that, with almost laughable regularity, at each of those interviews someone always asked you "What's your greatest strength?" And "What's your greatest weakness?" The result of uncoordinated interview sequences and ill-considered second opinions, is that with practice the candidate's answers get better, and the efforts of you and your colleagues backfire. The process backfires, not because of any inherent flaw in the multiple interview approach, but because the hiring manager is unprepared. The intent itself, "get another objective opinion," is sound, but lacks the planning to make it effective.

Let's step back and look at what you want to achieve and come up with a logical, objective, and time-efficient way of achieving that goal. It's a given that you want to make a good hire, but what constitutes a good hire? While this infinite variable depends on the unique needs of each job, there are certain givens that apply to all jobs. So, in analyzing what makes for a good hire, it is safe to say that you want someone who is functionally competent, someone who can actually do the job you hire the person for. In the interview process, you're looking to see if . . .

- **The person is able.** It is also probably safe to say that you want to hire someone who doesn't head for the hills every time something goes wrong.
- **The person is willing.** You want someone who is motivated, someone willing to take the responsibilities and the "rough and smooth" that goes with every job.
- **The person is a team player.** This is someone who acts with the best intentions of the group in mind, someone who can take direction, someone who *fits.*
- **The person is manageable.** By you, and those above you.

To put this into context, you want the interview cycle to gather enough objective information to enable you to make decisions on all candidates as to their abilities, willingness, and manageability. Remember, too, to look at skill sets—technical, interpersonal, and conceptual.

Thus, it becomes necessary to structure an interview, or interview cycle, that will gather enough information to make this decision. Now, while the duration of any interview, or series of interviews, will vary depending on the level or complexity of the job, you can contain the time and maximize the impact of person-hours with planning and preparation.

Planning the Interview Cycle

If you put adequate effort into developing a realistic job description for the position, you will already be ahead of the game. You will know the functions to be performed, the skill sets required to execute them, and hopefully have a profile of the behaviors you are looking for in your new employee.

You also know that in addition to hiring someone who is able, you are also looking for someone who is willing and manageable. For instance, there's no point in hiring someone who is really motivated by the job opportunity, but totally lacks the skills to get it done. To continue this line of thought, there's no reason to hire someone who is manageable but can't do the job or isn't motivated by the opportunity.

Your first step is to save time on those first interviews by screening out the walking wounded and the also-ran types as quickly as possible. You can do this quickly with a carefully scripted series of questions to determine if the candidate in question has those "must have" skills enabling him or her to actually do the job.

Structuring the Interview Process

As with most tasks you'll perform as a manager, interviewing works better when you have a strategy in place before you start. Otherwise, a disorganized interview process will leave critical questions unanswered by your candidates, and possibly lead you to make a bad hiring selection that will cause problems down the road.

The ideal structure for an interviewing "campaign" varies somewhat by the kind of position for which the candidate is interviewing and the nature of the management team involved. A team dispersed in many locations will use different tactics from a team that is side by side in a single building. Here are two strategic choices you'll want to make up front about your interview structure:

1. **Individual versus group interview.** In the case of individual interviews, the candidate has separate appointments with every member of the interview team—a one-on-one, usually twenty minutes to an hour, in person or by phone. The group interview, on the other hand, puts most or all interviewers in a room together with the interviewee. Each "player" has a role with a certain group of questions or issues to probe. The

group interview is usually less time consuming, and can be a better test of a candidate's poise and abilities in a real, "under fire" work situation, typical of an ordinary business meeting. Group interviews can achieve more honest assessments, because candidates cannot tell one interviewer one thing and another interviewer something different.

2. **Chronological versus behavioral questioning.** The traditional "chronological" interview style essentially probes experiences and skills as laid out on a resume, with questions such as what did you do at Acme Welding three years ago, why did you leave, what did you like best and least, and so forth. More recently—and particularly for higher-level positions involving extensive conceptual skills—interviewers and recruiters are turning to behavioral interviewing where the candidate is asked to "role-play" a complex situation—to think on his feet, make a complex judgment, and present it on the spot with reasoning. The candidate who does best wins the job.

Once you make these choices, deciding the timing, venues, and personnel involved becomes easier. You'll then want to start developing lists of specific issues and topics to address. It's a good idea to document these issues and give each member of your interview team a "score sheet," with the issue or topic and a space to write comments alongside. You might want to categorize these issues and topics somehow, perhaps into technical, interpersonal, and conceptual "buckets," or perhaps into a more detailed skill and behavioral framework (as we explain in Chapter 6). Does it make sense to use a performance evaluation framework to interview candidates? You bet.

From here, you're ready to organize specific parts of the interview process.

The Telephone Interview

A phone interview is a great time-saving tool for a busy manager. You skip the five minutes of meeting and greeting, and the small talk that always precedes a face-to-face meeting; and once you determine there isn't a match you can also skip the five to ten minutes it takes to get the candidate the heck out of your office.

Your only goal during a "phoner" should be to determine the essentials so that you invest face time with only viable candidates. You shouldn't try to probe the niceties of professional judgment, motivation, or manageability. Neither should you try to analyze the intangibles of chemistry over the phone. Generally, the telephone interview is done as an investigation of the candidate's work experience. The whole point of a phoner is to cut to the chase a lot more quickly. Once you have covered what you need to, you can say your goodbyes and move on, with a minimum of fuss, awkwardness, and investment by either party.

An effective phone interview requires that you have a clear picture of the information you wish to gather. Your job description will help you out with that. Once you have determined mandatory areas of core competence and experience, you can develop questions geared to gathering the required information in short order. For more details, *Hiring the Best* (Adams Media, 1994) by Martin Yate is a companion volume to this book, and recommended reading for anyone involved in the selection process. Along with a comprehensive and practical examination of the entire process, *Hiring the Best* contains hundreds of questions and interviewing techniques.

If you have an HR department, it will be accustomed to doing screening interviews over the phone. Going to HR with your analysis of what needs to be covered can only score you points by making its job easier. If you are new to management you can also go to HR and ask for input. You will learn from the feedback, and because HR is always involved in management selection and promotions, you will make yourself visible to an important segment of your professional public.

Delegating the Telephone Interview

Don't forget your existing employees in this process. You can also use the phone interview as a professional development tool for key employees; any member of your staff would regard it as a big plus to be involved. Because the phone interview is mainly used for fact-finding in very specific areas, and because you have developed which questions you plan to ask, it becomes a ready task for delegation. This will save you time, enhance the skills of your team, and demonstrate your coaching abilities. (Coaching is a much admired skill of the modern manager, and a topic we'll address in the next chapter). You will, of course, need to get the phone interview process down for yourself first, but once you do, with a little one-on-one training, other members of your team will relish picking up this responsibility.

Take time with your chosen delegatee and clearly outline the information you need. "Sam, I want you to see if these candidates are competent in these specific areas. Here are some questions I would ask to gather that kind of information. I'd like you to read them over, and see if they make sense to you. If you would like to change any of them or add questions of your own, that's fine, too. Look them over tonight and let's find ten minutes tomorrow and we'll role-play an interview to see how it goes."

The next day, you and Sam role-play a phone interview. Make a copy of a resume, give it to Sam, tell him to call you and you will role-play the candidate, basing your answers on the resume, and he will role-play the interviewer. Your goal here is to give Sam a successful experience in conducting a job interview.

Telephone Interview Strategy

A telephone interview should always be arranged at a time convenient for both parties. Unfortunately, this means that business hours will sometimes be out of the question, because it could embarrass a candidate to receive your call during work hours. When the phone interview must occur during business hours, always give the candidate the courtesy of initiating the call, because of the confidentiality issue. Often you will conduct these short interviews in the evening or on weekends, all the more motivation for keeping them short and to the point.

In all interviews, whether on the phone or in person, you need to guide the conversation but you don't need to dominate it. Every moment you are talking you are giving a candidate information about the kind of answers you want to hear, and you're not listening to responses or gathering information. *The rule of thumb in interviewing is to listen 80 percent of the time and talk 20 percent of the time.* Because there are fewer distractions with a phone interview, this is a good venue in which to polish the skill of controlling conversation with questions. You'll also be able to use that skill in many other management contexts.

The First Interview

How many interviews does it take to make a good hire? There is no precise answer to the question. However, for lower-level employees one or, at the most, two interviews should be sufficient. For professional and managerial jobs, a phoner followed by three carefully structured interviews, with at least one of them conducted by a third party, is usually sufficient.

This assumes that you know what you want to find out in each interview, that you have the questions prepared, and that you have an adequate array of questioning techniques, conversational control gambits, and interview approaches at your command. These techniques are all covered in practical detail in *Hiring the Best;* unfortunately, space forbids our addressing them further here.

When you wisely use another person as part of your interview team, you should choose that person based on his experience and competence. Use a staff member to do the phoner or a fact-finding first interview. Use a peer, a manager from another department, or your boss when you have whittled down the short list to one or two candidates after the first and second interviews.

The first interview should deal mainly with facts about ability. Are the functional skills present, and to what degree? How does the educational background support the experience? Does the employment history withstand scrutiny? In short, can the individual do the job? The phoner and the first interview are the major components of the winnowing process. Focus on ability and the candidate's relative interest in the opportunity, and select the best candidates. From there, subsequent interviews can be spent with functionally qualified and interested candidates.

First interviews should be short. Usually forty-five minutes to an hour is quite adequate for a first interview when you have a road map for the territory to be covered. Concentrate on questions that establish ability, and allow you to compare the relative merits of one candidate with another. Remember, although motivation and manageability are important, they don't have much relevance until you have determined ability.

You will want to determine the relative strengths and weaknesses of the individual's job-related and interpersonal skills, along with the extent of the individual's current responsibilities. If meaningful verbal or written communication is important to successful execution of the job's duties you need to examine such critical skills during this first meeting. Similarly if personal appearance and social graces are relevant criteria, you need to be evaluating them now.

This is the time to get all the knock-out questions answered, and to discover why the candidate wants to leave his current job, and why the candidate is interested in the functions and responsibilities of this job. If your company uses aptitude or skill tests, these tests are often administered as part of the process that accompanies this first meeting.

The Second Interview

Your second interviews should be restricted to candidates you are confident can do the job. Second interviews should deal with further examination of the functional areas: facts, judgments, depth and breadth of experience, and degree of appreciation for the long-term issues and challenges of the profession.

If you are coming in at the second interview stage, you should determine the candidate's ability to your own satisfaction. You won't have to spend quite so much time on the nuts and bolts, because you will already have received a comprehensive debriefing from HR or the staff member who conducted the first interview. You will simply requalify sensitive areas and address questions raised by the first interview; then you can concern yourself with motivation and manageability.

In most scenarios, you should address the candidate's comprehension of how the job and the department plays its part in helping the company make money. You should examine your candidate's ability to get along with others, his relative organizational and time management abilities, level of energy and stamina, and how he reacts and performs when the poop hits the paddlewheel.

If the interview goes well and the candidate looks like a real possibility for the job, you should consider checking references. Under the 1972 Fair Credit and Reporting Act, you need written authorization to do this. So if this isn't addressed on the company's standard application form (it usually is), make sure you gain that permission now. Also, make yourself a promise that those references will get checked by you or someone whose judgment you trust. Once in awhile, checking references saves you from making a terrible hiring mistake.

If you conducted the first interview yourself, you might consider using a peer manager to give you a second opinion in the second interview. At this point you should have a clear idea of what you want the peer manager to evaluate:

> Sally, I'd like you to have a look at my final candidates for the position of _____. They seem competent, but I'd appreciate your input. Here is the job description I've developed, and this is what I've learned, so any additional insight will be appreciated. I'd appreciate it if you could probe the following areas. By the way, I've already asked these questions . . . .

This way, you give additional interviewers a clear view of the task at hand and the information you already have, so that when they go into the interview they won't cover the same territory in the same way.

The Third Interview

You must cover certain items during the third interview. Be sure that the remaining short-list candidates understand how your company makes money and their specific role in this process. Explain what will be expected of people who join the company. Do this now when the candidates are most receptive; then later, during new employee orientation, you can hark back to this earlier conversation. Outline your department's mission and how you like things to run. Your goals and objectives form the umbrella for the future employee's responsibilities, and understanding them predicates any future success. A clear understanding of your expectations at this time will build the candidates' confidence in your leadership, the job, and the company.

The third interview in the cycle should revisit sensitive or as yet unapproached areas, and provide time for any "rubber-stamp" meetings, such as a courtesy meeting with your boss. This is a time for selling the opportunity and the company. Too often managers sell the company and the job to everyone who comes through the door, with the result that they waste time fielding follow-up phone calls from eager candidates they wouldn't hire on a bet.

Third or final interviews can also be done over breakfast, lunch, or dinner. A meeting in such an informal setting can also be useful in examining how candidates treat others at work, and how candidates are likely to behave with a client when representing your company. In this phase, you're examining character and enthusiasm, and how the prospective employee fits into the big picture.

Making the Hire

The hiring, reference checking, induction, and orientation of new employees is a topic beyond the scope of this book. Suffice it to say that the procedures for induction of new employees follow a standard pattern that has already been established at your company, and it is a process in which you will have little hands-on involvement. Just make sure you understand from HR (or in a very small company from the office manager) the standard company procedures, and follow them to the letter.

Although the recruitment and selection process is a complex process that warrants further study, after this chapter you should have a firm grasp of what it takes to make a good hiring decision. With a little additional study in this area you will quickly become a truly effective interviewer. This is a critical skill, because you cannot manage effectively unless you hire correctly in the first place.

Summary

As the essence of managing is getting things done through others, recruiting is undoubtedly one of the most important things you will do as a manager. In the long run, what you're able to get done (through others) depends on how well you choose your team. The team you build is likely to become the most lasting legacy or imprint left on the organization. Whether in hiring mode or not, the effective manager is constantly on the lookout for people who can get the job done, keeping track and cultivating them until the right opening comes along. When it does finally become time to make a hire, the Knock 'em Dead manager is willing to "go the distance" to make sure that the recruiting, selection, and interviewing processes are done with excellence and precision, with the appropriate help from others inside and outside the organization.

5 | Coaching and Skill Development

Developing employee skills brings benefits to everyone—follow these guidelines to coach your staff toward improved performance.

Management is all about you, more specifically what everyone wants from you. Your superiors want to know how much work you can get done through your staff. Your staff, in turn, expects you to defend, nurture, and champion them. As a manager, you are between the two; and sometimes it's the proverbial rock and a hard place. (Is *that* why they call it "middle management"?)

What Does Your Company Expect?

The company holds you accountable for your own productivity and that of your staff. Most likely very little about your responsibilities is carved in stone, and many of the skills that got you promoted can seem of little relevance. When you understand the importance of that amorphous directive to "get work done through others," you suddenly realize that there is a mountain of new skills to acquire.

You *are* up to the task—provided that you are prepared to continue the learning process that helped you reach this point professionally. Management is a learning process that will hold your attention for many years to come, and in large part, your continued ascent on the management ladder will rest on that ability to learn and to teach.

There is something special within you that has brought you to where you are today. You might call it competence, drive, commitment, or just burning desire. Whatever name you give this special something it is a spirit that brings you to work eager to meet its challenges, and ready to do whatever it takes to win the day. You know what it is that drives you, and management knows that you have what it takes.

What management wants is for you to clearly understand where the company is headed and then infect all your people with your same skills, commitment, and passion. Now your job is about becoming the energizer for your people, infecting them with the same burning desire to make something of their professional lives, and, in the process, enrich their personal lives.

What Do Your People Need?

While each of your employees has unique needs, there are some needs that most people have in common, including consistency in management and economic stability. Most of us also share a desire for work that . . .

- Is interesting.
- Provides the opportunity for professional growth.
- Provides the opportunity for financial growth.
- Provides the opportunity for personal growth.

Abraham Maslow, in his seminal *Maslow on Management* (John Wiley, 1998), wrote: "It is a fairly safe assumption that a prerequisite for enlightened management is a delight in novelty, in new challenges, new activities, variety, in activities that are not too easy, but all of these become sooner or later uninteresting and even boring, so that the search then begins anew for additional variety and novelty, work at a higher level of skill." In the book's context, Maslow is talking about the new style of manager most suited to getting the best out of his or her staff, and at the same time about the needs of all workers. Similarly, Harvard researcher Dr. David McClelland recognizes that all individuals have varying degrees of *achievement motive;* that is, people are motivated to outperform others, achieve high standards of excellence, and have a desire to innovate. The role of management is to *arouse* your employees' achievement motive so they can reach higher levels of performance.

Growth, Training, and Development

Most professionals recognize that success depends on competency in certain core skills, coupled with a desire to learn and grow. To succeed in management you must continue to grow in all the new skills of management, while at the same time understanding the needs of each of your people and helping them to grow professionally as well. Your personal commitment to your own development should be visible to your people. Your commitment to having all your employees approach their professional growth with the same level of dedication and enthusiasm will motivate the whole department. If it is safe to assume that each and every one of your reports wants to grow professionally, it only makes sense to help each one, as it is a central responsibility of your job.

This chapter is about the training and development of your people. We are not talking about the occasional motivational meeting, an odd training class here and there, but about the ongoing development that occurs every day as the department executes its duties. To emphasize the fine line difference between training and development, here are the definitions:

- **Training** refers to teaching the skills people need to do their jobs at an acceptable level today.
- **Development** means providing the skills people need to rise above the minimum required standards of the job. Development gives people a sense of satisfaction in doing their jobs well, and a feeling of progression toward their chosen career goals.

If you believe, as we do, that most people want to succeed and do a good job, why is it that so many managers seem to mess up? If you look at your own peers who may be stumbling, you'll realize that it is because they don't "get it," they don't understand, perhaps they don't make the effort to learn, and perhaps no one thought to teach them. The same applies to the group you have been managing. Perhaps the reason that some tasks are consistently screwed up by some people is that those folks never learned the right way of doing things. No one ever took the time to show them how to succeed.

Also, don't forget training your staff helps you to develop your successor, and at the same time helps you become more accomplished, which facilitates your next career step. Effective training and development of your staff are the means to this happy end.

Why Some Managers Don't Coach

The most common excuses are not enough time and too many other things to do. This usually comes from someone who prefers to work in a comfort zone. All too often, such managers are not really managing. They are doing the job they always did, spending time on their *own* activities, and when their staff experiences difficulties, these managers pick up the slack there, too, and do the job for them. These people are *doers,* not managers. They are not managing, they are not leveraging beyond themselves, and they are not getting work done through others. They do not train and develop their staff. They do not coach and nurture their people because of some silly reason like: "I'm scared someone will take my job."

No one will take your job, because you are not teaching anyone to do the job you are doing; you are teaching people to do the job you once did. You are now learning the skills of leveraging and influencing beyond yourself, which are far more valuable to the corporation.

Other "reasons" for not nurturing employees include:

I'm uncomfortable talking with employees about the need for improvement. Your people don't like screwing up, they hate failing, and they want to succeed. They are looking to you to help them achieve the goal of doing their job well. They know when they aren't doing a good job, so showing them ways to improve their performance will only improve your relationship.

I'm intimidated by the coaching role. You won't be the first and you won't be the last to feel uncomfortable in a new role. However, you wouldn't be a manager if you had not demonstrated that you can consistently adapt to new roles and challenges; this is just another new role.

No one taught me, so why should I teach others? The world has changed, and those managers who didn't learn how to coach and build the skills of their staff are almost all gone, with the remainder soon to follow. Getting work done through others is what management is all about, so coaching is at the heart of your job—end of discussion or end of your management career.

If I make good hires they won't need coaching. Everyone wants to grow, the talented people more so than others. If you hire well, those hires will expect to develop their skills under your command. If you don't help them to grow, they will quit. When a manager consistently loses staff through resignations this raises big black question marks, like thunderclouds, over that manager's legitimacy.

My employees won't be receptive. Simply not true. If you show the rewards of growth, both personal and financial, and lead—not coerce—people toward desired ends, they will listen. Your role is to deliver enhanced departmental performance to *your* managers, and coaching to increase your employees' skills is a far more effective way to achieve this than screaming for greater productivity.

There are no convincing reasons to ignore the development of your staff. However, that is not to say you will find coaching easy to face. The biggest obstacle is coming to terms with the necessary shift from doing the job yourself to helping others do it as well as you can. As a manager you have many overwhelming priorities landing on your desk everyday, and it is easy to put off until tomorrow the bigger challenge of employee training and development in favor of today's fire fighting.

There are organizational and management priorities (that quarterly report, for example) that take you away from the group. It is easy to rationalize that there is simply no time. This is not an acceptable reason; there *is* time, and you just have to make it. When you organize your time, you will be able to take care of all your priorities and develop your staff (we'll show you a useful tool in a few pages). Then as your staff grows you will be able to delegate more, and be available for those other management responsibilities that will earmark you for further promotion. It's a vicious circle, but one that spirals in the right direction.

Are You Coach Material?

Everyone goes through an adjustment period after arrival in the management ranks. The new job no longer has the clear-cut roles that your old job once had. You are no longer responsible for just your own productivity; now you are responsible for the productivity of a whole group of people.

Your staff needs to work together as a cohesive whole, with each member simultaneously committed to his own growth as an integral part of the success of the team. Such commitment rarely appears of its own volition—it requires a leader, or coach, to help each member, and the team, grow as a whole. Of the many hats you wear as a manager, that of coach is the one you wear as the default, removing it only when another hat is required for a moment.

You will still find yourself in the trenches doing what you have done so well in the past. Your goal, though, will be different. You will solve that problem or win that sale to set an example for a staff member as an exercise in learning and skill development for that specific individual or the group as a whole.

In general, you can divide your job into two roles:

- Managing the execution of the tasks for which the department exists.
- Improving the performance of the people who execute those tasks.

If you are intimidated by the idea of coaching others, it is easy to focus on the task issues of your job to the exclusion of developing your people. Invariably this leads you to do the work you are really meant to be managing, and in doing so, take over a subordinate's responsibilities because you can do it better. In other words, you *do* the task rather than manage its execution. It is this kind of approach that can lead ineffective managers to mutter, "if you want something done right, you have to do it yourself." This might be more comfortable in the short haul, but over time both you and your team will fray at the edges from the mounting frustration.

When you manage as a coach, you still get involved in tasks, but as a teacher, leader, coach, and cheerleader, and you become bent on seeing your people grow in ability. With this commitment your staff will increase their professional abilities and credit you with their growth. Thus, you will . . .

- Achieve more positive results with fewer resources.
- Have a happy, motivated staff.
- Have less employee turnover.
- Have more time for the rest of your job.

If you intend to manage as a coach, you must first ensure that the work environment is conducive to learning. You can do this by . . .

- Creating an open and trusting environment.
- Establishing reasonable standards.
- Being fair, honest, and open.
- Behaving consistently with all staff members.
- Establishing goals that are achievable.
- Allowing some flexibility in results and processes used to achieve them.
- Providing positive feedback in public, and negative feedback in private.
- Sharing the truth, because everyone has a need to know.
- Listening and offering ideas and suggestions.
- Being available with an empathetic ear.

In this process you will demonstrate your unwavering trust and belief in your people, which is noticed and appreciated. When people feel they are working in an emotionally safe workplace (addressed in the next chapter), they will open up to you and to each other. You will have more responsive workers, who will pull together into a cohesive whole. You may inherit a department that is in a total shambles but you can turn it around if you believe you can, and if you believe failure is not an option.

Set the Example

You need to exude confidence and pride in your team, because if you want your people to believe in success and their ability to grow and achieve, *they must see it in you.* As a manager you hold enormous sway and influence over your staff. In a very real way you are the "alpha wolf" who allows them to remain in the pack or can insist on their removal. This is harsh but true; you know it to be so from your relationship with your own managers; without their approval there is no paycheck come Friday, and that affects the relationship with your boss in an intangible but very real way.

Your people want to please you, they want to be like you, and they will model themselves on you no matter what model you choose to give them. Give them a model that believes in success and hard work, and they will adopt those beliefs. Offer a model of trust and commitment to personal development, and your people will gradually adopt these same traits. Create a trusting, winning, learning environment and everyone will benefit.

Create a Learning Environment

"Leader," "teacher," and "coach" are all terms that help describe the role of manager, and they all share a common core: to help people better themselves. The first step in helping the members of your team develop professionally is to create an environment in which they are able to learn and grow. This means an environment that is open and honest. If people are always watching their backs and are concerned about personal survival, they will not be open to expressing their own needs or to hearing the input they need to improve. *Open communication is essential!* When people have information, they feel included and can make better decisions; when they don't, they feel insecure and likewise withhold information that can be essential to you.

With open communication everybody wins; without it everybody loses. An environment of open communication is the bedrock of cooperation between you and your team members. When people cooperate they feel connected to a greater whole and are naturally more motivated to work toward the common good of the team.

The Golden Rule

When openness exists in a department, trust has the opportunity to blossom. As the manager you must set the tone, listen carefully, put your employees' needs before yours, treat everyone with courtesy and consideration, and, most of all, show that you care. It may sound trite, but it is nevertheless true: You can't go too far wrong when you treat your staff as you like to be treated. Always remember the Golden Rule.

This is going to demand that you are self-aware, because your employees look to you as an example for their own behavior. If you have fits and tantrums, expect your staff to mimic your behavior. If you demonstrate concern for others, and engender a spirit of cooperation by your concern for fairness and the truth, your staff will try to emulate your emotional maturity.

We all make mistakes at work, just as we do in our personal lives, and how others react to those mistakes predicts how defensive we will be in future interactions. Think of your relationships at work, with a manager who gives you a fair hearing and examines a given situation objectively. You will be open with that manager because you know you will be treated fairly. You also will tend to trust this person more, because you know him or her to be fair. This applies in the same way to your team's relationship with you.

Nothing but the Truth

The members of your department expect you to search for and honor the truth, rather than search for places to lay the blame. When you act honestly you create an environment where people will come to you with questions when they are unsure, or when they a see a problem looming. You create an environment where people can learn from asking questions, and where they aren't made to feel inadequate for not having all the answers.

When this trusting atmosphere is absent and people don't ask questions or seek advice, the first time you learn of a problem is when it becomes a catastrophe. When catastrophes occur, you need to remain cool, calm, and collected; analyze the situation with your people and come up with practical solutions together. Behaving, in other words, exactly as you want your people to learn to react.

Learn from (Your) Mistakes

Even the best employees can become discouraged when things go wrong, and this is where you need to step in to support, encourage, and help them over the hump. Let them know it isn't the end of the world, and show them how they can learn from the situation. A very effective technique for this is to share your own mistakes. It may sound crazy but it works.

> Jim, I know this stinks, but it isn't the end of the world. You know, about ten years ago something similar happened to me, let me tell you about it . . . and what I learned from the experience was . . . it didn't make the screwup go away, but I was better prepared next time so that it didn't happen again. What can we learn from what has just happened?

Effective coaching is more than reacting to circumstances; it's assessing both the strengths and weaknesses of the team as a whole and its individual members. In the last chapter we talked about having employees analyze their jobs and their skills (and where they wanted to improve) as part of developing an effective recruitment and selection process. People are usually quite objective about their relative skills and merits, so you can use this information to . . .

- Identify broad areas for skill development that affects the whole group.
- Identify pockets of need that affect more than one person but not the whole group.
- Identify individual development needs.

As a manager you are expected to develop your staff through coaching, yet it takes time and application to develop these critical coaching skills. Look at the coaches in the NFL or any other professional sport, and you'll realize that they didn't start where they are today. Invariably they started coaching as assistants, then as head coaches at high school, repeating the process at the college level, then all over again in the professional ranks. For these people coaching is a lifetime commitment to skill development in others, but most important, in themselves. While the context of your coaching is different from a NFL locker room, the essentials are the same. The more you work at becoming a coach, the easier the job will become.

Your coaching will fall into two distinct training and development categories:

- Training the skills that are needed to do the job today.
- Developing the skills needed to exceed these basic requirements.

If you haven't done it already, spend time with each of your staff members to discover what it is they feel good about in their work, and what it is they know they need to improve (we'll show you how to do this later in the chapter). While your people want to succeed, you can help them achieve their goals only when you discover where they need support. Your reward will be their motivation.

Teaching, training, developing, coaching, are all different ways of describing the process of developing human potential. Because developing coaching skills represents an ongoing process it is easy to justify putting it off in favor of some short-term emergency. However, *the ability to develop people's skills is possibly the single most important skill you can develop as a manager.*

Coaching for Results

Companies can indulge in long-range development plans, but as a manager you usually don't have that luxury. You hold a management title because of the company's belief in your ability to achieve results. Even if you are told that a turnaround, or substantive changes, are expected to take awhile, your employer is really looking for things to start happening about an hour ago, or at the very least your employer expects to see changes within a couple of quarters. Your employees will largely form their opinions of your regime in the same time span.

The way you make visible contributions to the bottom line is to impact productivity, and the way to do that is through skill development. Imposing your schedule of needed skill development programs on your department may or may not be on target, and will certainly meet with a mixed reception because it is imposed. Professional development plans are most effective when your people buy into and take ownership of them.

Skill development isn't just your responsibility; all your team members hold an equal responsibility to improve their professional skills. Most professionals already feel this responsibility from their need for peer respect, from a desire to achieve their own version of the American Dream, and from their awareness of their need for economic survival. Consequently, if you encourage your employees' involvement in development programs, you will meet with almost universal acceptance.

We say "almost" universal acceptance, because there are degrees in all things. You should look at each team member's development in an individualized context:

- **Employees who are highly skilled.** Some of your people will welcome development programs as an opportunity to garner the skills necessary to get promotions and raises. These are the highly motivated and career-driven members of your staff. They will make themselves visible to you, and their coaching is not only likely to be a joy, but may result in even closer mentoring relationships that last far longer than the time you spend working together in the department. We will discuss the differences between a coaching and a mentoring relationship later in the chapter.

- **Employees who seek recognition or more money.** Other staff members will welcome these skill development plans as a means for peer recognition and a raise. They are not going to be motivated to the same degree of achievement as some of their career-driven colleagues. This does not make them any less important in the success of your department. You should invest your energy in these people, too, but with different expectations.

- **Employees who aren't interested.** A few people may reject efforts to develop improved professional skills. These are the people you will gradually upgrade as time and opportunity allows—or you'll seek out other opportunities for them.

Just as your staff reacts to the opportunity for growth in different ways, they will also have widely ranging skill levels and motivations:

- Some will have both good skills and confidence in their abilities.
- Some will be less developed professionally, but be aware of their abilities and commitment, and have the confidence and a burning desire to succeed.
- Some will lack skills and confidence, but sincerely want to grow.
- And some, as we mentioned, are merely hanging out till retirement time.

In all except the last instance you will need to develop plans that respond to the needs of that specific individual. You should try to turn around the last group, but if you don't succeed you should gradually replace them with people who do want to be successful.

Company Direction Comes First

Identifying group and individual needs follows a straightforward process that involves meeting with each team member separately. From these meetings you can develop programs for common and individual needs. The more widespread the need, the more support you can expect from HR and the company.

Now, while the developmental needs of your employees are important and demand your attention, they demand your attention only to the degree that they are in alignment with the goals of your company. With larger companies the direction of the organization is probably clearly defined, which will make your choices of which skill areas to coach relatively simple. If you work for a smaller company you may well find yourself involved in the discussions that help set the company's course. In the process you will come to discover firsthand exactly which skills you need to develop in your staff if they are to help the company achieve its goals.

If you are not certain exactly what skills will most positively impact company goals, you should meet with HR, your immediate boss, and your peers in management to gather their insights. Even if you are certain, you should still do the same, because you will gain insight from the discussion, and confidence knowing that you are on the same page with other executives and have their support. Once you have a clear understanding of the company's needs, you should meet with each of your staff members to address their individual needs.

The sooner you do this with your people the better. If both you and your staff are new to each other, the conversations have a better chance of being open, because all concerned are starting a fresh page and want the relationship to go well. Those who had good relations with the last manager want good relations with the new manager. Those who didn't, hope that the new regime offers an opportunity for a fresh start in management relationships.

Building a Development Plan

Building an effective development plan is one of those opportunities that will occur rather frequently throughout your management experience. You'll spend far more time and effort recovering from a half-hearted effort at planning than you will spend doing the due diligence in the first place. Here are some steps toward creating the development plan:

1. **Talk with your staff about their existing skills.** Review existing personnel files before you meet with each employee. Build off of current or prior performance evaluations. Then start the meeting with a conversation about the evolving goals of the company and how they

affect the department's obligations. Ask your employee about how she sees the department's challenges in light of company goals. Then ask your employee to outline her job responsibilities and identify the skills needed to execute each effectively. Ask how she sees future professional growth, and what skills she believes are needed to achieve those goals.

2. **Address the strengths and weaknesses of each person on your team.** In light of the business, address existing skill sets and inquire how those skills might be developed further; then discuss new skills that need to be developed.

3. **Identify the steps you plan to take.** Let each worker know the process that you are going through to develop a plan to help everyone maximize their potential. Commit to coming back with a development plan to meet the person's needs, once you have met with everyone in the department and developed a clear overview of what the group, as a whole, believes its needs are.

4. **Follow through with HR and your boss.** Make that meeting with each of your staff members happen within thirty days. Imposing a deadline on yourself will force you to take action in developing coaching plans for group and individual needs. To do this you will first have to come up with a schematic covering everyone's needs, and then discuss the department's development needs as a whole with HR and your immediate supervisor. These discussions will give you insight from those who can make your plans happen, and inform you as to which company resources might be available to satisfy your needs. The discussions also add a dimension of commitment and seriousness to the process.

5. **Follow through with your staff.** Identify skills that only one worker needs to improve, common skills that two or three others need to work on, and common skills that the whole group believes need improvement. Follow through with everyone individually, and outline your plans for each desired area of development. *Make sure you get mutual agreement.* It helps to put the plan in writing, and to even get a signed commitment. Then outline your plan of attack for the group as a whole in a group meeting. Explain that following the one-on-one meetings you have identified areas where the whole group wants to improve, and outline what you think is possible. Also indicate that you will be meeting with everyone again to discuss individual programs.

Putting the Coaching Plan into Play

It isn't enough to say that you plan to help employees improve their skills; there has to be a means of implementation. Once a need for skill development is identified, a means of accomplishment must be delineated. This can range from your being available to answer questions on an as-needed basis, to other options such as the following:

- **Job shadowing.** The worker spends time observing someone accomplished in a particular skill or area. For example, the new salesperson might spend a couple of weeks making sales calls with your top sales people, before he goes solo.
- **Buddy assignments.** The trainee forms a short-term relationship with another employee possessing superior competency in the skill area. In this development scenario, the trainee performs the job with the ongoing advice and oversight of the senior staffer.
- **Personal study.** The employee improves skills by personal study via books, tapes, and videos. Most medium to large companies maintain formal training libraries situated within HR, to which you or a worker can readily gain access. If your company doesn't provide a library, try industry trade groups, bookstores, or query your colleagues. The Internet is a great resource. If you are still drawing a blank, try one of the resource companies such as Monad Trainers Aide (*www.monadtrainersaide.com*), which has been renting and selling thousands of audio and training videos for more than twenty-five years.
- **Formal training.** Training meetings can be run by you or a particularly skilled team member. HR may also sponsor formal training programs for your staff, or you can go outside to one of the many training and development companies that specialize in providing training services on an as-needed basis. Another excellent resource is professional associations, which often conduct professional development programs on an ongoing basis.

Making Coaching Stick

You should also assess how each worker is absorbing and applying new skills. There is little point in investing time, money, and energy in training your staff if the training has no impact.

Everyone is different in how they learn, and the rate at which they can absorb and apply new information and techniques. One person might pick things up after simply hearing a new idea; therefore, you should be sensitive to this individual being independent and a fast learner, and consequently not overtrain or smother this person with ongoing group training. Another individual might learn more slowly and need not only ongoing training but personal support as well. In this instance the formal training might be supplemented with job shadowing and a buddy assignment until the new skill is adequately absorbed.

No matter what approach you use; you must have an open door for your staff, and instill the feeling in them that they can come to you with questions. Whenever a worker needs your time, you must be available to that person. Even if your job requires you to be tied up eight hours a day, make sure that your door is open every day first thing in the morning, at lunchtime, toward the end of the day, and *any time* an emergency arises. Always answer the question "Have you got a moment, boss?" in the affirmative.

Remember—you must always be available on an equal basis to each and every one of your people. Some people find it easy to ask advice, others find it far more difficult to reach out. Showing a personal interest in and knowledge of your staff members as individuals will do a lot to break down barriers of distrust and nervousness. Your coaching must include reaching out, as you "manage by wandering around." You should regularly stop by everyone's office, desk, or cubicle to inquire after your employees' activities, or to simply say hello.

Tell, Show, and Involve

In the professional world of training and development there is a saying that goes: Tell me and I'll forget, show me and I'll remember, involve me and I'll be able to do it myself. The point of the saying is that the more involvement you can create in a learning experience, the better and more quickly it will be absorbed. All three of these techniques (tell, show, involve) have a place in your coaching bag of tricks, and used in concert will give you the most powerful in-department training tool available. This three-part coaching tool works in this sequence:

1. You share knowledge about the skill, and have the employee execute under your supervision.
2. You assign the employee to work closely with another staff member well versed in this skill (either as a shadow or a buddy).
3. You give the employee assignments that build confidence in the skill set area.

The coaching process doesn't necessarily teach each skill one at a time. While coaching can teach a continuing, ever-building sequence of skills, you can coach different skills and tasks in parallel. When you start a coaching process by sharing knowledge about the area to be coached, you don't stop once the buddy is assigned. Stay involved with the employee's development as you present more challenging assignments. You don't withdraw from sharing helpful information, nor is the buddy suddenly unavailable for help and advice. Follow a sequence to get the process moving, then continue to tell, show, and involve as the learning process moves forward.

Sharing Knowledge

There are many techniques for sharing knowledge. Some are focused on specific skill development, while others are geared toward increasing overall professionalism. Coaching for any specific skill should begin with first putting the skill in context of its importance to the individual job or position, the department, and the company as a whole. Here are the steps for sharing your knowledge effectively:

1. **You show how a task is performed.** Place yourself and the employee in the exact environment in which the job will be done. Reiterate the importance of the skill to the success of the job, and then execute the task as you explain what you are doing every step along the way. Give the employee actionable advice and phrases to remember whenever you can.
2. **The employee then executes the task under your step-by-step directions.** You direct, they do.
3. **The employee executes the task and explains what he is doing and why.** This reinforces both *their* confidence and yours.

When you need to share knowledge of a specific skill set, this "show and tell, do and tell" method, repeated as necessary, will often accomplish the task, or can be integrated with a larger coaching program.

Building Communication Skills

When teaching communications skills, this "show and tell, do and tell" process can be supplemented with role-playing. For example, if you are an HR manager you might role-play screening interviews; in customer service you could role-play handling a difficult or irate customer; and in sales you could role-play cold-calling a prospective client. When you want an employee to polish his communication skills, role-playing is a powerful tool.

In a role-play, your employee plays his role for his actual position, and you play the other party, such as the job hunter, the irate customer, or potential client. The role-playing allows your staff member to experience implementing the techniques he has learned, and experience a successful outcome. Let's stay with the example of an irate customer for a moment. There are countless causes for such a situation arising, so the customer service manager might do a number of role-plays presenting different scenarios, with each role-play presenting one significant challenge. After every role-play is completed the trainer gives encouraging input and advice on why things went wrong (if they did) and how to make a similar situation come out better the next time. Role-plays allow employees to put new knowledge into practice in a safe environment. Thus, role-playing is a great confidence builder.

Sharing Experiences

There's a fine line between sharing gems of wisdom from your professional experience and droning on and on about your war stories. The rule of thumb: *The experience you recount should always have a lesson embedded within it.* That lesson may be about the right or wrong way to do something, but there's a lesson.

You, more than your subordinates, know that success comes from hanging in there over the long haul and doing the job right no matter what the circumstances. Illustrative stories of your successes, failures, and observations can be inspiring to your staff.

> We had the same problem at XYZ company, this was the situation . . . and this was the solution we came up with . . . . Jason, I used to have the same problem until I tried a new approach . . . Have you thought of doing it this way . . . ?

Sharing your experience and wisdom through telling illustrative stories doesn't always have to be about how you slew the dragon with one hand tied behind your back; in fact, they should largely focus on how success results from applying specific techniques and professional behaviors. Small successes and lessons can be just as important—and often more useful—than the big ones. Sharing your failures with people in your group won't diminish your standing, either; in fact it will accomplish just the opposite. By sharing your failures your staff will be impressed by your openness and honesty and motivated to get past their own professional challenges.

Catch People Doing Things Right

As you get out and about in your department, dropping by cubicles and joining in casual conversations around the water cooler, your people will get used to your presence, giving you the opportunity to see them in action. As such, you will see them doing things well and also experiencing difficulties, sometimes with the job and sometimes with another person. Because you are out amongst your people, you have the opportunity to observe, encourage, share your experience, and give advice. One of the best things you can do for employee morale is to catch someone doing something well, and whenever you do, you should congratulate that person on it then and there.

Try to catch each member of your staff doing things well as often as you can. Apart from its obvious morale benefits, it opens everybody up to taking constructive advice when things don't go as well. Always try to start such conversations by asking the employee to relive the situation, and before offering your input, give your employee the opportunity to come up with ideas of his own.

> Is there anything you could have done to set it up differently? What other approaches are there that might have worked? Let's put our heads together on this and see what we can come up with.

Then you can add your ten cents:

> "You know, when this has happened to me, I always try to look at . . ."
> "I know that other people in similar situations have tried . . . and it often seems to work."
> "If I were in your position I might try to . . ."
> "Might I offer an idea . . . ?"
> "Have you considered . . . ?"

Having discussed all the possibilities, you want your employee to come up with a decision on how to handle the situation or problem differently the next time around. If the employee comes up with the answer (with your subtle help, of course), there is more ownership and commitment to its implementation. Remember, people who create tend to support.

Assign a Buddy

When you are helping new employees pick up essential skills or polish certain areas of the job to make them shine, using the buddy system can work very effectively. The buddy system simply means you assign the worker to a senior member of the team who has exemplary skills in the area in question.

You must choose the senior buddy with care. It must be someone who . . .

- Is doing the job successfully now.
- Can take the responsibility without letting productivity drop.
- Will experience the assignment as a reward and recognition.
- Has good people skills.
- Can take direction.

This last point is of particular importance. You don't want to assign a buddy who will undermine your authority or the way you want things done. Explain exactly the help you want, and how you want it given. You might even have the senior team member read parts of this chapter. When a buddy is chosen properly, the trainee gets close ongoing support in the hands of a competent team member who wants to make the project successful. This senior staff person gets to develop a new and valuable leadership skill; and you are seen to be developing people in a professional manner. To make this happen, first sit down with your senior staffer and explain the situation and set the ground rules:

> Brenda, we have a new kid onboard, and because of your expertise in marketing I'd like you to take him under your wing for a month. This is what I would like you to do: [outline the goals, what you have done so far, and how you would like Brenda to continue] and this is what I would like him to learn by the end of that time. [Identify the learning goals and how you will evaluate that new knowledge.]

You may choose to have your senior staffer take the trainee through the "show and tell" experience as part of the job shadowing/buddy relationship, as well. Even if the employee has already gone through it with you, repeating the process with another person will provide further opportunity for learning and hearing similar information in a different way. This in itself is a very valuable training technique; it is proven that the more times and the more opportunities a person is given to absorb information in different ways, the better that information will be implemented.

It is important to set time limits on the relationship so as not to overwhelm a valuable team member, or lock either party into an unproductive relationship. Setting time limits and deadlines also encourages results. If the relationship is to last more than a couple of weeks, you need to follow up with both parties on a casual basis.

You may want to rotate shadowing/buddy assignments by having the trainee spend time with more than one senior team member. This can . . .

- Spread the workload.
- Offer greater exposure to different techniques.
- Help the new team member build relationships.
- Help integrate the new team member into the team.

Throughout the duration of the buddy relationship you must monitor how things are progressing for the trainee; that is, what and how the employee is learning from the process. With the senior staffer you have two agendas: (1) You want to follow up on the junior staffer's progress and how your senior staffer is getting along with the responsibility; and (2) you need to keep a casual but very watchful eye that the senior staffer's other activities are not suffering because of the new responsibility.

Finally, recognize the value of a buddy assignment in training your senior team member for future management. In the assignment she will learn to coach others and get things done through others effectively, and will learn the job and department function from a different point of view—not just as a doer but as someone who gets things done through others.

As your coaching continues, the trainee in question will gradually pick up the new skills. She will have experienced the "show and tell" learning experience from you and perhaps other members of your staff. In addition, the trainee will have gone through at least one buddy coaching experience, and hopefully more than one. So, given that your trainee has a pulse, she is probably beginning to pick up the new skill set. As the skill develops, you need to build confidence by offering more challenging assignments, carefully analyzing the trainee's progress, and providing support as necessary.

Making Time for Time Management

For many employees, especially new ones, time management presents one of the biggest coaching and development opportunities. You'll run into two mindsets—people who simply aren't "programmed" to manage their time well, and people who are driven by the need to "do" and even to "impress" by taking on more than they can handle. Poor time management leads to poor or incomplete results, frustrated employees, and a frustrated *you*.

Time management coaching is tricky. First, the employee needs to recognize where people fail to make good decisions about time and why projects are late. Second, the employee needs to understand the value of using mechanical tools—calendars, day timers, and so forth. These tools are all a matter of personal preference, and aside from those people with extraordinary memories, everyone should use some form of calendar and "to do" list.

Finally, time management problems often stem from poor prioritization of work activities. As a manager you can help by identifying and divvying up tasks according to priority and importance. Lists of tasks and priorities for the department and individual employee might be categorized into A, B, and C priorities:

- **A priorities** are overwhelmingly important tasks that absolutely must be completed.
- **B priorities** are tasks that really should be completed tomorrow.
- **C priorities** are the tasks that need to get done when you have time.

They are all urgent, but because some are obviously more urgent than others, you start with the A's, followed by B's, and then C's. That way you know that even if you didn't achieve everything you set out to do (which is usually the case), at least you took a big bite out of your most important tasks. People who organize and track this way tend to be more productive and feel better about their efforts than those who don't. They go home at night knowing exactly what they are doing the next day, and are comfortable knowing they did their best today.

A Few More Developmental Tools

There are countless ways to coach and enhance the effectiveness of your people. Here are a few more ideas:

- **Let staff members run team meetings.** This will give them the opportunity to (1) put their skills into practice, (2) learn to lead, (3) react and respond, and (4) gain respect with peers. It is on-the-job training for not only their position and role, but also for management. It also gives you an opportunity to spend time on other things, and to see team members "in action." You may choose to rotate this assignment among team members.

- **Take employees with you, when appropriate, to interdepartmental meetings and to client meetings.** For most teams and individual situations, this is a good path to growth. Employees learn by observing, and generally feel more important and vital to the department's success—a critical component of personal growth. They feel more connected to clients and other departments, and gain the respect of those constituents.
- **Help your people network with other departments and other managers.** Introduce your people to other managers who stop by. Send your people to their meetings, and invite other managers' people to yours. Opportunities may subsequently develop where you can nurture that relationship and have another source of valuable input for your people.
- **If your people have training needs that you cannot satisfy, find someone who can do it, and offer to reciprocate from your areas of strength.** "Gain from exchange" is a founding principle of our economic system, and should be a founding principle of interpersonal relationships in the workplace. You have skills and experiences others can use, and they have skills and experiences that will be valuable to you.

When you help someone improve his skills, you increase his effectiveness and sense of self-esteem simultaneously. When you impact a group of people in this way, you develop a productive department and a reputation as an effective manager.

Remember—Not All Valuable Workers Are Superstars

It is easy in America's culture of winning to assume that anyone without the same burning desire as you is a slacker. This is a misconception you can't afford to harbor as an effective manager. Every department has two clearly identifiable groups—the super motivated who will do anything you ask and want nothing more than a good challenge, and the "walking wounded" who either can't or won't make anything more than a minimal effort.

However, there is a third, less readily identifiable group, those who plug along doing a reliable job, but who don't possess any real motivation to grow professionally. If you see everything in black and white it is easy to mistake these valuable employees as members of the walking wounded, simply because they are obviously not motivated by growth. It is a costly mistake to make, because these people could become the backbone of your group and your reputation, if only you learn how to handle them productively.

You can quite easily identify these middle-of-the-pack performers, the pluggers, from their personnel files. When you inherit a new department you should spend time in HR going over each member's personnel file. You will find that pluggers have often been in the job and with the company for a long time, and usually have good attendance records and steady reviews.

You can also get a heads up from how they are described by your boss, your colleagues, and the people in HR. You'll hear a plugger described like this:

- Likes the routine
- Reliable but not a superstar
- Doesn't complain
- Gets the job done, but don't expect her to stay past five
- Actually turned down a promotion

Put the pieces together and you have perfectly good employees who could be excellent if only they were motivated! And you are just the person to set a fire under them! Wrong, wrong, wrong, and a recipe for driving a valuable asset out of your department about three weeks before you lose the last of that prematurely gray hair.

Fortunately for you, there are plenty of good professionals who are not motivated by professional growth much beyond where you find them today. They aren't losers; they take pride in a job, but very often they have other things going on in their lives that take precedence. Often the job is a way to pay the bills, a means to an end that allows them to pay attention to the things that are important in their lives. Now if you can recognize the needs of these workers and don't expect them to be gung-ho zealots, you can secure a valuable asset. Here's how:

- **Show them respect for the reliable professionals they are.** Be thankful they are not back-stabbing others in an insatiable desire for success at all costs.

- **Appreciate their experience and dependability.** Be thankful that they don't need watching every moment of the day. These workers can be relied on to work steadily at their assignments, allowing you to use your time to develop other employees or otherwise further your department's interests.
- **Keep them busy doing what they are comfortable doing.** Sometimes you will be able to free up time for one of your superstars for a special project by reassigning some less interesting duties to a plugger.
- **Keep their workload manageable.** Remember, a plugger may not be late for work, but he is usually gone by five, too.
- **Don't press them to learn skills above and beyond those necessary to do the job.** They usually won't respond.
- **Recognize that sometimes people lack confidence and are threatened by learning, and as a result they sometimes learn more slowly.** When a new skill is necessary, perhaps because of the changing technology in the workplace, allow the time and resources necessary for them to pick it up.
- **Remember that pluggers are often undervalued and may carry a little resentment because of that.** Value them, and figure out roles to satisfy *their* needs, too. Once you are seen to value their efforts you can often win over a serious supporter for your cause.
- **Develop the plugger's qualities of reliability and steadiness in other people.** Because they are reliable and steady, they are often very good at the things they choose to do well.

So when it comes to coaching approaches like job shadowing or buddying, one of your steady, reliable pluggers might be just the person to deliver a solid learning experience. This also works because it provides them respect and recognition within their comfort zone. Because workers who fall into the plugger category aren't often seen leaping tall buildings at a single bound on behalf of their employers, they notice praise most often by its absence. Using pluggers in this way provides status and gives you the opportunity to praise their contributions.

One last word on pluggers: As a manager you are likely to be a driven and motivated person. As such, you will naturally gravitate toward people like yourself, even in relationships with your staff. You need to make just as much effort to get to know and find common ground with pluggers who perhaps don't share your particular approach to life. Just as you respond to those who take a genuine interest in you as a person, so do others.

Mentor versus Coach

Corporate jargon can get mighty confusing at times, thanks in large part to the verbosity of business writers trying to pad the mundane with jazzy catch phrases and important but amorphous words. This whole area of coaching is rife with this issue.

Teaching, training, tutoring, and coaching are, at heart, all the same thing; they each speak about helping someone grow. Perhaps the only real difference is that teaching, training, and coaching tend to speak about groups while tutoring speaks very much to a one-on-one relationship. So what's the difference between a coach and a mentor? A coach speaks and acts more toward the good of the group while a mentor speaks specifically to a one-on-one relationship. Many management treatments define "mentor" as a coach and "guiding light" from outside the department. But really, a good coach is a good mentor, and vice versa.

As a manager you have to coach your whole team, and to get the best out of that whole team you have to adapt yourself to, and build special relationships with, each person. In practice, you offer yourself up as a mentor to all comers in your department. So, as a manager you are there to coach everyone on a personal basis, and if any of those people reach out for a more intense tutor-student relationship, you will become a mentor.

You should read this chapter again, because everything in it applies to you, too. From recognizing the kind of person you are and the effort you are prepared to put forth, through the skills you have and the ones you need to develop, to the ways you can learn. Just as you strive to apply these techniques to improve the productivity of your people, someone else is striving to get the best out of you. Your boss may well have a number of employees, each of whom your boss will try to understand and help through coaching. Some of those will be special people especially open to input and self-improvement, and of these, a few may reach out for an even closer professional relationship.

Finding Your Mentor

Just as you expect your employees to make the effort to seek out a mentor relationship, so must you if you take growth and success seriously. One of those you mentor will possibly inherit your job when you move up, and when you move up it will probably be because you reached out to a senior manager for grooming. You can coach a person in skill development, but any success-driven person recognizes that skills are only part of the equation. The higher you climb, the more important your judgment becomes. Unfortunately, your good judgment usually comes from having bad experiences.

Management books talk about the lucky day when you find your mentor or, really, when the mentor finds you.

> Hey, Martin, I'm the CEO and it's a lovely day in the neighborhood so I thought I'd come by your pokey cubicle and offer to share all the wisdom of my success with you, my chosen one, my anointed. Whaddya think, kid?

You know, it may happen, just like winning the lottery obviously happens every week, but not to anyone we know. So, just as you wouldn't rely on winning the lotto for your retirement plans, don't count on anyone coming to you begging to be your mentor. As a manager you are open to anyone who comes to you for help, and the more they ask, the more you will help. That's your job as a manager and your ethical responsibility as a conscientious professional. You, too, should seek out this same personal advisory relationship for your personal growth. You look for these signs in your staff to identify people really committed to growth, so apply them in your own quest for a mentor. Here are some tips to attracting a mentor for yourself:

- **Seize every opportunity to learn and become a consummate professional.** Read books, watch tapes, attend seminars, and become part of your professional community.
- **Go for advice only after you have analyzed the situation and considered all the options.** Ask for advice only when it can be seen that you have done your homework, that you know how and when the problem arose, and what effect your own solutions would produce.
- **Seek respectful relationships with all of your superiors, and when asking for advice, act with professionalism and humility.** Think before you ask, and always place their needs and the needs of the business ahead of your own.
- **When you receive help, you recognize an obligation to repay the efforts on your behalf in some way.** You cannot expect a one-way relationship to last any longer than the summer love affairs of your callow youth. Your benefactor must know that you are thankful and willing in some way to return the support you have received. In doing so you are building alliances to increase your professional credibility and visibility.

- **Watch your prospective mentor with an eagle eye, looking not only for what she gets done, but how she gets it done.** Watch how she deals with people, how she deals with crises and setbacks, how she analyzes situations, and what criteria she uses for making decisions in different areas of her professional life. You will glean lessons from her successes and from her failures.
- **Seek career guidance from your mentor.** Talk about your dreams, and ask how the reality is likely to differ. Ask for suggestions for what you will have to do and what skills you will need to manifest those dreams. At the same time, don't expect your mentor to build a development program for you. Take this responsibility yourself. With your added insight, identify your needs and set about developing a coaching program for yourself (using the techniques we have discussed) to achieve your targets.

Summary

Whatever words and phrases we use to describe the development process, the goal is the same: professional growth for enhanced productivity. The increasing skill level of your staff and the resultant increases in productivity and efficiency will not happen overnight. Development is an ongoing process in the lives of professional people. Only slowly will your results be seen, but the effort must start now, today.

The essence of your job as a manager is to get work done through others, and coaching is the way you maximize your impact. Remember that the very techniques that help your people grow, will help you succeed as well.

6 | Performance Appraisal —And Dealing with Problem Employees

Evaluating your employees is a critical and often underemphasized part of managing the business. You must evaluate before you can develop, and must be able to change team players when necessary.

You may have grown up in some happily dysfunctional family totally unlike TV's *Brady Bunch.* Your team, the family you have at work, will have also its problems and challenges. Logically that's to be expected, because they are the people with whom you spend most of your waking hours. It is important to recognize that you are, indeed, the leader of what in many ways is a family group, and with that honor comes certain responsibilities. Not least among them is to keep everyone on track, for their own benefit as well as the common good. How you handle this responsibility will determine the health and well-being of your workplace family.

Leadership in family and leadership at work are tested when things aren't going as planned. In this chapter we will continue the discussion of nurturing your staff, addressing performance reviews and the subsequent action plan reviews, and then address how to deal effectively with troubled employees with a counseling/progressive discipline process. Although every manager hopes never to face it, we will also discuss the process of termination with just cause.

Evaluating Performance— The Big Picture

The vast majority of professionals put good effort into their jobs and work hard to be successful. The vast majority of professionals also put being appreciated for a job well done high on their priority list, and its absence is a major reason for leaving that job. You probably know this from your own experience. You also know from your own experience that performance reviews come too infrequently and all too often bear no relation to the efforts you have put forth during the year. So you won't be surprised to hear that, astoundingly, some studies claim that *almost half of all workers never receive a performance evaluation.* This lack of input after a year's effort is a clear signal of lack of appreciation.

So why doesn't management communicate better, why don't regular performance reviews happen, or when they do, why are they so often peremptory and inadequate? The *given* reason: not enough time. The *real* reason (in most cases): The majority of managers are afraid of their employees. They're scared because they have no ongoing dialogue with their people.

The performance evaluation is clearly a useful communication tool between manager and employee, a tool that recognizes good performance, offers an opportunity to correct poor performance, and allows coaching to progress on an ongoing basis. As such, performance evaluations are at the heart of all effective communications between worker and manager; without them, little problems turn into big problems, workers feel ignored, underappreciated, and eventually become alienated.

A Year-Round Job

For the modern manager, performance evaluation is really a day-to-day and year-round job. You might not always have the conversations that offer constructive input on a daily basis, but you should observe everyone's performance every day. When you notice a special effort—or a problem—discuss it with the worker when you can. If it isn't possible to do so at the time then make a note of the matter and slip it into that person's file for your next conversation. As you work through this chapter you will realize just how effective dropping a note in an employee's file can be in preventing management headaches down the line.

Those little notes you stuff into each file during the week not only become the basis for reinforcing success within the company, but they also document your commitment to playing by a clearly enunciated set of performance standards. This solid foundation gives your people a sense of security in that you have solid examples of good or "bad" performance (and not just vague recollections of issues) according to a set of rules and performance standards by which you expect everyone to abide.

Your tenure of authority in the work group depends on your effectiveness in getting work done through others, and that means keeping your employees on track and productive. Just as driving a car requires you to constantly look ahead and behind, adjust your speed, signal a change in direction, slow, stop, and reverse when necessary, so does developing your staff. Possessing the details of what has happened in the past is a key building block for structuring future action plans.

An Unwavering Responsibility

You need to set goals with each of your employees and help them plan how to get from where they stand today to where you want them to be a month or a year from now. Together you will plan the route and identify potential obstacles and develop contingency plans that will ensure reaching the mutually agreed upon goal. For the successful manager this is not a once-a-year occurrence; it is an ongoing daily, weekly, and monthly activity. Continuous monitoring of individual performance is what keeps your group as a whole on track toward departmental and company goals.

If you invest yourself in close, but unobtrusive, monitoring of ongoing performance, your more formal quarterly, semiannual, and annual performance reviews will hold no anxiety for you or your staff members. Evaluations will simply be an understood and accepted step in your management program, one that shows each person that her success is something of serious concern to you. This is a key element in demonstrating appreciation; it creates the kind of awareness that breeds loyalty in your staff (something we will be addressing in detail a little later in the book). Performance review meetings will hold no surprises because they are just formalized sessions recapping all the prior, and more casual, performance discussions you've had with your employees, and are now putting in context with goals for the coming period.

Standards and Performance Expectations

Your performance reviews need to take into account both standards of *behavior* and standards of *performance*. These standards allow large numbers of people to work in harmony, which is important because we spend more of our waking hours with our colleagues than we do with our family and loved ones. These standards are the ones that allow everyone to feel they are on a level playing field, where the bounds of acceptable performance and behavior are defined. Without everyone willingly abiding by such standards no workplace can be a productive and happy working environment.

While the majority of people find it easy enough to treat others as they would like to be treated, maintaining acceptable job performance standards doesn't always come so easily. In earlier chapters we laid the foundations for good communication between you and your reports. In Chapter 4 on recruitment and selection you evaluated the responsibilities of each job title in relation to overall department and corporate goals. You asked your existing staff to write their own evaluations of job performance requirements, then aligned those evaluations with corporate reality, and subsequently discussed them with your employees both individually and as a group.

You achieved consensus with each team member on what it took to be successful in a specific job. You subsequently established individual and group coaching initiatives to help group members maximize their professional potential. You built a department plan and used it to set standards, and a framework for objective performance analysis during a given period of time (you'll learn more details about this process in Chapter 8). Taking these steps dramatically increases everyone's chances of success.

Where do standards come from?

Most often, standards are directed by the needs of the business, and are a result of the planning process (see Chapter 8). But in some industries, organizational bodies beyond your control set those performance standards. Healthcare, education, law enforcement, government agencies, and certain other types of organizations frequently have whole areas of their performance standards set by outside accreditation or oversight functions. If you are in an industry or profession governed by such overriding considerations, these overriding considerations must be adhered to above and before all others.

Organizing Performance Review Meetings

We discussed the importance of regular performance reviews in the last chapter, but referred to them as coaching meetings. In many ways the two are the same. Both are opportunities to sit down one-on-one to review performance and plan benchmarks for future efforts. A performance review meeting is wider in scope and perhaps more formal, but essentially it is no different. In this section we talk about the organization and structure of performance review meetings that will serve you well as a basis for all private interactions with staff.

The opportunities you create for private communication with your employees will largely determine your success as a manager; when your employees see you are paying attention they realize you care about their success.

How Often and How Much?

It is typical to talk about annual performance reviews as being tied to salary raises or the lack thereof. They happen once a year because raises come but once a year, and there is no way out of them. We are not alone when we tell you that the frequency of such meetings is entirely inadequate. Semiannual performance reviews should be your minimum goal, and once a quarter is ideal. You'll see by the end of this section that this is not an onerous burden; rather, it is something that over the long haul will make your job easier and your presence as a manager more effective. It's a case of a little short-term pain for a lot of long-term gain. Like going to the dentist on a regular basis, the more you go the less that has to be done.

The more time you invest in the development of your people's competency, the better your efforts will be recognized and rewarded. At minimum you should hold some form of review meetings with each employee once a month, and as you become involved as a coaching manager this will become a natural occurrence. Consequently a more formal review once a quarter or every couple of quarters will be a natural step for both of you.

In planning and organizing performance review meetings, you examine individual projects, just as you do in the more frequent monthly meetings, but now you expand your purview to include overall performance in all aspects of the job. The broader the range of topics, the more carefully you must plan and organize the event. When you learn to organize and execute these carefully focused meetings effectively, you develop skills that you can apply in the larger scope of your general management interactions.

One-on-Ones

Many managers supplement the formal, company-specified annual review with a somewhat less formal, but still structured, one-on-one review. The manager schedules time (even by phone, for remote employees) to review not only the employee's task performance, but also to give feedback on the job done as a whole. Often, these meetings are an hour or less, and occur monthly. One-on-ones not only serve to update the employee on performance, but also serve to update the manager on what's going on, usually in a broader context beyond specific task details. In short, not only do they function as performance feedback tools, they also serve a vital role in general communication, particularly in decentralized, complex, fast paced environments where regular communication is a challenge.

Preparation, Preparation, Preparation

You will find it useful to have a general schematic for performance review meetings, which you can customize to the individual. Preparation should include these elements:

- **Goal of the meeting.** You want to review the performance and productivity in each of the worker's areas of responsibility; the worker's commitment and comfort level as a member of the work group; and the worker's adherence to company standards.
- **Desired outcome.** You want the worker to understand that good work is recognized and appreciated, that support is available for challenging situations, and inadequacy or slackness doesn't go unnoticed. Given these points you want both of you to leave the meeting with a positive outlook toward the future and an overall plan for implementation that takes you both to the next formal review meeting in ninety or 120 days.
- **Your role.** You guide the conversation through accurate and careful recall of the employee's performance, and ask stimulating questions. You must plan your observations and questions in a way that will bring the two of your toward consensus on plans for the future.
- **Employee preparation.** If you meet regularly with your staff, the trepidation of these formal meetings will be much diminished; however, your staff member will still be nervous. To minimize this, alert your employee to the date, time, and nature of the meeting, give him or her an outline of the areas you plan to address, and explain what to bring.
- **Follow-up strategy.** How will you follow up on commitments made? This should be simple, because you will agree to follow through on your mutual commitments in your regular weekly/biweekly/monthly follow-up.

Keep Your Objectivity

In preparing yourself for these meetings you need to be aware of your personal preferences and feelings. Here are two common pitfalls:

1. **Comparing one employee you particularly like to another for whom you have no particular feelings.** This will color your objectivity because you should be comparing this person to the requirements of the job, not to another person. Be especially careful when reviewing people who are like you and have similar interests; you are likely to unconsciously color their performance in a more positive light. At the same time be equally careful reviewing employees you don't like on a personal level; here your objectivity can be inappropriately colored in a negative fashion. Remember that differences in personality and outlook on life are what give your department real strength and balance.

2. **Going too far to avoid conflict.** Most of us don't like sharing unpopular views when they might cause friction or confrontation. If you know you are not good at sharing the not-so-palatable news, then try role-playing with a peer or someone in HR (not your spouse at home unless it's mutually agreeable!). You'll get practice and valuable feedback, learn to share the information more effectively, and turn a weakness into strength.

Here again, dropping notes into a personnel file gives you documentation to back up your arguments on difficult topics. For example, instead of saying "you have been coming into work late most mornings and leaving early most afternoons," which is nonspecific and will lead to an argument, you can instead cite specific dates and times and have the documentation to back it up. Just as in making business presentations—and remember, a performance appraisal *is* a type of business presentation—*preparation* is the key to avoiding pitfalls.

The Performance Evaluation Process

Your company may well have an evaluation process that you are required to follow. If this is not the case, it isn't a bad idea to create some standardized format to ensure you will be evaluating everyone based on the same criteria. Depending on the complexity of tasks your employees perform, this may be a single sheet of paper or a more complex document. What it should address are all the aspects of work that affect performance as an individual and as a contributing member of a team.

It isn't a bad idea to create a form that you can make notes on and subsequently place in the personnel file. Nor is it a bad idea to offer this form to the employee a week beforehand, requesting that she review it, answer the questions, and return to you no later than forty-eight hours prior to the scheduled meeting.

This is a win/win technique. Your employee knows what's going to be addressed and has an opportunity to make her own statements well in advance, which will greatly reduce her nerves at the meeting. You will also find that most people are pretty honest, given the opportunity and motivation. With the completed form in your hand forty-eight hours before the meeting, you have adequate time to strategize your approach, knowing exactly what the employee is thinking.

Most companies have evaluation forms, but if you need to develop your own, don't skimp on it. It will help you do a better job, and it will make you shine in the eyes of your superiors as a leader who is in touch with the staff. The form should start off with standard biographical info about the employee, and it should be specific about the time period covered.

Beyond this "header," the evaluation should cover specific topics. Some will be standard, some may be unique to an individual's job (as in safety, special communication skills, etc.). There may be a ranking or scoring measure, then a few blank lines for written comments. The section for written comments may be divided into two sections: review of past performance and accomplishments, and a development plan for the upcoming period.

Making the Grade

You might also consider at the end of each performance review a simple ranking system along the lines of . . .

- Excellent
- Above average
- Acceptable
- Needs improvement

Or . . .

- Consistently far exceeds job expectations.
- Consistently exceeds job expectations.
- Consistently meets job expectations.
- Occasionally does not meet job expectations.
- Consistently does not meet job expectations.

These "grades" or ranks will apply to each individual area being evaluated, and may be used to judge the employee's overall performance. They should match or fit into the wage and salary administration framework of the organization.

Understand that if you rank anyone below excellent in any area you need to justify it, and you should come up with initiatives to help the person improve in that particular area. At the same time beware of grading people too high to avoid confrontation; that slightly troubled employee may, at some point in the future, need to be terminated (more later in the chapter). A termination can be countered with a wrongful dismissal suit because all extant evaluations show you marking the employee as above average.

Areas of Performance

Here are some topics relevant to performance review in most professions. You can customize them to your own unique needs.

Job Responsibilities and Performance

- Does the employee clearly understand his responsibilities as you have jointly defined them?
- Does the employee achieve what's expected within those responsibilities?
- Does the employee understand how the job relates to other jobs and how his job contributes to the whole?

Technical Competence

- Does the employee possess the skills required to do the job effectively, and does he apply them well?
- Does the employee utilize technologies to the level required by the job?

Work Quality

- Is the employee's work accurate?
- Has the employee made adequate personal contributions to the success of the department by effective execution of responsibilities?
- Are there positive or negative opinions of the employee's work from coworkers or customers?
- When mistakes are made, are they subsequently corrected or is assistance sought?
- Are the same mistakes made on an ongoing basis?

Judgment
- Does the employee make sound decisions in areas that affect job performance?
- Does the employee manage multiple or conflicting tasks well? Does he prioritize tasks well?
- Does the employee seek assistance when necessary?
- Does the employee understand the environment in which he operates? In which the business operates?

Dependability
- Are project deadlines regularly met or missed?
- Does the employee effectively track project or work status?
- Is the employee punctual coming to and leaving work? Attending meetings?
- Is the employee dependable?
- Is the employee organized in his approach to the working day and the projects at hand?

Teamwork and Professionalism
- Does the employee treat coworkers with respect?
- Does the employee get along with members of another sex, race, or belief system?
- Does the employee adhere to any necessary company dress policies?
- Is the employee's work area organized, clean, and professional?
- Is the employee professional with customers, clients, and the public when representing the company?
- Does the employee adhere to all company policies and procedures?

Communication
- Does the employee communicate with others effectively? When necessary?
- Are written communications adequate? (Layout, grammar, syntax, tone, etc.)
- Are verbal capabilities appropriate to the needs of the job?
- Is communication with peers, customers, and management appropriate?

Initiative
- Are there instances that exemplify a commitment (or lack thereof) to the job's responsibilities and the success of the work group?

- Does the employee raise problems or suggest solutions?
- Does the employee identify needed tasks and perform them, or wait until they are brought to his attention?
- Does the employee come up with ideas to improve productivity, workflow, teamwork, or the like?
- Is the employee a self-starter, or does he wait for instructions?

Customer Satisfaction
- Does the employee understand the needs of his customers, internal or external to the work group? The organization?
- Does the employee work to satisfy those needs? Is the employee committed to customer satisfaction?

This may be more or less than you need to address performance review of your people. Doubtless you will need to customize the questions to your departmental needs and word them in a way that can comfortably be given to an employee. You may start with a standard company form and amend it. You might want to run it by HR along the way.

How Long, and How Much Detail?

It may seem as though you could write a book on every employee, given how much information you have collected on each one. In fact many performance reviews—particularly for higher managers—might include five, six, seven, eight pages, or more. The trend today is to summarize and hit the highlights, and generate something in the range of one to two pages. This crystallizes what's really important to tell the employee and what the employee needs to work on. It still allows for greater detail to be conveyed verbally in later evaluation sessions. And as a matter of practicality, because today's manager may have twenty or thirty people to review, writing long, detailed evaluations simply takes too much time. The rule is, do whatever it takes to get the performance review done efficiently and effectively. Remember, less can often be more.

You might also consider giving the evaluation form to new employees early on in their employment with the company, perhaps as part of company orientation or as you begin the ongoing coaching dialogue. In one of those early meetings you might offer the form, saying something like this:

> Jack, we will continue to meet informally every week [month] during the year so that we can stay on top of things. However, once a quarter [every six months] we will have a more formal meeting to review activities for the last period and plan for the new one. What will happen is that I will schedule a meeting with you and give you this evaluation form for you to complete and return to me a couple of days before the meeting. I'm giving it to you now because it will give you a pretty good idea of the kind of things we value here at Last Chance Electronics.

In this approach your actions do double duty: They prepare employees for the evaluation process but, moreover, they pave the way for employees to do well with the company. It always helps employees to know what will be looked at and what will be judged. At the very least, providing such a form early in the employment relationship gives employees a very clear picture of acceptable levels of performance throughout the landscape of their job responsibilities.

The Action Plan

Without specific plans nothing gets done. With them, you have clear short-term goals, a means of reaching those goals, and a means of measuring employees' success at completion. As a wise man once said about management: People don't respect what you expect; they respect what you inspect. Follow-through is the key ingredient in helping your people grow.

It is all too easy to overload your people with professional development plans. Overall performance improvement may be as small as developing a single new skill for a highly competent employee. Or it might be something as elemental as giving a staff member the organizational foundation on which to build success through regular performance evaluations.

It takes time to objectively evaluate the needs of each of your employees, but by investing the time in observation you will not be making the mistake of teaching a person how to run when that person needs to learn how to walk first. Action plans focused on small goals, and when implemented in small steps, give you the best results. If someone cannot manage her time effectively and is unable to prioritize activities as effectively as you might wish, there is no point in developing action plans to increase productivity by 25 percent, because the foundation for her success (prioritization and organization) is lacking. You build a house on solid foundations and you build from the ground up, brick by brick, allowing time for the mortar to set before you build higher.

Managers who engage in focused ongoing dialogue with their reports invariably benefit from improved group performance. This is why we have put such emphasis on mechanisms to facilitate these conversations. These mechanisms of focused dialogue with your people are a core competency for any leader. Because your communication will be structured, focused, and frequent, the meetings themselves become a normal, stress-free part of the work week. Because the great majority of working professionals want to succeed, those with clear direction, and an atmosphere supportive of their success, will work harder and do better in their jobs. The result is that over time your regular meetings with individual staff members take on an energizing life of their own.

This is not to say, however, that skills won't need to be improved or deadlines met. To this end there is an aspect of every meeting you hold with an employee, or group of employees, that should focus on the planned activities that will help your employee reach the agreed-upon goals of the meeting.

Goal versus Task Orientation

Some people are naturally goal oriented, while others are task oriented, allowing tasks to fill and often overflow the time allotted to them. That Thursday deadline is barely met, or often missed, with accompanying excuses and requests for a few more hours or days for completion. Helping your people focus on *results-oriented* activity, rather than just activity for the sake of itself, will increase your department's productivity. Avoid situations like the sales-person who invests inordinate time in developing tracking mechanisms, to the exclusion of making sales calls.

Some staff members will need to learn that every activity must be geared to some tangible result that can be measured in days or weeks. You achieve this awareness, not by making speeches, but through the ongoing meetings you have with each of your reports, where a planning dimension focuses on achieving quantifiable results by specific deadlines. To better understand how you can help a staff member improve a necessary skill set, let's take the example of the task-oriented worker with poor prioritization and organization skills. Once the weakness has been identified from documentation of rushed projects and missed deadlines; you can offer a solution:

Jack, it is clear we need to work on time management and prioritization skills. I want you to read this book on the subject. It's a quick read and I found it very helpful. Why don't we meet in two weeks and share what we learned from the book. Focus on techniques you could adopt to help you plan your day's activities better, and help you develop some new ideas on how to prioritize your workload. Once we have a better handle on how you invest your time, you'll be much more productive and experience far less stress and frustration.

Organization and prioritization are foundational skills that any task-focused worker should develop, but the example takes us far beyond the specific skill to be improved. In this short exchange you not only identified a development area, you put forth these concepts as well:

- Provided a development goal
- Provided an action plan
- Provided a training resource
- Confirmed a target date for follow-up
- Identified that progress would be analyzed
- Sold the goal, highlighting the benefit to the employee—the "win-win"
- Committed your help and involvement in reaching the goal

Now to take this example from the specific to a more general application you follow these steps when coaching for improved productivity:

1. **Identify a results-oriented goal.** In our example, the goal is to enhance a core competency that would improve productivity.
2. **Detail the goal and time frame.** In our example it is to develop specific techniques for improving time management within two weeks.
3. **Provide an action plan.** In this instance the plan is to read a book to learn new techniques and customize them to the employee's needs.
4. **Set a deadline for follow-up.** In our example, the plan is to meet two weeks from today to review what Jack learned and what he is going to do differently in the future.
5. **Measure a tangible result.** You tell Jack you want him to focus on techniques he could adopt to help plan his day's activities better, and prioritize his workload. Two weeks from now there will be an improved blueprint for organizing activities.

6. **Identify mutual benefits.** You tell Jack that once he can invest his time better, he'll be much more productive and experience far less stress and frustration. Jack's improved productivity will reduce *your* stress and frustration as well. This is a win-win situation for both of you.

7. **Demonstrate your involvement and commitment.** In our example, you are saying to Jack, let's share what we have both picked up from the book. In other words, this is something I tried and it worked for me; we'll talk about your ideas and I'll share my ideas from the same training source that worked for me.

There is no hard and fast rule on the number of action plans an employee is capable of handling at any given time. It depends on the worker and your identification of the skills that need to be developed. Choose your targets for improvement carefully and be sure that your goal is clear; that the plan is based on specific actionable steps; and that the plan is focused on measurable results.

In the next section we address follow-up on the performance action plans you set. Good management requires you to keep track of your worker's efforts to execute the improvement plan, and the results he achieves.

Progress Reviews

Progress reviews are simply the meetings you hold with employees to follow up on the performance action plans you set. In a number of the larger companies the subject of the progress review is the set of action plans, or "deliverables," previously committed to the organization and/or to you, the manager. Such "deliverables" may be improving a skill, tracking a project's development, or making progress on any other ongoing activity for which specific plans have been set.

Progress reviews can be one-on-ones, which we described earlier. These meetings follow the same procedure of looking at what has happened since the last meeting, assessing the current situation, and making adjustments for the future based on those discussions. These meetings should be short and to the point, and depending on the complexity of the matters under discussion, can run anywhere from five minutes to an hour. Here is how one might go:

1. **Set the frame of reference.** "Jack, we are going to review progress on the following items."

2. **Get the facts.** You should then let Jack proceed with his analysis of progress on each of the topics you have agreed to address in the meeting. Ask questions as Jack talks, but only to gather further insight into the status on each of the deliverables. If you are not clear on a point ask for clarification. However, this is not the time for you to editorialize; just listen and learn.

3. **Summarize and confirm.** Restate what you have heard and ask for confirmation that what you heard is correct. This ensures that you have a clear understanding of the status of each of the issues under discussion.

4. **Offer your analysis of the status on each agenda item and where matters stand today.** Look at what you feel has gone especially well and why, and look at the areas that didn't go as smoothly as planned and discuss both. If new variables have arisen to affect execution of your jointly made plans, these should be factored in.

5. **Construct an action plan for the next period.** "Jack, we'll be meeting again in three weeks right at the end of the month. Where do you think we'll be then on each of these items?" Ask for Jack's suggestions for what he believes are the next steps in the project or skill development experience, because in so doing you build Jack's analytical skills and sense of responsibility.

6. **Add your insight and together agree on the next steps.** Once everything is agreed upon, get in the habit of reviewing the plans and having Jack jot them down; then at the end of the meeting say, "Jack, remember to e-mail me the plan at the end of the day." This way Jack will twice write down his commitment, and twice give you his commitment to follow the plan—once in person during the meeting, and once when he sends you the written version. This process gives your employees much more ownership and commitment to follow through.

Take your team through these processes for a year and you will have a team that knows how to analyze, plan, and execute in almost all situations.

Beware of Overpromising

Because employees want to please or impress their managers, they sometimes tend to overpromise. You should be aware of this and not be reticent about scaling back Jack's promises for the coming weeks. Overpromising always sounds good but can lead to more damage if promises aren't kept. Remember, your goal is to build confidence as you build competency; small steps will get you there more quickly over the long run.

Dealing with Unwanted Behavior

Until this point we have looked at your employees as capable and motivated by success. Sadly this may not always be the case. There will be times when a worker simply cannot come to grips with the job, or behaves in unacceptable ways. In these situations the nature of your meetings will gradually change, as you engage in a process of *progressive counseling* or *progressive discipline.* These processes aim to turn around unproductive employees, while at the same time recognizing the potential for termination. As such, while you continue to coach for improvement, you sometimes must also proceed through verbal and written warnings, thus laying the groundwork and documentation trail that will allow you, if necessary, to terminate an employee with just cause.

Terminating an employee is probably the worst job any manager has to do, and it is just as rotten an experience for the worker, too. Sometimes a terminated employee becomes angry enough to initiate a lawsuit against the employer for wrongful dismissal. This doesn't happen very often, but as a manager you don't want your shirttails flapping in the wind. In this section we go through the essential steps of a discipline process that is fair to all concerned. You should, however, make a point to sit down with your HR department or an immediate supervisor and get clear company policy guidelines on how your employer likes to handle these situations.

Progressive Discipline

A progressive discipline process is the fair way to treat troubled workers; it's important because everyone in the department will observe the way you treat a coworker. It also ensures that your company has adequate documentation of the good efforts made to help employees do their job satisfactorily. The paper trail you create along the way is the written record of your efforts, and properly done will protect your employer's interests.

Progressive discipline involves a series of meetings, following the same essential format as your other meetings to monitor progress; it is merely the tone that gradually changes. To start, you will hold regular meetings to discuss progress on skill development or behavior adjustment. At these meetings, you will suggest and seek agreement to plans of action that will improve skills or change observable behavior. You will also set dates and times of subsequent meetings and have a clear agenda for those subsequent meetings.

Then as time progresses, if improvements are not made, you begin to introduce a stronger progressive discipline to those meetings, notably discussing the consequences to a lack of improvement in essential skill sets or professional behavior. There are a handful of rules for the progressive discipline process to ensure that you do the right thing by your employee, while at the same time protecting your company from a lawsuit:

1. **Communicate that there is a problem.** First of all, the employee needs to understand that there is a serious problem that potentially threatens his employability with the company. If this is something addressed in the company policies and procedures manual, show the appropriate pages to the employee; note that you did so and place the dated note in the personnel file.

2. **Be specific about the problem.** The employee needs to understand exactly what the problem is. Therefore you must break down the problem into parts. "You don't seem to get along with the others," is far too vague. As is, "You need to improve your productivity." Be clear and specific, not only about the nature of the problem, but also how to turn things around.

You will need to carefully rehearse what you intend to say in these meetings, and as you do, ask yourself if the explanation is clear enough that the employee could recite it back to you. The employee needs to know what the problems are, how they can be fixed, and that not doing so adversely affects his employment prospects, coworkers, and the health of the department.

3. **Determine appropriate time frame for turnaround.** There needs to be an adequate period of time for the employee to turn the situation around. This is determined partly by the complexity of the problem. For example, tardiness is a cut-and-dried situation where immediate improvement can be expected in most circumstances. An exception? Perhaps that worker is a single parent and needs some help in juggling the child-care issues, or perhaps the worker has aging parents who have regular medical appointments. Just as the nature of the problem affects the time for turning around the problem situation, so does the complexity of the issue. You need to be fair to the person in question and you need to be seen as fair by the rest of your staff.

4. **Spell out the consequences of inaction.** You are only in this situation because the worker in question is having serious performance or behavior

problems, to which he did not respond from previous coaching efforts. If you aren't specific, your wake-up call may well be misconstrued as a snooze button. So saying, "this just isn't good enough, you need to improve," or "if you don't change I'll have to take additional steps" isn't good enough. You need to be specific and say something like, "You need to increase the number of calls taken per hour, otherwise, I will have to replace you in the call center and transfer you to shipping."

Here is an example of a progressive discipline meeting that covers all four steps:

> You are late to work two to three mornings every week, and always on Monday. You leave early two to three times a week and always on Friday afternoon. You have called in sick either before or following every public holiday during the last year. The department cannot function properly unless everyone pulls their weight. This specifically includes putting in a full day's work five days a week. Is there any reason why you can't come in those days? If not, I expect you to be on time from now on. If you continue to be late, this tells me you are not taking your job here seriously.

Make Sure the Worker Takes It Seriously

Act on the assumption that the worker in question wants to do well but doesn't appreciate the seriousness of the situation. This will allow you to be direct and supportive.

> Michael, this continued tardiness is a serious threat to your ongoing employment here at Double Dip Accountants. You potentially have a great future ahead of you, and I would like that future to be here with us. However, you must come to work on time and put in a full day's work. Do you think you can make the necessary changes? Good, because if you can't, I will have to give you a written warning which would be followed by termination of employment. Am I making myself clear? Excellent. Today is Friday; let's meet next Friday at 4:30 P.M. to look at how things have gone in the intervening time.

In being direct and supportive, you are . . .

- Clear about the problem.
- Clear about the solution.
- Clear about the consequences.
- Clear about the process if things don't improve.
- Clear about the follow-up.

Be Fair to All

Your application of progressive discipline leading to termination must also be fair. You would treat a tardiness problem with a brand-new employee somewhat differently from how you would treat the same problem with an employee who has been with you for ten years. The difference would be in the patience you show the long-term reliable employee. However, you cannot single one person out for a particular problem, and take no action against other employees who are behaving in the same way.

The disciplinary actions you take should also be in keeping with the way this type of problem is typically addressed in your company. The moment you identify a problem requiring disciplinary action, talk to your boss and to HR about the way such an infraction is normally handled.

From Verbal to Written Discipline

In many instances a clear verbal warning about a performance or behavior problem will be enough to begin the turnaround process. You should note the circumstances of the verbal warning in the personnel file.

There are usually five steps in a progressive discipline procedure that can ultimately end in termination:

1. Deliver a verbal warning.
2. Write a letter of intent.
3. Deliver the first written warning.
4. Deliver the final written warning.
5. Terminate the employee.

Of course, there are factors that could foreshorten or extend this process, such as the type of problem the employee is experiencing, past performance track record, length of service, and your company's usual way of handling similar offenses. You cannot start the progressive discipline process with a final written warning because someone is late to work three days in a row. On the other hand, severe infractions such as harassment or violence against other workers can often begin with a final written warning.

The written warnings and your proper documentation of them in the personnel file is an important step you must take as a manager to protect your company in the event of a lawsuit brought by an ex-employee charging unfair dismissal.

More Info on Complex Terminations

The area of employee termination and protection against lawsuit is complex to say the least. As soon as any such issue raises its ugly head, take immediate counsel from your HR department and your immediate supervisor. Two books that delve into these areas in comprehensive detail are *25 Essential Lessons of Employee Management* by Dennis L. Demey (Facts on Demand Press, 2001), and *The Hiring and Firing Question and Answer Book,* by Paul Falcone (AMACOM, 2001).

In documenting problems and offenses in an employee's file and in written warnings, you need to be careful with language. Anything you put in writing can and will be discovered by an employee's attorney and used against you. The rule here is not to become hysterical, editorial, or judgmental in your writing. For example, if an accusation of harassment has been made against an employee, you do not necessarily know that it, in fact, actually took place. What you do know is that an accusation was made. Consequently you must not accuse the employee in writing of harassment, but you can state that a *coworker* has made the accusation; it is not for you to make legal judgments.

Written warnings of imminent termination can leave an employee feeling very threatened. Imagine having to read this: "Failure to improve in this area will result in further action up to and including termination of employment." Taking this step puts pressure on everyone involved. You're better off not to go here if you don't have to.

Letter of Intent

There is an intermediate step that you might consider using on occasion as a "shot across the bow," to warn an employee that the next steps will be written warnings followed by termination of employment. This step is sometimes referred to as a "letter of clarification" or a "letter of intent." It is a way for an employer to put in writing that things are not going well, and that more serious actions will be taken unless there is significant and immediate change or improvement. For example:

> It is necessary for me to clarify management's feelings on the issue of your continued tardiness. Despite numerous discussions about your continued lateness in coming to work, and frequent early departures, I have noticed no change in your pattern of behavior in this area. I want you to know how serious this matter is in the eyes of company management. I have to advise you that if there is not a change in this pattern of behavior, disciplinary action will be taken. Those actions will include formal written warnings followed by termination of employment if we cannot remedy the situation. This letter itself is not a written warning. I just want you to understand the importance of turning this situation around and what the next steps will be if these changes do not happen.

With a letter of intent, you clarify the company's position and displeasure, and identify what the next steps will be so that there can be no misunderstanding.

Written Warnings

Written warnings themselves, should be direct and specific, identifying the problem:

> The tardiness has to stop. You must come to work on time, at 8:30 A.M., every day.

Or . . .

> As a customer service representative, you are aware that company standards require you complete a minimum of ten incoming calls, as measured by our XYZ telephone router, per hour.

Or . . .

> Conversation, language, and jokes that demean another person's race and religious beliefs are unacceptable.

Most important, you must spell out the next steps, if things don't improve:

> This is a written warning that continued conduct in this manner will warrant one final written warning, followed by immediate dismissal. You must make immediate improvement in this area. Failure to do so will result in a final written warning followed by termination of employment.

Some authorities recommend including a sentence or two that makes it clear you have encouraged employee input:

> I would be eager to hear any ideas you have to improve this situation. I encourage you to write down your ideas of ways you can improve your productivity, and then share them with me.

To Sign or Not to Sign

Usually employees are asked to sign a written warning, although it isn't necessary from a legal point of view. There is the idea that by signing, the employee is formally acknowledging a problem, and in doing so, might ultimately take responsibility for improving the situation, and at the very least provides proof that the employee has received due process.

The employee may sign, or may not; either way is okay. The employee also has the right to take the letter away for review. The important thing is that you document in the personnel file all that occurs. In the event the employee refuses to sign the letter of warning, simply ask another staff member to enter the office and witness that the employee has received the letter but does not wish to acknowledge its receipt with a signature.

Even in these difficult circumstances, try to be aware of the employee's emotions. For example if you do need that witness, don't use a coworker. Arrange for someone from HR, your boss, or another manager to be available. The employee in question can sometimes be in denial about his role in these unpleasant circumstances; the employee can quite possibly feel victimized, angry, or hurt. Being aware of this, you should make every effort not to further compromise the worker's sense of personal integrity.

Time to Terminate?

There are several categories of behavior that can warrant disciplinary action and ultimately termination:

- **Sustained performance inadequacy.** An employee can't seem to handle crucial aspects of the job, and is unable or unwilling to develop the necessary skills for adequate discharge of duties.
- **Inappropriate conduct.** This applies to conduct with coworkers and clients, and includes but is not limited to dishonesty, committing crimes while at work, endangering or harassing others verbally or physically.
- **Substance abuse on the job.** We would stress that you be particularly careful with the issue of substance abuse in the workplace. There are some instances of substance abuse that are covered under the Americans with Disabilities Act, which protects the employee from termination in certain cases. If in doubt, consult with your HR representative or corporate counsel.
- **Company policy infractions.** Company policies are put into place to ensure smooth running of the business and a safe workplace for everyone. Theft, fraud, or disclosure of confidential information or documents, or violation and/or noncompliance with extant policies must be addressed.
- **Chronic absenteeism.** Your policy manual clearly states the work week and each employee's obligations to adhere to its guidelines. Poor attendance of events within the workday, such as meetings or training sessions, or chronic unavailability by phone or e-mail, can also require discipline.

Reasons for Termination

In management, the only way you can lead and expect your troops to follow is to care about doing the right thing. Once you have concluded that there is no other option left (and you have clear documentation of giving the employee due process), you have to take action. To postpone the inevitable does no one any good. You must, however, take the time to talk to HR and/or your immediate management to ensure that you are adhering to existing company policy, working within the law, and have all your documentation in order.

There are a number of careful steps you must take in terminating an employee in order to protect yourself and your company. Follow them, and this distressful procedure can proceed with the most minimal pain possible for both parties. Ignore these steps, and the potential for frustration and litigation increases dramatically.

Step 1: Is Termination Legally Defensible?

Our legal system recognizes that we all have a right to work, and that this right may not be taken away without just cause. You establish just cause, in concert with your HR department and/or senior management (never take this action arbitrarily and on your own), by the documentation in the personnel file, where you have kept track of all meaningful interactions with the employee over the length of your relationship. That file will document the content of all the meetings you had together, and will include the steps you took in your progressive discipline process. If you did your job well, the documentation will show that you have helped the employee identify problem areas and consistently offered all reasonable accommodations to help the person improve his performance or change an inappropriate behavior. If you have any questions about the legitimacy of your action, or whether you have adequate documentation, take counsel from HR or senior management. If no one in your company has expertise in these matters, we advise you to take outside legal counsel.

Employment "At Will"

In addition to termination for just cause, you need to be aware of the concept of "employment at will." Employment at will is codified in the legal systems of many states, and refers to the circumstances where no contract exists as to the duration of the employer/employee relationship.

On the face of it, at-will laws would seem to imply that, where no contract determining length of employment exists, both the employee and employer could terminate that relationship at any time for any reason. In practice, whereas the employee can resign at any time, matters are not nearly so clear-cut for you as the employer.

As a practical matter even if you work in an at-will state, you are strongly advised to prove just cause for any termination. This means you always come back to documentation of just cause. In other words, ensuring that the employee clearly understood the problem, had adequate opportunity to remedy the situation, and was made fully aware of the consequences of failure to remedy.

Be aware of specific circumstances of behavior and performance for which you are forbidden by law to terminate an employee. These include the following:

- Substance abuse recovery: Awareness of an employee's involvement in a twelve-step or other substance-abuse recovery program.
- Personal financial problems outside the workplace, such as bankruptcy.
- Disclosure of medical conditions, including HIV.
- Disclosure of innumeracy or illiteracy, dyslexia or other learning disorders.
- Membership in a union, or other lawfully recognized organization, or organization activities related to membership in such organizations, so long as they occur outside the workplace and working hours.
- Pregnancy or childbirth: There are specific laws you should discuss with HR just as soon as pregnancy becomes an issue in your department.
- Military service. Time away from work necessitated by compulsory military service.
- Worker's Compensation claims.
- Protesting unsafe working conditions, or reporting of illegal activities of the company.
- Discrimination based on age, race, sex, religious beliefs, or other areas covered by Title VII of the 1964 Civil Rights Act.
- Immediacy of vesting in pension plans; that is, terminating an employee shortly before she becomes eligible to receive a pension.

These are all extremely sensitive areas where you should seek appropriate advice immediately and before proceeding too far. The same holds true in cases of accused sexual harassment. There can be innocent parties on each side of these claims and both must be given due process and treated with fairness. Likewise, proceed carefully with issues of misconduct on the job, accusations of hostility and violence, or complaints of unfair treatment or discrimination by a member of the management team. If you get dragged into any of these areas, either within your department or by a third party, seek counsel of HR and/or your immediate management before you take irrevocable action.

Step 2: Verify That Your Action Is Unbiased

You have to determine if your action is unbiased. Your reason for terminating one employee must be a reason that you apply in the same fashion to all of your other employees. If it isn't, there is a chance the terminated employee will try to prove discrimination through legal action. You can avoid embarrassment and cost to the company by conscientious discharge of your responsibilities.

Step 3: Consider the History

An employee's employment history with the company must be considered, as must the seriousness of the offense. A fifty-five-year-old employee, just becoming eligible for full retirement benefits, who is summarily dismissed for tardiness is surely a case for immediate legal problems for you and the company. In other words, the punishment must fit the crime, and the punishment must be taken in context with the length and quality of the employee's history with the company.

Step 4: Make Sure the Employee Understood the Problem

There must be clear evidence that the employee understood the problem and its seriousness, and also that the employee was given adequate time, opportunity, and support to solve the problem. This is especially important in cases of competency in discharging duties. The way the law looks at this is: You hired this person and in that procedure had adequate opportunity to ascertain that person's competency. Documentation should confirm that you spoke clearly about the need for improvement and offered support in improving skills in the substandard area.

When the employee is caught in misconduct that clearly transgresses company policy or otherwise endangers the safety of other workers, the case is more clear-cut. An employee caught drunk or under the influence of other illegal substances (be careful to ascertain that it isn't the case of an employee having an adverse reaction to prescription medication), being violent, threatening violence, or harassing other workers leads more directly to termination. Nevertheless, the steps to termination should always be taken with the endorsement of company management.

Check and Double-Check

Once you have determined that termination is the only reasonable course open to you, check and double-check that you have covered all your bases:

1. There must be a clear paper trail in the employee's personnel file that documents your efforts to help the employee remedy the problem.
2. It must be clear that you have communicated the problem and that the employee understands the seriousness of the issue.

3. It must be clear that solutions to the situation have been offered to the employee.

4. It must be clear that adequate time for solving the problem has been allowed. (Solving a tardiness problem requires far less time than picking up a new workplace skill.)

5. It must be clear that you are being fair and that this employee is being treated no differently from other employees.

Your employee should also have received the opportunity to discuss the situation and offer his/her interpretation of the circumstances to a third party within the company.

Your next step is to plan the termination meeting.

Carrying Out the Termination

Once the determination to terminate has been made and approved through your normal channels you need to execute your decision as swiftly and cleanly as possible. Because this is invariably an unpleasant task, you may look for reasons to put it off. There is endless discussion on the topic of the best day and time to hold a termination meeting,

The arguments go that Monday terminations are best because the employee has the whole work week to get a job hunt started; if you fire someone at the end of the week, he will mope all weekend. On the other hand, Mondays are worst because the employee will have to wait all week for the help-wanted section of the Sunday newspaper. In fact, Fridays are best because the employee will have the weekend to think things through, read the want ads, and get off to a fresh start with the job hunt first thing Monday morning. And so it goes, for every argument there is an equally convincing, or equally air-headed argument to the contrary.

The fact is, there is no perfect time, because every person has a different reaction to such an event. Consequently your procedure is simple: Plan the termination meeting for as soon as conveniently possible after the decision to terminate has been made. Get it done, and get on with the future.

If the day doesn't matter, can the time of day matter? Actually there is considerable convincing logic for holding the termination at the end of the business day. At the very least, if you hold the meeting earlier in the day you create an opportunity for the employee to throw a wobbly in front of the remaining staff, and the staff to spend the day in post-game analysis. You might also have a corporate policy that requires employees to pack their belongings under supervision and be escorted out of the building. So an end-of-the-day termination offers less potential for humiliation of the employee in front of former colleagues; and with fewer people around there are greater odds for privacy, and less chance of workday disruption.

Planning a Termination Meeting

When you have determined a date and time you need to take a dry run through the process with someone (ideally someone in your HR department) to be sure that your plan adheres to all existing and relevant company policies and procedures. Most authorities concur that you should have a witness attend any termination meeting. It will give you moral support, help keep you on track, lessen the chance of hysterical outbursts, and provide you with a corroborating witness in the event of litigation.

In Writing?

Then comes the question of whether or not to put the termination in writing. The three divergent opinions on the matter run the whole gamut:

- Some companies believe that the less that is committed to paper the better. In the event of litigation, carelessly worded termination paperwork can only serve as ammunition to opposing counsel.
- Other companies provide a single sentence letter essentially stating, "As of this date you are no longer an employee of XYZ Company."
- Then, of course, there are companies that provide a detailed written explanation of all the reasons for termination. This might include performance reviews that demonstrate the problem, progressive warning documentation, and records of other disciplinary action and efforts of rehabilitation. Such a letter has no room for error (based on its potential for use against you in legal action), and because the detail required can take an interminable amount of time to prepare. Because of its legal ramifications, once completed to your satisfaction it should really be run through corporate counsel. It all adds up to time and money.

A Termination Checklist

You will need to develop a checklist of items to retrieve from the employee, such as keys, computers, cell phones, credit cards, and the like. In an age when every employee has a computer and access to many company records, stopping computer access is a logical step to take, because you don't want ex-employees compromising company secrets, client lists, and so forth. In practice, it really needs to happen from the very moment of the termination, because it takes an distraught employee only takes a few clicks to wreak untold havoc with complex databases. Your company probably already has a policy and procedure in place for this; if not, it is an issue that needs to be raised with HR and IT.

You will also need to make a list of items to pass on to the employee, such as copies of noncompete clauses signed at the time of initial employment and information on COBRA insurance so that coverage can be extended while the employee is job hunting.

You will need to prepare final wages if you are required to pay such wages at time of dismissal. Such requirements can be stipulated by city, county, or state. Take the time to learn what the correct procedure is for your location either from HR or the payroll department. No matter what has been written about work being purely for the love of company and profession, money is the real reason we work. It is a touchy subject, and you don't want to give a disgruntled employee just cause for righteous indignation in the courts.

Termination Day

If you follow the progressive counseling/discipline guidelines we have outlined, no termination will come as a total shock to any employee. An employee will have had numerous meetings with you where the problem areas have been addressed and the employee has been given opportunities and time lines for improvement.

In preparation for termination, you need to script your statements carefully, and stick to it, even if the person in front of you gets emotional. If this happens, sit quietly and wait for the person to regain composure; don't get drawn into commiseration or unscripted conversation. This is another reason it is useful to have a witness there. It keeps you aware that you are under scrutiny, too, and need to stick to your guns.

Plan for a meeting that lasts no longer than ten minutes, and use the self-imposed time constraints to keep yourself concise and to the point. Longer than this, and you are editorializing and doubtless digging yourself into a big hole by saying too much. This is not a progressive discipline meeting, replete with further negotiations and deadlines; that time has passed. The two of you are now engaged in the ritualistic breaking of a relationship. Your role is to be courteous and considerate of the other's feelings, but also to make it clear that there have been problems, they have been discussed, and commitments to resolve the issues have not been satisfactorily met.

You should clearly state that, compliant with company practices, policies, and procedures, because of problems with discipline/conduct/productivity, you are hereby terminating the employee's employment effective on a specified date. If you are required by policy to give two weeks' notice, you can still give the notice but tell the employee her employment effectively ends immediately so that she can get a job hunt underway in the ensuing notice time. Don't go into the details beyond a simple statement of reason for dismissal! The employee will invariably have seen this coming, and if you have been fair and open in your dealings may well accept your comments without discussion. This is one of those instances where the less you have to say the better.

If you do have to go into further detail, state that you have made the employee aware of certain productivity/skill/conduct problems, have asked for them to be rectified, have encouraged improvement, and offered (if applicable) resources for the same and a reasonable time frame for improvement. Consequently you must now (don't say you have no choice, because this can then immediately become an issue) terminate employment with the company. Then cover the following matters:

- Explain the procedures for gathering personal effects and returning any company items that might be used in a home office, or are otherwise not present at your place of business.
- Outline payment of final monies due, including investment, retirement, and insurance issues.
- If there is outplacement assistance or an exit interview procedure conducted by HR, mention that it is the next step in the procedure and, if necessary, walk the employee over to the HR office for formal processing out of the organization.
- Wish the employee well and bring the meeting to a close. You might chose to tell the employee that you will announce that he has left the company, but that you will say "in deference to John's privacy, it is inappropriate for me to discuss the reasons."

Healing the Team

A termination doesn't happen in a vacuum. Coworkers will have seen it in the offing, and, given the time it takes to legally execute a termination, have probably been wondering if you were ever going to take action. It isn't appropriate to ignore the event as if it didn't happen; you have a responsibility to bring closure to the team and focus everyone on the future.

Hold a meeting and make sure your staff understands that the ex-employee was treated fairly, and at the same time, you be careful to protect the privacy of the terminated person. Speaking ill of the departed employee might get back to him or her and form part of a legal action for defamation of character. It is enough to announce that the person in question has left the company as of today/yesterday, and that the parting was amicable. To give everyone a chance to allay personal fears without turning the meeting into a post mortem, say at the end:

> I think it is best to focus on the tasks we have in hand and not speculate on the reasons that caused Jack to leave the company. However, if any of you have any questions let's handle them on a one-on-one basis. With Jack gone we will be immediately looking for a replacement and have ads running this weekend. If any of you have referrals, or if you have any input about the type of person we should be looking for, I'm interested in hearing from you.

It isn't a bad idea to give everyone a busy day to get their minds focused on the present and future. To this end you might tell the team that, on another topic, management is looking for an update on progress with a particular activity or project, and that you'd appreciate a quick review with everyone during the course of the day. Turn those ensuing very brief meetings into a review of current activity and encouragement for continued good work. Why is this a good idea? After a termination, everyone has passing worries about their own status. Giving staff members a chance to remind you of what a good job they are doing, and giving them positive reinforcement will set their minds at ease and get them to focus on their work.

When an Employee Resigns

Employees can resign for any number of reasons: Better professional opportunity, more money, and personality conflict are the most common. The resignation can also occur because the worker is retiring or has been encouraged to resign. When an employee resigns, this lessens the company's obligations—a position you do not want to compromise by careless handling of the situation.

If an employee walks out or quits at a moment's notice, there is little you can do. However, most often an employee will give a normal two weeks' notice. How you handle this invariably depends on company policy. If the employee has not been a morale problem and assures you of an intent to complete the notice period with good effort and no intention for departmental disruption, it is usually best to let the person work out the notice period. In doing so you are seen by the rest of the team to be acting responsibly toward an employee who, in turn, has acted responsibly toward the company. This is especially important if the company policy manual stipulates that it requires a two-week notice of resignation.

What Goes Around Comes Around

It is a good, long-term career strategy to treat everyone as you would like to be treated yourself. Over the long haul of a career you will notice that while you may start your career as a miniscule "peon" in a large profession, over the years you increasingly become visible as a member of a much smaller professional community. You never know whom you will meet again down the road.

When an employee resigns, that person is doing so at her will and this lessens the company's obligations for unemployment benefits as mandated by the state. If, however, an employee resigns with two weeks' notice, and you then require that person to clear out her desk and leave immediately, you have, by that action, changed the resignation to a termination. With termination, the employer has more responsibilities to the departing employee in terms of due process and unemployment liabilities.

It is a good idea to apprise yourself on company policies in this area. Also, if you are considering encouraging an employee to resign as a face-saving offer to avoid imminent termination, you should discuss it with HR first and make sure that the employee in question is aware of the ramifications of resigning. If possible, seek out legal counsel. Laws change and are subject to interpretation.

Summary

In this chapter we continued the discussion of nurturing your staff, addressing performance reviews, and dealing effectively with troubled employees with a progressive counseling/progressive discipline process. In the process we addressed an important aspect of leadership, that of helping your people through troubled times with a caring but strong hand. You will use this skill again and again over the years. We will continue this discussion of leadership in the next chapter.

Part III | The Leadership Challenge

This section teaches you how to guide your team toward accomplishing the right goals for the organization while building your reputation as a leader along the way.

7 | What Does It Mean to Lead?

Through building trust in you, good leadership motivates your workers to put the extra effort into doing what's right for the organization, and makes the team function in harmony.

Success in management is a challenge for everyone. Frequently you arrive on the scene because you have profession-specific—not necessarily managerial—skills, and then have to succeed with a completely new set of responsibilities for which you have little or no direct experience. At the heart of those responsibilities is getting the work you previously did yourself performed by many others.

True, a firm hand and a big stick can get the job done. But is that the way you want to go? Is it the path to success? Only so long as you maintain a persistent, watchful eye on your charges. Turn your back, and your team members have little motivation to produce for "management"—naturally perceived as the enemy. This is where leadership comes in.

If there is a more abused word in the lexicon of business language we don't know it. More purple prose, verbal diarrhea, and obfuscation have been employed in "explaining" leadership than any other concept in business. If you have read two management books you have read two different definitions. If you have read six books you probably have half a dozen conflicting and smoky definitions swirling around in your head. The problem: Some people try to separate the concept of leadership from the concept of management. Others look at leadership and management as the same. The reality is, both of these approaches oversimplify and miss the point.

What Is Leadership?

In effect, management and leadership are inextricable, different sides of the same coin, if you will. Management sets the table and puts food on it, and may deliver a mandate that participants eat. Leadership gets the participants to eat *willingly.* Leadership without management will fail, for there will be no food on the table to eat. Likewise, management without leadership will also fail, particularly in the long run, for sooner or later, participants refuse to come to the table. *Leadership in the workplace is simply the application of a number of learnable behaviors that make people eager to follow your direction.*

Lead for Success

When people are eager to follow your direction you feel confident that they are giving their all, even when you are absent. Successful application of leadership skills means that your team of employees has taken ownership of the success of their jobs; and given how the majority of workers genuinely want to succeed in their professional lives, you are already more than halfway there. When you apply the behaviors we talk about in this chapter, your team will follow wherever you lead because they believe that you will lead them to success, both yours and their own.

Don't believe for a moment the claptrap about love of profession and company being a worker's most important motivation, although professional self-respect does play a role. When dealing with people's motivations for making an effort, don't stray too far from the concept of enlightened self-interest, that is, a self-interest that is motivated by mutual benefit between you and your employer. We all work because we have to make a living, we have to make a living because we have responsibilities outside of work, and we have dreams for fulfillment in our lives as a whole. Company and profession are important motivators only to the degree they help us realize our life dreams.

A manager, who can show people a path to professional success (and thereby get them closer to personal success), will become a leader with eager followers. So a central pillar of your success as a manager is to create a workplace environment where your people can experience success in their own professional lives. Grasp this and you grasp the essence of leadership.

Follow the Winner

People do not willingly follow losers, so when people follow it is because they believe they are following a winner, someone who will not jeopardize their well-being, and someone who stacks the odds for success in their favor. If you can engender the belief in your people that you have their best interests at heart, that you will steer them clear of danger and guide them to success, you will have a department full of people who believe in you as their leader. *Good leadership means letting everyone know (1) you're in charge and (2) that you're confident in the outcome.*

Leadership Is Learned

Leaders aren't born "ready to wear" right out of the box, as we sometimes hear. Yes, we do have those globally known examples of born leaders, but invariably if you probe beneath the biographies you will see that they also had warts and behavioral quirks that they overcame to achieve greatness. *Leadership is mainly a learned set of behaviors.* And, you will be no different, because you have it within to become a leader. You just have to look at the leadership skills you already posses and continue to polish them, and be able to recognize the behaviors that you need to develop. A lot of leadership skills are picked up through experience and through emulating the behaviors of other successful leaders.

Enlightened Self-Interest

Your success and the success of the company is important to all members of your team only to the extent that it can impact their own self-respect and chosen path to success in life. To lead your team, you may require skills different from those that earned your promotion into management. Largely leadership skills are all about persuasive influence in your human interactions. Leadership behaviors can be learned and will have a guaranteed effectiveness when applied diligently.

Your enlightened self-interest requires that you understand that some of the very things you demand in your own life are equally important to others. You already know what they are from your own perspective; now you have to look at them from the viewpoint of a leader, someone who facilitates others' success. Your people need to understand that . . .

- **You will not lead them into danger.** You need to understand the challenges and obstacles facing the department and chart a course with achievable goals that lead to success.
- **Your need for departmental cohesion will lead to personal success.** People will work toward the common good only if it is not in substantive conflict with personal good. People will accept short-term pain for long-term gain, but only when they can see the connection.
- **They will gain professional self-respect from working with you.** People need to feel respect for themselves and the work they do every day. Your interaction with them and the environment you create enables this.

- **Your path will lead toward their successful professional future.**
  People no longer can trust companies to provide a secure long-term professional future, but they will gain the career development building blocks they need to succeed.

Leadership is about winning the hearts and minds of your reports. After moments of heroism, soldiers have often said that they were not fighting for God and country, but to help themselves and their buddies survive, that it was the right thing to do for the people who believed in them and needed them. So to advance your own agenda for success you will need to be seen as putting the interests of your people ahead of your own. When you do this, the individual members of your team will work together for the common good because the common good also results in personal gain.

Fortunately, the changing landscape of corporate structures provides ample opportunity for empowering your staff to meet your needs while serving their own. The last twenty years has seen a dramatic restructuring of the corporate hierarchy, with far fewer levels of management, and the advent of workplace tools that put far more information and power to act in the hands of all workers. This flattening of corporate structures offers opportunity for workers at all levels to unleash their energy and creativity on behalf of the company. The opportunities are there; you just have to nurture them.

The Golden Rules of Leadership

The more things change, the more they remain the same. Corporate America has a necessary love affair with improving competitiveness, and this leads over the years to an endless parade of new management strategies. These strategies immediately devolve into training programs for management and the troops. All too often they comprise little more than a new lexicon of impressive-sounding business jargon, that on deconstruction defies meaning. There isn't a management or productivity approach that, at its heart, doesn't say to treat your people as you would like to be treated yourself. Workers' expectations at work, and their commitment to work, is a direct result of the way they are treated by management.

People don't follow a company, they follow a boss who is fair, logical, decent, honest, optimistic, and focused. If company policies and procedures are also supportive it only adds to the commitment. Your job then is to engender a working environment that enables people to be their best and to self-actualize the professional part of their life dreams. Support your people and they in turn will support you. This then is the underlying theory of practical leadership. Now, let's look at how you put it to work in everyday management.

Good Leaders Are Good Followers, Too

When you join the ranks of management, you can succeed or fail; it depends on how well you grasp the company's expectations for your department and the role it plays in achieving corporate goals. There is no point in leading your troops in a direction at odds with the company's mission.

Just as your enlightened self-interest is going to require you to interact in a supportive way with your staff, you must interact in the same way with your superiors and their goals. In most management situations, learning to lead requires that *you in turn follow your leader.* Helping your leader be successful will help you achieve success. If you have been around in the professional world long enough, you will have observed how companies develop inner and outer circles, and that those in the inner circles all tend to grow together as a group. This isn't accidental; they are all enlightened professionals whose self-interest has been served by contributing to the common good. On the one hand you are the general of an army of soldiers—your department. On the other hand, you are a soldier in another general's army.

When you land in a management position, it is because you are the best choice from a field of candidates, not the only choice. Many considerations played a part in that decision, but with every promotion into management there is a boss who believes you are the one with whom she can best work; you are the one who will make her look good. You are chosen because someone believes that in becoming a leader you won't forget your role as a team player and follower on the management team.

As you read through this book, you will note a recurring theme that says if you help others succeed, they will help you succeed. Most of this is said in discussions about putting your staff first, but you need to apply the same approach to your boss. By putting management's needs first, you put your own needs for success first, too.

Getting on the Same Page

Before setting out to lead your team down the path toward success, it is a good idea to first make sure you have all the proper roadmaps you can obtain from your own managers. But don't expect your managers to have everything all mapped out! This is a common mistake. Just the same, you should first establish agreements and open lines of communication before setting out. You need to make sure you are getting the inputs needed in order to lead in the right direction, and do it efficiently.

Your talks with your own managers should cover such topics as organizational goals, history, successes and failures, strengths and weaknesses, opportunities and threats (remember SWOT from Chapter 3?). You should get clarity on budget and resource issues. Finally, you should agree on communication style, frequency, and means. If your boss expects a weekly written report, don't come back with irregular voice-mail messages from crowded airports. Not only will such "disconnects" impede your relationship with your boss and the organization, but even more dangerously, your team members will quickly pick up these disconnects, and start to wonder whether religiously following your lead is the right thing to do.

Elements of Leadership

Because leadership is a combination of art and science, a set of behaviors rather than a checklist of to do's, it is difficult to meaningfully compartmentalize the many aspects of leadership. Irregardless, the following are—in our experience, anyway—the most important elements and traits of effective leadership.

Establish Order and Routine

It may seem sort of "back to basics" to say that you need to establish a structure and MO (modus operandi) for your team and the team's role in the organization. But it's important to remember that people don't do well without some structure. There may be some temporary successes in "chaos," but eventually, things go off in unintended directions, people waste effort or see efforts go unrewarded, and sooner or later, they look to jump ship. However loose and informal, people want some structure for communications, presenting results, and, where necessary, performing day-to-day operations. The successful leader feels for the *minimum* amount of procedure and protocol necessary for people to achieve successfully, then makes sure it is in place. The rule is . . .

- Create structure, but not too much structure.
- Structure should be the minimum necessary for people to achieve.

Take Responsibility

As a leader and as a manager you take responsibility for the cumulative output of your team. Thomas Edison, having had a hand in the creation of the majority of our modern conveniences (including electricity and recorded sound and vision), is arguably the most visionary leader of modern times. He had this to say about success in the business world: "Success is 10 percent inspiration and 90 percent perspiration." Let's apply that to vision and leadership. Edison had the idea of electric light (visionary in more ways than one), but his success came from turning the idea into reality. This required driving himself and his team for two years and through almost 2,000 failed experiments to create an incandescent lightbulb. The idea was important and without it the reality never would have come to pass; however, the payoff came from his leadership (that 90 percent perspiration) in seeing the task through to completion. Good leaders take complete responsibility for the success—and the failure—of the team. Further, they get deeply involved in that success or failure. If they don't, they lose the confidence of their teams and their organizations. The lesson here is . . .

- Be totally responsible for both success *and* failure.
- Keep the end in mind.

As a middle manager you must have the vision to appreciate the big picture, and your mission is to energize your people to work together toward its realization. Workers will believe in your leadership if they believe you to be capable, honest, enthusiastic, and having their best interests at heart. Good leaders keep the end not only in their minds, but also in the minds of their teams. They don't get lost in details, or "lose the forest in the trees." As a good leader, you must . . .

- Keep the big picture.
- Show enthusiasm.
- Don't get lost in details.

Be Forward Looking

As we've already emphasized, effective managers know their business and the internal and external influences that drive success. While keeping the end in mind, successful leaders always look ahead through their scopes to see what lurks on the horizon that might impede or enhance success. When leaders get good at this—*and good at interpreting these signals proactively into action—*

they gain the confidence of their teams. Teams that are constantly sideswiped by surprise "storms" lose confidence in their leaders. When the leader does a good job of looking ahead, people feel more safe and secure, and can focus more on their jobs and less on the distracting "what-ifs." Good leaders make careful observation of all stimuli inside and outside their team and learn to anticipate. They also share what needs to be shared; many leaders fall down when they correctly interpret signals but don't share them with anyone. Finally, good leaders always look ahead and avoid dwelling on past mistakes—or successes. A forward-looking leader . . .

- Makes careful observations.
- Anticipates problems and opportunities.
- Lets go of the past.

Break Down Barriers

It is often said, and we agree, that the role of a manager is to create an environment in which his people can succeed. This is indeed a critical component of leadership, because the leader who continually removes roadblocks and eliminates distractions and other sources of "pain" that get in the way gains the confidence of his team. These roadblocks can be organizational or technical, internal or external. Good leaders make sure their teams have proper resources to do their job and the proper authority to use them. They make sure their own managers and peers have bought into what they're going to do, so that team members don't run into unexpected roadblocks as they pursue their objectives. The leader who breaks down barriers . . .

- Creates a success-oriented environment.
- Gets proper resources and buy-in.

Create an Environment of Openness and Involvement

People who sense their leaders are "one of them" tend to follow them with more enthusiasm. Distant, aloof leaders tend to be perceived as not caring or not even aware of what's going on, engendering a downward spiral of discontent and disrespect. As a leader, you want to be involved, which requires a sometimes delicate balancing act of staying close to what's going on without being perceived as meddling, or picky, or, worse, mistrusting. Ask constructive (as opposed to critical) questions about what people are doing. Try to learn from them without being perceived as "investigating" their performance. Take a hand at doing their tasks. Ask if they *like* doing their tasks, and what they don't like about them. Try to find out how they would do it better. And always—*always*—keep lines of communication open. Discard all notions of rank and privilege in communication; be on a first name basis with your employees and always let people know you are open for conversation. This open-door policy engenders the communication you need to manage your team, as well as trust and honesty, the "lifeblood" of your relationship with your reports. A good leader . . .

- Stays close to what people are doing, but doesn't meddle.
- Establishes an open door policy.

Assign Jobs Effectively

We already discussed the hiring of team members in Chapter 4. Now we're talking about picking the right people for jobs within your team, matching talent and expertise to requirements. This can be a critical and oh-so-tricky role of leadership—assign too much or too little to team members, and productivity and morale will suffer. People generally like to be challenged and like to achieve. But they don't want to take on too much work or too much risk; sooner or later the discomfort gets to them. So the trick is to challenge people without overburdening them, and to let them clearly know the importance and, where appropriate, the reward for their accomplishments.

Good leaders match jobs to persons, not persons to jobs. If the job or task is changed too much to shape the needs, skills, or work habits of the employee, sooner or later the wrong things will get done at the wrong time or with poor quality to the detriment of the whole organization.

Good leaders don't just stop after assigning tasks. They work to ensure that everybody is keeping pace. If someone is struggling or holding back the whole group, the good leader works with that person to help him get up to speed. The good leader avoids the temptation to "beat up" that person, because that person will leave, and others will soon wonder about the consequences should they fall behind. Good leaders strengthen—not break—the weakest links.

Finally, good leaders learn to rotate responsibilities to develop people, avoid monotony, and to ensure team capability if an individual is absent or incapacitated. Good leaders assign jobs effectively by . . .

- Matching talent and expertise to requirements, and people to jobs (not jobs to people).
- Rotating responsibility.

- Ensuring everyone is keeping pace.
- Shoring up the weakest links.

Set Expectations Clearly

Good leaders set good expectations, and they make those expectations clear to their teams. As an employee, you know what is expected, and you know the consequences of achievement and nonachievement. You know where you stand. Good leaders communicate their expectations and consequences well, and follow through on them consistently. Unclear expectations lead to guesswork and unproductive behaviors on the part of employees. Further, lack of clarity tends to brew resentment as employees toil under uncertainty and get "jerked around" after missing unclear targets and having to constantly adjust and rework their efforts. Clear expectations expressed in the form of clear goals, measures, strategies, and personal objectives go a long way, as do efforts to communicate and revisit expectations periodically. Don't change expectations without notifying your team. As a good leader you should . . .

- Set clear goals, measures, and consequences.
- Communicate them effectively.
- Apply them consistently and always follow through.
- Revisit and reinforce expectations, and adjust them when necessary.

Delegate Effectively

Delegation is one of the most important tools you'll learn as a leader. Delegation gets complex tasks done, spares your time, and develops your people. A manager still fixated on being a "doer" will immediately say, "the staff isn't capable," or "I don't have the time to babysit them," or "I'll have to do it myself in the end anyway." These are all excuses to hide insecurity about losing control, which is a misconception about your role as a manager. Your role is to help your employees grow to the point where they are as competent and motivated at their work as you used to be in the job. Your role is not about control; it is about developing a team of people who can be relied upon to do the work well and take the right actions at the right time and for the right reasons.

You cannot manage a group of employees and do all of their work for them, any more than you can micromanage the activities of each individual. When you make people's decisions for them or take over when things get tough, you take away people's opportunity to show initiative and gain the satisfaction of having conquered a new skill. (Remember how good it felt when you finally managed to ride a bike without training wheels?) If you make others' decisions, your staff will see you as someone who has no faith in their professional abilities, and will sit back and let you do all the work. We'll cover the important strategies and mechanics of delegation in a separate section later in this chapter. Good leaders . . .

- Identify tasks to delegate.
- Delegate them with clear authority, responsibility, and expectations.
- Empower their people.

Confront Problems Directly

Good leaders confront problems directly, resolve them, and implement the resolutions without missing a beat. Ineffective leaders let problems distract or consume them, they lack focus, and they may become so distant that the rest of the team loses faith. Team members relish an environment where leaders get and stay in front of problems, work their best to solve them, and avoid, at seemingly all costs, passing problems on to the team. Where would the famous Lewis and Clark expedition have ended if Lewis and Clark hadn't been good at resolving problems?

Problems emerge not only from outside but also from within teams. Good leaders take responsibility for all problems, and learn to deal quickly and proactively with all. They get close to—not back away from—problems. If a team member is causing problems with the rest of the team, good leaders get close to that team member to try to "restructure" their attitude and performance. And, just as good leaders look to the future to set direction, they also let go of the past when solving problems, and they don't let the problems follow them around. Finally, good leaders recognize that special challenges and problems, when solved without adverse consequence, should be recognized and rewarded. People who aren't rewarded for solving problems or anticipating them soon start to not care. So, when it comes to solving problems, as a good leader you should . . .

- Take responsibility.
- Pay close attention inside and outside your team.
- Let go of the past.
- Create pride, and reward your people for handling challenges.

Excel in the Face of Crisis

It is said that true leadership is shown under conditions of stress and duress. In times of success, employees are happy, so seemingly anyone who does the basics and provides a few positive "strokes" along the way can lead. When times get tough, however, leadership "men" are separated from the "boys." People get stressed, best efforts fail, resources are lost or are not available in the first place, and heretofore secure confidence may be lost. The relationship between team members can deteriorate as much or more as the relationship between the team member and leader.

In conditions of duress, leaders must make reinforcing team confidence "job number one." Team members who lose confidence in the leader start to lose confidence in the entire effort, and shift to no-contribution or even negative contribution in a heartbeat. When confidence is lost, employees soon look for the lifeboats and care little about the success of their team, and care only about their own survival. Good leaders make the effort to preserve or restore confidence. And this must happen through actions and truthful statements, because false or exaggerated admonitions soon become known.

Maintaining confidence most often requires action, not just words. Good leaders get involved and may often get into the trenches to assure the outcome. They bail out the boat, and just don't stay on the bridge barking out orders. They share the pain as well as the gain, and they see the situation, as much as possible, through team members' eyes. They offer historical perspective. ("When I was in this situation before, here's how we proceeded . . . ") They defer, when appropriate, to the advice and experience of team members, and aren't afraid to admit when they *don't* have the answer. And, as in many other aspects of good leadership, they are able to let go of the past. If something needs to be changed, they change it. Good leaders go down with the ship, but only after they've tried everything. To excel in the face of crisis, a good leader . . .

- Reinforces confidence.
- Gets (and stays) involved.
- Is strong, but defers to advice of others when warranted.
- Makes necessary changes.

Build a Leadership Style

Books have been written on the subject of leadership style and how it fits into organizational climates and settings. Every leader will develop a style—a consistent pattern of attitudes and behaviors that, sooner or later, become a "norm" for people to deal with. As a leader, you should try to be consistent in style and in what you require of your people. Don't enforce the rules to the letter one day and cut a lot of slack the next. Don't ask for a written report one week and expect a summary in the hallway the next.

Be aware that different leadership styles arouse different behaviors in people. High achievers need a nurturing, highly empowering environment; basically, you give them the resources to succeed and leave them alone. People with strong affiliation motives (that is, the need to build strong relationships) want to work as teams in job assignments and need consistent feedback. Some people want highly structured work environments and are uncomfortable unless you continuously keep things running by the rules.

Organizational climates are just as different as the people who work in them. Some organizations focus on product and technical excellence and require a lot of laissez-faire, light-handed, achievement oriented, nurturing leadership, while others operate in highly competitive, low margin, rapidly changing environments and may focus more on process and cost control to survive. In the highly competitive organizations, the climate dictates a more autocratic, heavy-handed, "governing" style of leadership.

You will have to decide what leadership style works. Your own observation and discussions with your mentors will help decide what style works best in the organization. Your ultimate leadership style will evolve as a blend of what's required and what comes to you naturally based on your personality and approach to business. So long as what's required and how you approach the responsibility are somewhat consistent, you shouldn't have a problem; if way off the mark you may be in the wrong job. And the key word in this discussion is "evolve." Your leadership style will evolve over time through experience and learning on the job what works and what doesn't.

We will expand on leadership style later in this chapter but for now please keep these three basics in mind:

- Always be consistent ("ABC").
- Recognize differences in people and organizational climates.
- Learn continuously, and let your leadership style evolve.

Element	Description
Establish order and routine	• Create structure, but not too much structure, minimum necessary for people to achieve
Take responsibility	• Be totally responsible for both success and failure
Keep the end in mind	• Keep the big picture, and be able to describe to others as a "vision" • Show enthusiasm • Don't get lost in details
Be forward looking	• Make careful observations • Anticipate problems and opportunities • Let go of the past
Break down barriers	• Create a success-oriented environment • Get proper resources and buy-in
Create an environment of openness and involvement	• Stay close to people but don't meddle • Establish an open-door policy
Assign jobs effectively	• Match talent and expertise to requirements • Match people to jobs, not jobs to people • Rotate responsibility • Ensure everyone is keeping pace • Shore up the weakest links
Set expectations clearly	• Set clear goals, measures, and consequences • Communicate them effectively • Apply them consistently; always follow through • Revisit and reinforce expectations; adjust when necessary

Figure 7-1. Elements of Leadership

Element	Description
Delegate effectively	• Identify tasks to delegate • Delegate them with clear authority, responsibility, and expectations • Empower your people
Confront problems directly	• Take responsibility • Pay close attention inside and outside the team • Let go of the past • Create pride and reward your people for handling challenges
Excel in the face of crisis	• Reinforce confidence • Get (and stay) involved • Be strong, but defer to advice of others when warranted • Make necessary changes
Build a leadership style	• Always be consistent ("ABC") • Recognize differences in people and organizational climates • Learn continuously, and let your leadership style evolve

Figure 7-1. Elements of Leadership (continued)

> **The Greatest Leader That Ever Came on to God's Earth, Bar None**
> Historians have long recognized the outstanding leadership skills employed by Sir Ernest Shackleton, the British explorer who, in 1915 and 1916, led his team to a miraculous recovery after a shipwreck in deep Antarctica. After the wreck of the *Endurance*, Shackleton calmly led a crew of twenty-seven men on an 800-mile trek across ice floes and through danger seldom seen, let alone dealt with, by humans. The entire crew survived. It is widely felt that under almost any other explorer's leadership, the entire crew would have perished. Crisis leadership? You bet! Recently, management scholars have begun to recognize Shackleton's excellence. He employed an uncanny mix of crew selection, team building, and many of the leadership techniques outlined in this chapter to pull it off. Required reading for any manager is *Shackleton's Way*, by Margot Morrell and Stephanie Capparell (Viking, 2001).

A Recipe for Delegating

As mentioned earlier, delegation is one of the key elements of leadership, with multiple benefits of (1) expanding your power to get work done, (2) allowing you to focus on "bigger picture" things, and (3) developing your people. Here we take a closer look at this critical management and leadership skill.

The Essence of Delegation

When you believe in your ability to groom people to new heights of professional competence, you will be only too eager to see them strut their stuff, because their competence signals your success and readiness for your next professional step. Successful delegating finally arrives when you trust your people with a task, and when making them look good makes *you* look good.

Delegation begins with the execution of small tasks, but progresses (as rapidly as the employee demonstrates ability) to the assignment of projects with real importance to the success of the department. More than anything, delegation for you means relinquishing the right to make every little decision, and conferring that decision-making authority (in a controlled manner) on your staff. It can be scary to give people work to do they haven't done before. Wouldn't that mean you have to stand over them every step of the way to make sure the assignment is completed to satisfaction? On the contrary—delegation requires that you have faith in your people, and faith in your ability to stack the odds in favor of their success.

Delegation doesn't mean that you relinquish control or responsibility. Rather, it means that you let members of your staff share the responsibility of making their jobs and the department a success. Managers who delegate actually *increase* their influence over staff. The cumulative effect is to create a unifying sense of common cause among your employees: As each employee grows and makes real contributions to the overall success of the group, everyone takes pride in being part of a winning team.

You hire your staff because you believe them to be capable professionals; delegation is the opportunity to prove yourself right. Until you reach the ranks of upper management, the staff you manage will usually be people who do work similar to that which you did not so long ago. By hiring them you have already signed off on their basic competency and motivation to succeed. Even when staff members are inherited, perhaps all they need to really shine is the opportunity to show that your belief in their success is warranted. In short, your employees are competent professionals who want to succeed and grow, and with your help they will—and help your career in the process. Deny your people the opportunity to grow by refusing to delegate, and as they leave in droves you will prove to management that you are not leadership material. Believe in your people and everyone's career will prosper.

It would be nice to say that delegating will also immediately decrease your stress levels, but it won't. In fact, as you learn to delegate you will act like the proverbial cat on a hot tin roof. This is no different from the nervousness you experienced before as you conquered a new skill. As you learn to apply the techniques of effective delegation, the nervousness will gradually change to excitement as you see an energized staff and a more productive department emerging.

The Art and Science of Delegation

Successful delegation requires that you choose carefully what to delegate, and to whom, as well as how you implement and monitor the process. At the same time, this is a process that you must apply to every member of your team in equal measure, according to her capabilities. You suit the assignment to the person, basing your decision on the assignment's suitability in helping the person grow, rather than overwhelming her. As a manager you have plenty of assignments at all levels to delegate, but not all your responsibilities are suitable or even desirable for delegation.

You start by taking inventory of all the different tasks that are involved with running the department. Make a master list of all the things you do daily; then add the weekly, monthly, and quarterly responsibilities, and finally the long-term projects you have been assigned by management as supplemental to your regular responsibilities. List everything that takes up time during your day. The next step is to divide all your responsibilities into three master lists.

Responsibilities You Can Completely Delegate

This would include much of the detail work that comes your way. While logically a good choice for delegation, it is emotionally a difficult one because these very tasks are likely to be ones that you can do so well they make for easy work. However, the detail work and repetitive tasks of the department are also likely to be backbone skills for each of your staff members. Your job is to multiply yourself by bringing others along toward your level of competence. Just as learning to clean your room and brush your teeth were essential building blocks of your self-reliance and socialization skills as a child, the detail of the work process are building blocks for your staff's professional development. Look for "time gobblers," like . . .

- Preparing schedules.
- Checking results, numbers, and data.
- Preparing administrative, production, and other reports.
- Gathering information.
- Researching online or offline.
- Tracking budgets, expenses, and expense reports.
- Planning, scheduling, and organizing meetings.

Delegating these tasks frees up your time for more important duties and provides a growth opportunity for everyone to polish a skill, learn a phase of the business, and get visibility among other departments.

Development and Coaching Opportunities

If your excuse not to delegate is that you cannot rely on anyone to properly complete any or all tasks of this nature, you have simply identified some good opportunities for coaching. You should always be developing your people to eventually assume your role and responsibilities. *If you cannot delegate, then you have coaching to do.* If you do coach, you must delegate to judge your effectiveness, and if you can't coach and delegate, you can't lead.

Responsibilities You Can't Delegate or Delegate Completely

In these areas, all too often it is easier for you to do the job rather than to delegate it. But know that when it comes down to it, about the only management responsibilities you cannot delegate to some degree are progressive discipline and termination. Further, it is difficult to delegate those tasks that are simply too big to delegate; that is, those jobs that need to be broken down into parts. Until a person has the full picture and can run that particular job from start to finish, you can delegate the different components of the job. Apart from these considerations, when you have a well-selected, trained, coached, and empowered staff, in theory, anyway, you can delegate almost anything. If you can't delegate it, you should contemplate a development path that will allow you to delegate it *eventually.* When your team can substitute for you not only to accomplish a task, but also to represent you at presentations and in conference calls, even in selection and interviewing, you know that you've done your job. Further, you've enabled yourself to move onward and upward. Remember that delegation is a golden opportunity to help your people grow, and to free up time for yourself.

Develop Your Team's Skills Through Delegation

When you have no idea of someone's capabilities, start with smaller assignments, ones that won't have any serious impact on the bottom line or cause company activities to come to a crashing halt if they are improperly executed. In the early days with new reports, one of your overriding responsibilities is to determine the capabilities of each team member. However, once you know the competence level of each of your reports, the task is not to delegate jobs just to the people who can do them. This would do neither you nor your employees any good because . . .

- You would not be developing the skills of your people.
- The employees would not be learning anything new.
- Your best people would get overworked and feel put upon.
- The rest of the team wouldn't get a chance to grow professionally.

If you aren't sure where to start, take time to look objectively at your own skill-development path. You learned simple tasks, then picked up the parts of the bigger jobs until, over time, you developed a solid grid of professional competency with which to tackle any job that came your way. You can use this personal frame of reference to help your people follow their own paths of professional growth.

There is no shortage of tasks to delegate. With the exceptions of progressive discipline and termination, just about everything you do in the department can be delegated in part or in whole. If you make this your goal, one result will be a department of motivated, highly competent people. A second result will be gaining the time to do your job without losing all your hair. And a third result will be clearly marking yourself as a man or a woman ready for further promotion.

Practically speaking, you start finding out what everyone can do by delegating the simpler tasks first. You should tell the team your intentions.

> I want everyone to build new professional skills this year, and by the end of the year I want this to be the most smoothly operating outfit in the company. If we work together to do this, we'll have the most fun and get the best raises the company will afford us. I gradually want everyone to be capable of handling every single responsibility this department holds. Some of the things we have to do can be really exciting, and some of them are the mundane, but that goes with the territory. It's work we have to do, and if we have to do it, I want us all to take pride in doing it well. That's what will mark each of us as true professionals. It's what will make us stand out as individuals and as a group.

There are a number of considerations for delegating any task, including:

- **Who has the time?** Really, no one does, but if your people understand the big picture they'll make the time.
- **Who is interested?** If you find people who are consistently "not interested," you may still have a good team to accept certain delegated tasks. (See our discussion about pluggers in Chapter 5.)
- **Who can already do this job the way you want it done?** If the answer is no one, then you start with the most qualified person for the job and coach that person in exactly how you want the task done.

Once your people can do a particular task the way you like it, you can use them as surrogates for yourself in training others in this task. It will free up your time, and give your best people experience in coaching others in skill development. It is this process that will help you institute succession planning within your department. This is important for your professional growth, because you cannot hope to get out of this job and into another one until you have found a replacement.

Effective Delegation: A Few More Pointers

Delegating is more than a science; it is more like a practiced craft at which you will improve steadily over time. Here are a few more pointers to consider as you start down the delegation path.

One common mistake made by new managers is to delegate tasks *only* to the people who can already do them. You should try to avoid this pitfall. That doesn't mean everyone must always be doing things they haven't done before. Far from it, the efficiency of your team depends on people executing tasks they are competent to perform. Where does your department suffer skill gaps? The functional areas in your department where no one or only a couple of people are competent become areas for immediate attention.

If there are no resources but what you have in the department, recruit the couple of people who are competent in the skill gap area and explain the challenge. You can buddy the competent players (yourself included) with those who need the skill, and if it is a department-wide weakness you might choose to use yourself and your chosen warriors to run training programs along with the one-on-one buddy training.

It is important that you analyze all tasks in the department and make every effort to bring each of your people along at the same speed. By that, we mean learning new tasks suitable to their stage of development while at the same time being able to pull their weight with the things they already do well. If you are conscientious in this and regularly keep open lines of communication with each team member, you will avoid the petty jealousies and ego conflicts that dog many managers' days.

In some cases, you will need to proceed gradually, not just "throw tasks over the wall" to others. For example, when you do get around to having your people represent you at meetings as part of the development process, you should take them to the meetings a few times as observers, prepping them beforehand and debriefing them after. Later you can take them with you to make parts of your presentation. This not only develops the person's skills, it gets the others at the meeting used to the person's presence and willing to accept him or her as your emissary. And everyone, including the employee, feels that you're standing behind the employee in her development.

Managing the Delegation Process

The way you institute and manage the delegation process is a critical coaching skill, and a foundation of your success. The way you delegate tasks and responsibilities should be aimed at maximizing the odds of success for the employee with whom you are working. The process is logical and will quickly become second nature. This is how to delegate a task to an employee:

- **Put the job in context.** Identify the task to be done and its time lines and deliverables, along with its role and importance in the department and the business.
- **Define the resources available** to get the job done.
- **Confirm the employee's understanding** of the desired result (and the process if necessary) and how you will measure the results and the acceptable time frame for completion.
- **Establish follow-up procedures and a time line.** Reinforce to the employee what you expect, by when you expect it, and what levels of completion are to occur in the interim.

Every delegation project should start with the employee learning about the job and why you have chosen him or her to do it. Your tone should always be motivational, tying the assignment to the overall professional growth of your employee. Your opening statements should gain the employee's full attention, and offer motivation to do the job well.

Begin by explaining the task in simple brushstrokes and tie it into the bigger picture of what role this task plays in the overall success of the department's activities and the business. Follow this with a step-by-step explanation of the execution of the job, if necessary. When you believe your employee has a grasp of the task at hand, apprise the employee of all the things that can go wrong, and what to do in the event of complications. This is a very important part of your delegation process because employees tend to see you as a parental figure in some ways, someone to be pleased, someone whose opinion is important to them. That's why, all too often, people don't ask questions when they are unsure, or when things go wrong, because they don't want to upset or disappoint the parent figure. At this point in the discussion your employee should be fully engaged in the process and wondering about resources, budgets, and time frames.

When you delegate tasks that run within the normal activities of the department your discussions often focus on adjusting work priorities and training. Sometimes an assignment may require a change in the person's workload schedules, but most skill development projects can probably be integrated with minimal disruption. And sometimes skill development takes more than a quick explanation and on-the-job training. When the task requires some ongoing coaching while the employee picks up the new skill, you can either do the training yourself or assign someone competent in this area to do it for you. In this latter instance the buddy/trainer you assign is a separate delegation project, and you will need to "train the trainer" in how you want him or her to pass on those skills.

You should be aware that just as there are common-sense approaches and building blocks to completing any task, there are countless ways of putting them together, too. It's unlikely that anyone will do any job just as you do it. Your employee needs the opportunity and *space* to find her own way of putting those building blocks together. These are the building blocks you need to provide your employee:

- **Information.** You don't need to be the sole source of information for a delegated task. Make an effort to explain the availability of certain other people to ask for advice, and places employees can go to gather needed information. The more sources of input an employee has, the better he will learn the job at hand.
- **Level of authority.** We've known employees who score plum assignments and then set about assigning their coworkers to help with the work, in effect delegating the task themselves. This understandably upsets the other employees. You need to be clear about the levels of authority that go with any delegated task.
- **Empowerment.** At the same time you need to grant the level of authority that allows the employee to get the work done without conflicts with other workers. Make sure the employee knows what authority he has, and make sure others within and outside of the department you interact with *also* know the nature of the delegated task and responsibility.
- **Behavior.** Explain clearly the type of behavior you expect to see, and behaviors likely to cause conflict and resentment with other members of the team. Delegation and related empowerment can cause conflicts within and outside the work team if not handled properly.
- **Time lines.** Clearly outline when you want the project completed, or the time frame in which you expect the new skill to be developed. In deciding on time lines and deadlines, factor in the learning curve and time for setbacks and problems to be resolved.
- **Resources, a.k.a. budgets and expenses.** As a manager, you hold fiscal responsibility for your budget. Many of your employees, especially the younger ones, have no concept of this. Be firm about the limits for expenses and at what level approval must be sought for expenditures.
- **Quality of deliverables.** Another important aspect of successful delegation is making sure that your delegatee has an absolute

understanding of what the results of her work should look like. You need to emphasize the quality of the work you expect to see, and illustrate it with examples whenever possible. Don't allow for any surprises here, because the employee can lose confidence in accepting another assignment, and the rest of the organization can lose confidence in the employee.

It is important to lay out the tasks you delegate in a clear and logical fashion as we have described, but that doesn't automatically mean your employee has grasped what you've said. You should confirm understanding of what has to be done, how it has to be done, what the result should look like, and the acceptable time frame for completion. You should review the assignment and the quality and performance factors involved, along with the time frame and deliverables you expect to see at the "end of the day." This is the only way you can be sure that your anointed hasn't misunderstood you and is preparing to charge off at full tilt in the wrong direction.

It isn't a smart idea to ask a closed-ended question like "Do you understand the job?" All you will get is an affirmative. Instead, ask an open-ended question that requires a detailed explanation of the employee's understanding. (For a deeper discussion of conversation control techniques, see *Hiring the Best: How to Staff Your Department Right the First Time* by Martin Yate [Adams Media, 1990].) You can ask for the employee's explanation of the assignment at the time you assign the job, or you might consider giving your worker the rest of the day to think things over and come back to you.

> Carole, this is an important assignment. Why don't we meet first thing tomorrow morning and you can ask me any questions that have come to mind, and then give me your understanding of everything this job entails?

When you are comfortable that your employee has a good handle on what is expected, the next step is to establish how and when you will follow up with each other to ensure that activities stay on track. If the delegated assignment is brand new to the person, you should conduct more frequent progress meetings, perhaps as often as once or twice a day at the start. Then as time goes on, the meetings can become less frequent. When your employee knows beforehand when, why, and how you will follow her progress, the employee won't view the meetings as your lack of confidence, and will consequently be more open.

> **Your "Outlook" on Tracking Delegated Tasks**
>
> If you delegate tasks on an ongoing basis to a number of people, you will need some kind of tracking mechanism so you don't get hopelessly lost. Losing track of everyone's activities will say to your people that you can't keep a grip on things. If this happens your efforts at delegation will not only fail, but may well negatively affect the overall quantity and quality of work as well. If you don't have a chosen tracking system already, or a system specified by your employer, check out Microsoft Outlook (which comes bundled with most computers), because this has a good task-tracking capability.

Developing a Leadership Style

We touched earlier on the need to develop a leadership style consistent if not totally congruent with your organization, the nature of your department's job and role, and the individuals involved. Here are some more attributes and factors important to developing a successful leadership style.

Set Reasonable Expectations

Every time you delegate work, you raise the bar on your employee's performance. So, as we discussed in Chapter 5 on coaching skills, you need to tailor your approach to the employee involved. We all have different learning approaches, so some of your people will learn more quickly than others. Some will want you to hold their hands, while others will want to run with the ball. As a manager, you need to develop the ability to recognize these different needs in your employees and have the flexibility to accommodate those needs to enhanced productivity. Be flexible in setting expectations, yet firm in requiring results.

Establish Regular and Productive Communications

Perhaps the most important thing to remember about the delegation process is communication with the employee. With good communication you'll hear about problems before they arise, or before they explode and ruin everyone's day. Communication will help you catch your people doing things right, which offers you the opportunity to motivate them with your recognition and praise. The result will be their enhanced self-esteem, a feeling that their efforts are recognized, and a growing impression of you as one damn good manager.

Lead with a Light Hand

Good communication with each person in your group is different from micromonitoring their every move. When people don't feel they are trusted to do a job they know only too well how to do, they will do only what you tell them to do, nothing less and nothing more. Productivity and morale will plummet, and they will see to it that mistakes are made, and that those mistakes will be made by following your exact instructions. A department in this shape is not a pretty sight, and is fortunately an experience you can easily avoid. It starts with faith in something that you know but cannot see. In this instance we refer to the fact that most of your hires are competent professionals who want to do a good job today, and who want to grow professionally.

> **Facilitation Est Très Facile**
>
> Facilitation is a good concept to remember. It comes from the French word "facile," which means "easy." As leader, you will often find it more effective not to lead and "command" your team directly but rather to facilitate their arrival at the right decisions and actions themselves. As we said in earlier chapters, people who create tend to support, and by facilitating teams, individuals on those teams will feel better and more supportive of their decisions. You are still there in the background to guide, answer questions, and provide input when necessary. As your team gains experience, the facilitation approach indeed is easier for everyone.

Lead by Example

Actions speak louder than words, so make sure you set the tone of leadership with your behavior by . . .

- Doing things the right way and for the right reason.
- Doing things the fair and honorable way.

Consistently show, explain, and train the right way to do things

Don't Give Fish—Show People How to Fish

Always help your people help themselves, and help them to do well on their own. Not only will this approach relieve you of many task burdens down the road, but it will ensure your people will develop, and in the long run, are happy with their assignments. Too many managers—especially new ones—make the mistake of giving their people "fish" instead of "teaching them to fish." "Fish" might satisfy the need, but once done, neither your employees nor you are better off than before.

You may start your tenure as a manager with few superior performers in your group. As you apply the common sense from these pages to your efforts, one good performer will become a handful and the handful a whole department. Your goal is to create a department full of high performers who "learn how to fish" and can be trusted to do the right thing, at the right time, and for the right reasons. It will take time to elevate everyone's skills to the level you might desire; nevertheless, skill elevation should be the primary focus of your management activities. The sooner you start to really *lead* your team, the sooner you will reach your goal of creating a self-directed work force, freeing your time for more important matters.

Be Consistent

No matter what, always be consistent. Managers who continuously change expectations—or leadership styles—are simply moving targets for their employees. Missing those targets is frustrating and altogether unnecessary. You may "experiment" with different leadership tactics over time as you develop your style. When you can, it's a good idea to let your team know when you're experimenting with something. Otherwise, they may perceive you as wishy-washy or worse—totally unpredictable. When people perceive leaders this way, they start to look out for themselves, and if the perception continues, they strive to break away from the team. On the other hand, when you lead and delegate consistently, your team will start to work together more cohesively as a unit. As a leader you can accelerate this process by orchestrating team projects that require everyone to work in concert with one another.

Remember, Leadership Takes Time

From a management perspective, taking a leadership approach to your duties can change attitudes quite quickly; but you can't expect to see improved results in the same time frame. Improved efficiency and productivity will come as a result of your leadership attitude but never as quickly as you might like. Your job as a manager requires you to have the tenacity and resilience of the long-distance runner. While the short-term gains you see will be pleasing, you must create the work environment that will nurture the arrival of the more tangible results: improved quality and deliverables.

Nothing will help this more than a calm, orderly, and predictable work environment. There is enough drama in everyone's work life without an atmosphere of mayhem at the office. When your people experience their workplace as a friendly and safe place to be, they will concentrate better on their jobs, and on their personal development. This does not mean creating the rule-ridden atmosphere of a Communist gulag. Rather it means creating an environment where people know what is expected of them, and can appreciate the resources and support they have to make a success of their work.

This in turn requires that people receive the coaching necessary to understand and execute their jobs in a competent fashion. Through the ongoing communication strategies we have discussed in the book you can demonstrate that you care about your employees' success. You will achieve this by the way you listen, observe, show, teach, delegate, encourage, and direct the activities of your people. Most of all, you will do it by showing your faith in their abilities, by providing these tools and the space and opportunity to do the work themselves. As a leader you will facilitate individual success by creating the correct environment in which it can happen, and directing the activities which allow it to happen. But you must let your people do the work. You are a manager and leader; you are no longer a doer, and you most certainly cannot do everyone's work for them, unless, of course, you want to fail.

We want to do everything we can to ensure your success with practical approaches to leadership that will work whether you are working in a small company of twenty employees or less, all the way up to an international conglomerate. While there will always be distinct differences between such roles depending on the size of a company, there is still much in common.

Summary

Leadership is all about swaying people to your vision of the world and getting them to perform willingly and energetically toward that vision. At the heart of every management job is the challenge of welding a group of disparate individuals into a cohesive whole focused on a common goal, because they see achieving that common goal as a contributor to individual success. Good leadership skills are learned, and contain a rich variety of personal traits and exacted principles. The rest of Part III of this book will further explore key elements of good leadership—in particular, planning, decision-making, and motivation.

8 Heading the Ship in the Right Direction: Setting and Managing Goals

By building a logical strategic plan, help your staff accomplish what they set out to do and help your organization become a winner.

If you fail to plan, you plan to fail. This statement is the quintessential epigram of every manager who ever managed. How the phrase originated is unknown. Regardless, it prevails as a core management theme of all those who've been there and done that in some form. Read it carefully and then read it again.

The core message might have been uttered by management philosopher Yogi Berra: "If you don't know where you're going, you probably won't get there." Your organization will flail in different directions, *reacting* (and pay note to *that* word, too) to different and opposing stimuli, like a ship at sea with no engine or rudder, simply bobbing in the waves. Few people succeed in situations where they just plain don't know what's expected of them. Everyone—no matter how independent or self-sufficient—needs at least a little structure. They need some goals, some "ends" in mind to work toward. Without direction, people get confused and often work against each other. Productivity falls, effort is wasted, and morale suffers, because if there is no "there" to ever get to, nobody can be rewarded for "getting there."

Granted, there's much work to be done before developing and achieving goals. Basic organizational structure and management skills keep an organization running, and an organization must "run" before it can be guided somewhere. Your basic management skills and organization structure provide the vehicle—a machine—to get somewhere. Goals and strategic plans provide the "chart" or "map" to establish where you're going, and to show how you're going to get there. This chapter covers goal setting and strategic planning to achieve those goals.

What Are Goals and Strategic Plans?

Managers and employees fall over this terminology all the time. What are goals? Strategies? Tactics? Objectives? What's the difference? Is it possible for one group's tactic to be another group's objective? Why do many management teams seem unclear about when and how to use these terms?

The reality is that there is some overlap. Structured planning is indeed complex. What may be a tactic for an organization, may be the central focus or goal for an individual work group in the organization. "Develop an effective TV ad campaign" for a new product may be a *tactic*—a tactic to achieve a goal of becoming more profitable as an organization by introducing new products. But if you're running the advertising department, this organizational tactic becomes your department's *goal,* which will likely require you to carry out your own "local" set of tactics.

Structured Planning: Goals and Strategies

The differences between goals, objectives, strategies, and tactics should become clearer as we go through the chapter. To start, we offer the following framework:

- **A *goal* is a high-level *business* objective.** Accomplishing a goal should lead to a direct and visible improvement in overall business financial performance—increased sales, increased profitability, increased return to shareholders. "Increase net profit percentage to 7.5 percent for the year" is a very high-level goal. "Increase our service organization's profitability to 15 percent for the year" is one level lower, but still probably qualifies as a goal. As we'll see, goals are specific, quantifiable, and have specific time frames. There can't be too many of them in a focused organization. Goals become the *why* for all strategies and tactics outlined in the strategic plan. Everything in a strategic plan must, in turn, tie back to a goal.
- ***Strategies* are the list of "whats" to achieve a goal.** What few things will we do to achieve the goal? "If the goal is to achieve 7.5 percent profitability for the year, we will focus on a critical few strategies: build market share for Product X, raise prices on Product Y while lowering them on Product Z, cut costs in production process 123." All of these,

taken together, achieve the goal. Strategies answer "what are we going to do?" Goals answer "why are we doing it?"

- *Tactics* **map out the "hows" to achieving a strategy.** If "reducing costs in production process Z" is a strategy toward achieving the profitability goal, then there will likely be several tactics, such as finding a new supplier for subwidget A, and outsourcing the cleaning crew.
- *Objectives* **become** *personal* **goals tied to a business goal, strategy, or tactic.** Therefore, objectives appear in your personal goal statement, development plan, and evaluation. They represent what you as an individual (or your individuals, as part of your team) are supposed to accomplish.

Good structured plans, rather than being a "mishmash" of goals, strategies, tactics, and personal objectives, have a clear hierarchy. Goals are at the top, with strategies to fit the goals, tactics to fit the strategies, and objectives to (usually) fit the tactics. Objectives may also fit to strategies or even goals, particularly for management-level individuals, who may be responsible for entire strategies or goals within the organization.

Goals and Strategies: How Many and What?

As structured goal setting is carried out, it's often good to remember that "less is more." Clarity and simplicity in structured goals is important, so that organizations can remember what to do, internalize it, proceed without confusion, and focus. Reducing the number of strategic goals to a minimum also helps make sure there are enough resources to *really* get something done. An organization trying to achieve ten or twelve goals at once is not likely to succeed. In fact, if there are ten or twelve stated goals, usually one of two things is happening: (1) some of the goals are really strategies or tactics, and/or (2) there is a heck of a lot of dissent and politicking going on during the goal-setting session!

Ideally, an organization should have fewer than five goals, and two or three seems to work best. As many Japanese management practices were imported and popularized in the 1980s, so came the idea of Hoshin planning (from the Japanese term "Hoshin Kanri," meaning management compass), where one or, at the most, two major "breakthrough" strategic goals are identified for the organization, and then everything is tied back to those simple goals. Everybody

Strategic Planning Element	Description
Goals	• High-level business objectives • Usually tie directly to market or financial performance • Should be fewer than five; two or three are best • Define "why" we do everything else
Strategies	• Identify the critical few "whats" done to achieve a goal • Can be many, but two or three are best for each goal
Tactics	• Are the "hows" to achieve a strategy • Can be many per strategy, as many as needed to clearly set direction • Can be amended or changed as results come in • Can specify a finished result or end with an investigation or evaluation
Objectives	• Are usually *personal* goals, tied to business tactics, strategies, or goals.

Figure 8-1. Stategic Planning Elements

had a copy of the Hoshin goals posted in their office or cubicle, and they may as well have been tattooed on everyone's forehead! They were simply ingrained into the organization's psyche and culture, and formed the frame around everything that was done in the organization. While this may seem a bit extreme, it really does capture the essence of good goal setting and structured strategic planning to support those goals.

Each goal, in turn, probably should have a few strategies—key directional change items that need to occur in order to make the goal. Again, too many strategies will spread organization resources—and resolve—too thin. Too few may not get the job done, or may indicate that a strategy is really a *goal* in sheep's clothing. Remember, goals represent change in an overall business performance area; strategies represent initiatives for action—for directional change—to achieve the goal. Like the fable of Goldilocks—too many or too few initiatives will spoil the porridge. Three goals—with three strategies each, nine in all—is a comfortable working paradigm for most businesses.

Tactics are where ambitious, detail-crazy managers can go nuts. There may be many tactics needed to achieve each strategy. Some tactics may require completed action, others will be investigation only. Regardless, there's no "right" number of tactics; the number of tactics is simply driven by what it takes to best achieve the strategy. Generally, the more tactics you can plan up front as the strategic plan is developed, the better. But tactics—unlike goals and generally unlike strategies—can be amended as you move forward, discover new ideas, and measure results. And, like tactics, personal objectives are as numerous as required to achieve a structured goal—but naturally, you can't overload your people.

What Makes Structured Planning Work?

There is, of course, a big difference between plans that work and plans that don't work. Plans that don't work produce the wrong results, confuse people, and waste time. We've all been part of organizations that seem to spend more time *planning* than *doing*. Ready, aim . . . ready, aim . . . ready, aim.

There is no single formula to successful planning, although quite a bit has been written about it and many platforms of "pop" management culture, such as Hoshin planning, have emerged and had their day. We don't mean to belittle the contributions of these methods; indeed, a great deal of what they offer works, or at least helps. But our point here is that there is no single, guaranteed recipe for achieving a good, effective, well-structured organizational plan. Just as people are different, different organizations respond differently to different things. Some organizations have simple, well-contained goals and strategies, while others are very complex and interdependent.

That said, there are some basic rules and processes that should be followed in all planning exercises. To be effective, plan elements—whether they be goals, strategies, tactics, or objectives—should possess some fundamental characteristics in order to be understandable, actionable, and measurable. And there are some basic principles to follow in the planning process that can make or break the value of a plan. Let's explore these fundamentals further.

Planning Elements

Of course, the main idea of creating a plan is to create a framework for success that works to help the organization or business grow and be successful. Otherwise, it simply wouldn't be worth doing. Plans that, once developed, are simply stuffed in a drawer, allowing business as usual to go on, are worse than worthless because they clearly show what you *didn't* do! The idea here is to come up with something that really helps employees, peers, and upper management understand *what* you are going to do, *why,* and *how.* (If your plan doesn't do this, do not pass "Go" and do not collect $200!) The plan must be *actionable*—that is, it must specify elements that are understandable, realistic, and, well, *doable.* Finally, a plan that has no *measurable* outcomes will leave your team and others scratching their heads. (Well, did they succeed? Did they do what they said they were going to do? Hmmm . . .)

So, how do you construct a plan that makes the grade, that is understandable, actionable, and measurable? Here are a few pointers for building planning elements that work. Plan elements should . . .

- **Be specific and measurable.** There should be a specific action or achievement implied in the statement, with a specific measure. The measure can be a number, or a specific "yes/no" criterion, but it needs to be there. "Increase production from 100 to 120 units per day" is specific and measurable.
- **Identify and address a key result area.** Stand-alone plan elements usually don't work. They should be tied to other plan elements up the chain. A tactic without a strategy is a tactic that probably doesn't need to be done; likewise a strategy without a goal probably isn't needed either. Some personal objectives may be linked to one's own development rather than organizational goals and strategies, so linkages may not be necessary there. But a casual outside observer should be able to clearly see how different plan elements are linked at different levels. The above production strategy/tactic to increase production to 120 units per day doesn't work standalone unless there is a goal/strategy to reduce unit cost or to increase production volume.
- **Be challenging but not too difficult.** This seems obvious, but is often forgotten. Goals, strategies, or tactics that aren't achievable, don't get achieved or get achieved only at excessive personal or organizational cost. Never forget about potential effects on employee morale and retention.

Likewise, elements that are too easy might get accomplished, but don't do much for job satisfaction, or your track record as a manager if they are too prevalent. Goals should be realistic and sufficiently challenging. At the same time, extended goals tied to "extra credit" rewards provide extra challenge, and can lead to greater results without undue stress.

- **Document assumptions.** Complex planning elements, depending on yet-to-be-known events or outside influences, should document assumptions. If increasing production to 120 units per day depends on delivery of a key machine or realization of enough orders to sell those units, say so.

- **Specify time period.** Measurable objectives without a time period in which they are achieved have no basis to be tested for accomplishment. The strategy or tactic to increase production from 100 to 120 units per day needs to specify by when. June? August? End of the year? Which brings us to another point. Your plan should have a specific time horizon in its entirety. This year? Calendar year? Fiscal year? Is it a two-year or five-year plan? Some plans may have elements with different horizons—long- and short-term—but should be clearly specified as such.

- **Have ownership.** Good planning elements always have owners—individuals in the organization primarily responsible for carrying them out. (Delivering an organizational planning element becomes an owner's personal objective, too). It's okay to have more than one owner, but one owner works best for accountability. If the goal, strategy, or tactic is very complex or involves many resources or organizational units, you, as manager, may take ownership. But don't do this too often because your team members like to see their names on important stuff, too (at least they should). Spread the ownership—and the opportunity for recognition—around.

- **Be linked to recognition or rewards.** As a motivational tool, plan elements can be linked to some kind of reward, particularly for individual objectives. If a department meets a goal, executes a strategy, successfully accomplishes a tactic, and if individuals meet an objective, some form of recognition and, where appropriate, reward always helps. It makes people feel good about themselves and about starting the long climb toward pulling off next year's plan.

- **Deal with possible consequences.** Be careful when constructing a plan element to deal with possible negative consequences, and clearly spell out how the consequences will be dealt with. In the example of growing units per day from 100 to 120, realize there could be a negative consequence to quality or possibly even cost. So the original statement "increase production from 100 to 120 units per day" probably should have added something like "while keeping defects to less than 1 percent of production" or "without working overtime." Organizations with goals that are too one dimensional or simplistic, without considering all possible business issues or consequences, may fail.

Planning Elements Should	Explanation
Be specific and measurable	• Specific numerical measure of "yes/no" success criterion
Identify and address a key result area	• Link to a specific goal of business issue
Be challenging but not too difficult	• Not too easy, not too hard. Achievable with effort
Document assumptions	• Keep record of critical points of data or history used as basis for the plan
Specify time period	• When to be done by, including progress reviews
Have ownership	• Assign responsibility to individual or joint owners
Be linked to recognition or rewards	• Plans with motivational elements work better than those without
Deal with possible consequences	• Address possible risks and downsides; plan elements must make sense in total business context.

Figure 8-2. Requirements for Good Planning Elements

A SMARTER Acronym

In business, there's an acronym for everything, and strategic goal setting is no exception. As a rule of thumb, goal setting should be SMARTER:

Specific
Measurable
Acceptable
Realistic

Time definite
Extendable
Rewardable

Upshot (in case you missed it): smarter managers set SMARTER goals.
(*Source:* Carter McNamara, Ph.D., Authenticity Consulting LLP)

Organizing Your Planning

It may seem a bit trite and, well, pedantic to talk about how to organize your planning efforts. But many managers fail in this area, not because they fail to do it, but because they don't recognize or make time for the necessary steps to produce and deliver a *good* plan. It takes discipline. Poor management of the planning process can lead to insufficient or disconnected plans. Plans may not be "bought into," and plans that aren't bought into usually don't turn into results. It all starts with developing and following through on a good planning process.

The complete interdepartmental corporate planning process is beyond our scope here. In fact, it is the subject of several books, and many large companies have specific individuals or even departments assigned to developing planning frameworks and making sure individual teams develop good plans that link with the needs of the business. As we said, we won't go into that level here, and we'll assume that at least some of your goals are handed down from above.

Strategic Planning Meetings

The structured planning process usually kicks off shortly before the beginning of a relevant time period, usually a fiscal or calendar year, or a quarter, or some other horizon. The first step, of course, is to clearly define that horizon, so all folks in the organization are on the same page as to the task ahead.

It is important to start the planning process *after* key results from the previous period are mostly, if not fully, known, and before much time has passed in the time period you're planning for. Since planning often drives resource commitments (as in budgets), it should precede the formal budgeting process in your organization. There is usually some wiggle room to adjust plans even after budgets are set, but the major goals and strategies should be in place. Seems obvious? Believe it or not, some companies make a complete mess of this timing, with budgets set in stone months before planning is even attempted.

The Organization Offsite

The strategic planning process usually is kicked off with an organization-level dedicated planning session. "Dedicated" usually translates to "offsite," where key managers get together, review performance, identify key challenges, and appraise strengths and weaknesses. Along with good food, lots of voice-mail messages, and break-time entertainment, the managers work their way down to a few goals and maybe a few more strategies. The SWOT (strengths, weaknesses, opportunities, threats) tool identified in Chapter 3 works well here, too. The goals and strategies emerging from these sessions are usually fairly high level and often involve many departments together.

The Department Plan

Once you have a good picture of where the organization wants to head, and the nature and focus of this year's big goals, you can kick your planning process into gear. If your organization doesn't bring any formalized goals and strategies to you in writing, you may have to spend some time with higher-level managers trying to ferret these out. It's usually a good idea; otherwise, you may waste a lot of time constructing a plan that is out of sync and ultimately rejected.

Whatever you get to work with, share it with your group. Just as you did at the organizational level, find time away from interruptions and daily chores to deliver the information to your people. It's incredibly hard to think about the "big picture" and what makes sense for your department, say, a year from now, when you're interrupted by a guy from your shipping department with a crushed box asking, "what should I do with this?" Even if a long lunch is all you can afford, go somewhere, take a flipchart, and have a focused and results-oriented meeting.

Participation Counts

In Chapter 3 we mentioned the notion that people who create tend to support. In no area is this more true than in the planning process. Outline the performances, challenges, and goals of the business; then throw the door open to your team. Identify and discuss alternatives openly. If you make your team feel part of the process, they will *be* part of the process, and will eagerly participate in the delivery of the plan once it's finalized.

Brainstorming is a favorite technique for structured plan development. In brainstorming sessions, the floor is opened to ideas that address a particular goal or solve a problem. So that there is no psychological pressure or risk, people are allowed to throw anything out there that they please, and all ideas are considered. No ideas are rejected offhand. The openness of the brainstorming session encourages equal participation in the result, and gets new ideas out there that might otherwise be reluctantly held in. Running a good brainstorming session is a trait of a good manager.

Always encourage your team members to think as though it were *their* business. What would they do if they were the owners or top managers in the business? What would they like to see as customers? As shareholders? Getting people to think this way not only empowers them, but may bring out fresh ideas.

Flesh Out the Structure

Random thoughts and ideas may be good, but they will have much more effect if thoroughly thought out. It's a good idea to take one goal, identify all strategies relevant to that goal, then all tactics relevant to the strategies. The order may not be that important, but you want a consistent train of thought, not a "shout session" where one person adds a tactic to Strategy No. 1 while another person is adding a Strategy No. 4 to Goal No. 2. You want to create at least a few strategies or strategic alternatives for each goal, and some tactics and tactical alternatives for each strategy, otherwise the plan looks empty to others, and perhaps skewed to one goal or business issue.

If you can't flesh out a structure completely, put in placeholders identifying what you need to do and by when. Frequently it is necessary to collaborate with another department to complete a plan. Make sure you follow through—many plans get started and never completed due to time constraints.

Document the Plan

This may also seem pretty basic, but in real organizational life, many plans don't get documented properly. As you work through your meeting, take good notes. Then, using either your organization's or your own construct, publish—yes, publish—your plan and distribute it to your team and other interested stakeholders. A neat, well-written plan says that you have your act together, and it brings clarity and motivation to your team.

There are many ways to present plans. Usually they are constructed in outline format, with the goals as the top level, then strategies, then tactics, and sometimes stretch goals and personal objectives. So Item I may be a goal, and Item I.3.2 is a tactic supporting Strategy No. 3, which supports Goal I. Indents are helpful so that people can see how tactics are subordinated to strategies and upward to goals.

Each item or planning element (goal, strategy, tactic) should have a descriptive phrase ("increase net profitability to 7.5 percent"), a measure, a time frame or due date, an owner, and identified linkages (particularly if it is a strategy that supports another department's goal). There should be a blank column for "status" or "progress," which will be filled in during status reviews.

Validate the Plan

Again, it seems simple, but validation is where many otherwise good planning exercises come to grief. You can have the best offsite meeting and create the most beautiful, neat, multicolored plan documents, but if these plans aren't validated and sold to those who need to be sold, so what? Make sure you take the steps—attend meetings, set up meetings, get onto key manager calendars—to show your plans and get them blessed. A plan that doesn't have a managerial blessing on it won't get funded or supported by the rest of the organization, and eventually will fall flat on its face within your team.

Be sensitive to the needs of others as you validate. Conducting a three-hour meeting with the general manager to show every detail of a plan for your receiving department might not go over too well. Learn to isolate the highlights for presentation to way-upper managers or others (including your family at home) who might be tangentially interested. Become skilled at the "elevator speech," the simple one- to two-minute highlight-capturing spiel done in the elevator or hallway.

Review the Plan

Recall a cardinal rule of business: plans are useless if they are simply stuffed in a desk drawer upon completion (or before completion). They must become the governing set of commandments if you will, for the period's business activity. Most businesses review plans at least quarterly, sometimes monthly, sometimes at other intervals as the nature and precision of the plan dictates. At that review, plan element owners may stand up and talk for a few minutes about the item they own, and how it's progressing. At this point, the "status" column at the far right-hand side of the plan document gets filled in. Often this column is coded with an indication of "done," "on track," "slightly off track," "way off track," or "not started." For tracking, managers might use a date for completed work or the estimated start date for work not yet started and a green/yellow/red scheme for on track/off/way off. Since colors don't photocopy well, some managers use smiley, straight, and frown faces or some other visual symbol. These visuals are good for keeping up with performance for the plan overall.

Though status review is the main result of this exercise, the review process goes further to amend and adjust the plan. It is obviously disruptive to make wholesale changes to the plan, but where new tactics or even strategies become evident, they should be incorporated. Likewise, those that don't work or are replaceable with better ones are removed. But be careful—the plan review is *not* the time to chuck the entire plan out the window and start afresh! If people get that idea, your planning process will go entirely for naught.

The PDCA Cycle

In the era of total quality management (TQM) in the 1980s, managers spoke of a PDCA, or a plan-do-check-act cycle, for achieving improved quality and better business results. Naturally, the cycle starts with a *plan,* as explained in this chapter. It could be a department or business level plan, or a plan built around a specific task—say, replacing the multicolored widget-painting machine. Once the plan is in place, the organization sets out to *do* what's in the plan. Then it is *checked*—results are assessed against the plan. Once results are evaluated, the *act* phase starts, where course corrections are made. Of course, these and relevant learnings become part of the next plan, and the cycle starts all over. PDCA cycles can be a full year or more at the business or department level, and can occur several times a day "in the trenches" of business operation. PDCA usually starts out as a formal exercise in business discipline, becoming second nature eventually not only for managers but everyone in the business.

Solving Specific Problems

The "normal" planning process is usually an annual exercise, but certain events in business require the development and tracking of very specific plans constructed around the specific event. If you're planning to move a facility, a plan will be constructed around that, usually with goals, strategies, and a lot of tactics. Owners, time frames, status reporting, and all of the other planning "mechanics" apply.

One-time plans can also be "course correction" plans. If the business goes off track, say, or if costs are out of control, a plan can be constructed using the strategic planning framework to deal with just that issue, and amended to the formal, annual planning exercise. This separate plan may have its own review cycle (perhaps daily, in a "war room" meeting format), and will usually soak up a lot of time and attention. Generally these "one-timers" last only a portion of a planning year. If they grow in importance, or fail to be solved, they should normally be integrated with the standard planning process the next time around. Too many one-timers going on constantly is distracting.

Contingency Plans

Really good plans have contingency plans—that is, if things in the business environment change, here's Plan B. Companies in the high-tech industry (well, most, anyway) got pretty good at this, because customer needs, emerging technology, and supply chains changed so fast. A complete contingency plan, with its own goals, strategies, and tactics, might be laid out and stored away just in case something big changes in the business environment. As a good manager, you should always think about contingencies and "what ifs" that might affect your department's plans, and if you document plans to handle these contingencies, so much the better.

Scenario Plans

Closely related to contingency plans, scenario plans document what strategies and tactics will play out, say, if sales are 120 percent, 100 percent, or 80 percent of expectations. Scenario planning may be done as a separate exercise, or imbedded directly into the original department plan (often better).

Long-Range Plans

Most organizations do long-range plans—two, five, even ten years out—particularly at top management levels. Long-range plans create visibility to alternative business strategies and environmental scenarios that otherwise might be lost. These plans are particularly important input to capital acquisition, hiring, and construction plans. Most middle managers don't get too involved in this process but may be called in to advise. Outside consultants may also come in, which is something we *don't* like to see for traditional organization or department planning! It's always good to keep a finger on the long-range pulse, given that sooner or later your plans—and your job—will have to fit in. Long-range planning documents can be fantastic educational tools to learn the dynamics of the business you're in, because they contain a lot of industry information about the marketplace, competitive cost structures, and so forth.

The Ten-Step Planning Process

Long-range planning requires a careful look at the crystal ball, including many external factors you may not think much about in your day-to-day business. You can use the goals/strategies/tactics/objectives framework, but it usually helps to put some structure in front of *that* structure in order to identify the right goals and to set the right structured plan for the immediate planning year. For this, many corporate business planners use the ten-step planning process as a tool to develop structured plans for longer periods, say, two to five years:

1. **Statement of purpose.** A generalized global statement about how you see your business in five years: "Become the world-class supplier of end-to-end computing solutions." Okay, without the jargon: sell more computers and services than anyone else on the planet.

2. **Five-year goals.** Specific goals to support the purpose: "Achieve market-share leadership in the United States, Europe, and Asia by 2004." "Double the size of the services business by 2005." "Achieve 10 percent net profit margins each year."

3. **Description of customers and channels.** Describe your customers and sales channels, emphasizing trends and change. Try to visualize what will change during the planning horizon, and what their needs will be five years from now.

4. **Description of competition.** Similar to step 3, but for competitors.

5. **Description of necessary products and services.** In light of your customers, channels, and competition, what products and services will you have to provide to achieve your goals?

6. **Plan to develop necessary products and services.** What business changes and resource commitments will it take to bring the necessary products from step 5 to market?

7. **Financial analysis.** Project the financial results for each year (sometimes known as a "pro forma" financial plan).

8. **Potential problems.** Identify the risks and issues apparent in steps 3 through 7. This becomes the basis for specific strategies and contingency planning.

9. **Recommendations.** Pretend you're a consultant—distill steps 1 through 8 into a clear set of recommendations for what the business should accomplish and what the priorities are.

10. **Develop first-year strategic plan.** With steps 1 through 9 in place, you're ready to build your plan for the coming year, using the process outlined in this chapter.

The ten-step plan becomes the guiding hand in putting the current year's structured plan together. Throughout the process, document each step carefully. You are documenting both known facts and assumptions, which should be checked periodically. Not only does the ten-step plan become the guiding template for managing each year's planning activities, it also serves as a terrific educational tool for your team members and employees new to the business.

Individual Development Plans

Development plans were first covered in Chapter 5, so we won't open the topic up too far here. Individual development plans are, naturally, geared toward the need of the individual, not the organization. They usually have some objectives that are tied to the goals, strategies, or tactics in departmental plans, and to some personal goals that transcend or lie apart from business goals. Good development plans for the individual mix business achievement and personal achievement goals related to training, personal growth, and capturing new experiences in the workplace.

What Causes Bad Planning?

Sometimes, to learn what works, you need to examine what *doesn't* work. There are many pitfalls in the planning process. Many are obvious, many are quite subtle. We'll discuss seven of the most common.

Insufficient Planning Skills

Many managers—particularly new or inexperienced managers—don't understand the importance of planning, or more often, think they do, but don't. They don't understand structured planning—how planning elements need to fit together—or the difference between a good and poor planning element. Some great plans, no doubt, have been constructed on the back of a napkin with only one other department member present, but such informality and incompleteness invites trouble.

As a manager, you need to think through the planning process. You need to study the successes and failures of others in your organization, and learn to study your own. If your organization has a formal planning process, by all means *learn* it and use it. If it doesn't, you might find yourself experimenting with different processes or borrowing from the successes of your manager, mentor, or peers. Good planning is an art that is learned continuously, and won't be perfect the first time around.

Lack of Commitment

Loosely translated—certain organizational death. Plans created just to fill paper and to satisfy the corporate planning manager just won't cut it. Without a plan, your team will sooner or later settle into 100 percent reactive mode, ready to jump ship when something better comes along (usually another department or outsourced organization). While business was slow paced and simple enough to get along without detailed planning 100 years ago, it really doesn't work today. "Don't have time!" you say? "Gotta make time," we say. Your plan doesn't have to be elaborate and it doesn't have to produce half-inch thick documents—one or two pages often will do—but it should be done, bought off, and committed to.

Poor Information or Assumptions

Good planning requires research. *Why* did the business fail to meet expectations last year? Don't just focus on the symptoms—get to the problems. While we don't encourage "analysis paralysis," it is worthwhile to spend time to get the story right. Plans based on too many assumptions and too few facts lack credibility and often steer the ship in the wrong direction. A miss once in awhile is probably okay, but blaming poor planning on bad information or assumptions won't work for long.

Short-Term Focus

People who can think only about short-term, day-to-day results may succeed in the short term but will usually come up short in the long term. Good managers do both—they simultaneously keep up with the short term and plan for the long term. Some organizations have short-term, month-to-month, or quarter-to-quarter focus in their genes; they just can't get away from it. It's your job, as a Knock 'em Dead manager, to keep at least a little of the endgame in mind.

Internal Focus

Like short-term focus, excessive devotion to internal issues without recognition or consideration of external forces may succeed for a while, but not for long. It doesn't matter if you produce 120 units per day if nobody wants to buy the units. Good planning is both internally and externally driven.

Dependence on a Planning Department

Big companies have planners and planning departments, although this may be less true as more diverse responsibilities are landing on the modern managers' shoulders every day. These planning departments may regulate the format and planning process, and may serve to link structured plans together—or they may go further to facilitate planning sessions and do your plans for you, too. Regardless, you can't throw your planning over the wall to them. Some managers may recognize this "service" as a convenience and a great relief of time. We believe typically this is a bad idea; you should learn the planning department's process and stay involved in the actual planning as much as possible. (But don't become a maverick and avoid the planning department completely—that will usually reflect badly on you sooner or later.)

Poor Validation

Probably the number-two plan killer, behind lack of commitment, is lack of validation. In some sense, these are related. If you fail to get your plan validated, you probably won't get the resources you need. Moreover, others in the organization will start "picking on" your plan and going out of their way to identify why it doesn't fit into the overall organizational goal structure. You find yourself quickly paddling upstream for resources and cooperation, and sooner or later your own team starts to jump out of the boat. Always make sure your plan is viewed and "rubber-stamped" by the important business players around you.

Summary

Failing to plan is planning to fail. As a manager, you need to create structure around what you intend to do. Why? So that (1) your activities fit into overall business goals, and (2) your team has a structure and framework in which to operate. Structured planning means creating a hierarchy of goals, strategies, tactics, and personal objectives that all fit together to achieve a common business purpose. Goals answer why, strategies answer what, tactics answer how, and objectives take planning elements to an individual employee level. Plan elements—specific "line items" in your plan—must be specific, measurable, assigned, and owned; set up to occur in a specific time period; and linked to the rest of the plan.

A good plan makes the rest of your management job easier. It provides a necessary framework to monitor performance. That framework helps you to communicate with your employees, peers, and senior managers, and to accomplish what you intend to accomplish. To end this chapter with another phrase, made popular by the International Standards Organization "ISO9002" business quality standards system: Say what you do, and do what you say. Planning allows you to say what you're *going* to do, then provides the necessary guidance to *do* what you say.

9 | Making the Right Decision

Ready, aim . . . ready, aim. Making quick, effective decisions in today's business climate is more important than ever. Here are a few thoughts on how to pull the trigger.

Management expert Peter Drucker once said, "Wherever you see a successful business, someone made a courageous decision." Indeed, if you go through the motions of planning, organizing, staffing, training, team building, and acquiring resources, you've prepared yourself to achieve and deliver results to the business. Now comes the true test—making the decisions necessary to guide the business into battle—the marketplace. Many managers fail because, while they are excellent at preparation, they cannot make a decision—be it a good one or a bad one—when the critical moment arrives.

In today's fast-paced, competitive business environment, quick, accurate decisions are more important than ever. Good managers must recognize when they *need* to make a decision. Often, they must be able to make that decision with imperfect information. Then they must *communicate* the decision effectively, and follow it up. Failure in any one of these steps can lead to trouble.

We should point out that decision-making does not only occur on the tactical "battlefield"—it also occurs during the preparatory steps of planning, organizing, and staffing. Bottom line: Managers need to learn, and get comfortable with, a decision-making and problem-solving process. It needs to become part of your *thought* process. As a manager you will repeatedly be called upon to "think on your feet" and make important decisions without the luxury of adequate time and information. There is no concrete decision-making process. Every manager does it differently at different times, depending on his own style, preference, and the nature of the decision being made. Different tactics may be used depending on the type and importance of the decision. In this chapter, we'll share a framework and some tools to help guide decision-making and problem solving.

A Seven-Step Decision-Making Process

In the last chapter, you learned about a ten-step long-range planning process. In this chapter we discuss a seven-step process for decision-making. Indeed, having a structure can break down what seems like a gargantuan task into smaller, easy-to-follow steps. Using these seven steps will make it easier for you and for the other people you work with.

The seven-step decision-making process goes as follows:

1. Define the situation and problem.
2. Identify knowledge gaps and constraints.
3. Develop alternatives.
4. Analyze alternatives.
5. Select the best alternative and identify why.
6. Implement the decision.
7. Evaluate the decision.

Step 1: Define the Situation and Problem

Believe it or not, this first step can be one of the hardest! Bradford F. Spencer, Ph.D., a behavioral management consultant, observes, "Once most CEO's and top managers recognize the problem, they can shoot it dead. The hard part is recognizing the problem." More often than not, great amounts of management and team effort go into solving the wrong problem, or into dealing with a symptom while the real problem goes untouched.

Careful work must go into investigating the situation and the real problem at hand. The trick is to find the right issue or problem at the right level. You can't solve world hunger, but you may be able to do something with surplus food in your own household.

Issues and problems need to be taken apart to find root causes. The perceptive manager will try to separate symptoms, problems, and root causes. Again, you may do this on paper. Over time, it becomes a natural thought process, which you'll not only do yourself but also impart to your team. Any decisions that can be made without your intervention will keep the business moving faster, create greater employee satisfaction, and reduce the burden on you.

Symptoms, problems, root causes. Sounds simple, but often it's hard to separate these. "Low productivity" is usually a symptom of something else. A superficial investigation may come up with "employee absenteeism" as the reason, which many managers will try to remedy with threats and "big stick" mandates. Or, some deeper probing may find a root cause, buried deep somewhere in morale—*why* are people not showing up for work? If you try to solve the "low productivity" or "employee absenteeism" issues straight on, without pursuing underlying causes, you might come up with something like "work more overtime" or "buy an expensive machine" or "outsource" as a decision. If you look deeper into the root cause, chances are that you won't jump to those solutions, but might look at your reward structure, working conditions, employee teamwork, and other possible reasons for the real, underlying cause.

To get at root causes, collect facts and data to the extent allowed given the time allotted. One of the key skills in making decisions is to be aware of the time you have to make the decision, and to be able to manage the depth of investigation and analysis accordingly. Talk to people close to the problem. It's good to talk to a few people "inside" the problem area and others who may observe it from the outside. Don't be afraid to ask lots of questions. It's expected of you. Try to get at not only the quantifiable or "hard" facts, but also the qualitative "soft" factors that might be influencing the situation. Think large and small, internal and external. Depending on the size of the issue, you might find it worth calling a short meeting with those involved to identify the situation, including the symptoms, problems, and possible root causes. For larger decisions, it's good to write down your analysis of the situation. Obviously you can't do this for every little decision that gets made. But it helps.

Step 2: Identify Knowledge Gaps and Constraints

In management practice (and in many other endeavors), knowing what you don't know is almost as important as knowing what you do know. Keeping a balanced perspective on the unknown is important, for it is here that human nature can take different people on widely divergent courses. Some will "jump to conclusions," preferring to ignore the unknown, and get a quick decision behind them based only on what they *do* know. Others will continually try to get more information, ponder, and resist deciding because they aren't sure about Factors X, Y, and Z. Obviously, while such a course may make sense for some kinds of important, deep decisions, such "analysis paralysis" falls far short of the mark in many situations. Obviously, as a manager, you should take an approach that mostly lies between these two extremes. You must make a quick assessment of . . .

- What you know.
- What you don't know.
- What it will cost in terms of time and money to find out the unknown.
- What the downside risk is of proceeding without knowing the unknown.

You may find this intimidating, but if you think of it in this framework, eventually, through experience, you'll get good at identifying and understanding knowledge gaps.

You also must keep your decision-making process within the confines of known constraints. Obviously, employee morale, and thus attendance, and thus productivity, might go up (at least for a while!) if you double everybody's pay. But there are constraints to doing this and other solutions. You should know what the constraints are in terms of resources, money, company rules, policy, laws, and ethics before you even begin to consider the decision. If you aren't sure what the constraints are, this becomes another element in your fact-finding.

If you work your decision in a team meeting, be careful not to allow the discussion of knowledge gaps and constraints to become an "excuse" session. With particularly difficult or "sticky" issues, there will be a tendency to "look for shelter"—that is, to find a reason *not* to decide. Some people are comforted by excuses such as "not enough information" or "can't possibly do that," because it postpones the inevitable. Be sure that, while these concerns should be adequately addressed and tested for validity, they don't get out of hand or put your whole team into "analysis paralysis" mode.

Step 3: Develop Alternatives

Now we get to the "fun" part of making the decision. You've collected the facts and clarified the situation or problem down to the root-cause level. Now it's time to put on your thinking cap (or collective thinking caps, if in a team) to come up with possible alternative courses of action to address the situation.

This is where your creative juices are engaged; where you have an opportunity to think both inside and outside the box. Involve your team. Remember that people who create tend to support, and that many minds in a room usually think of more things than a single mind. So it's good to get a variety of thought into the alternative-generating process if time and resources allow. You don't want to miss your deadlines or monthly production targets because everyone on your team is spending too much time cranking out alternatives.

Brainstorming is a good technique for generating alternatives. Your brainstorming may be with yourself in the shower or while sitting in traffic on the way into the office. Or it can be (and usually is) a group exercise. We briefly mentioned brainstorming in the last chapter as an open idea-generating forum. The rules of brainstorming sessions include . . .

- It's an open forum where all ideas are heard and documented.
- No ideas are eliminated.
- No evaluation is made during the session (but perhaps just after).

Remember that while it would seem efficient to sort and filter some of the ideas before they even make it onto the "idea board," that tends to intimidate team members and stifle thoughts that may indeed be valuable. It also turns meetings into arguments. Good managers keep the brainstorming sessions completely open, but lay the groundwork by defining the problem and constraints clearly, and setting a definite time limit so that the session avoids going into the wee hours.

The idea of brainstorming, or any other team alternative-generating process you decide to use, is to get varied inputs, eliminate blind spots, and achieve greater solution validity and acceptance (people feel part of the process). But also be aware that there are downsides to using meetings or group sessions to generate alternatives. First and most obvious, it slows things down. While you may want to get team input, you don't need a brainstorming meeting to decide what time to hold your weekly staff meeting. Don't involve too many people— more than four or five individuals starts to get cumbersome. Once again, people with outside perspective, perhaps from another department, will supply new angles and enrich the thought process.

After generating the alternatives, narrow the list down to no more than four or five ideas for careful analysis and decision-making. Choosing between fifteen or twenty alternatives is just plain cumbersome. You may choose to narrow the list down yourself, or to make it a team exercise.

Pareto Analysis

Pareto analysis is a tool and a fundamental way of thinking that will help you narrow down alternatives, set goals, and solve problems. Italian economist Vilfredo Pareto realized that approximately 80 percent of the wealth is controlled by 20 percent of the population. He went further to realize this is true not only in Italy, but in most societies. He and others further realized this principle applies to almost *everything* in business. Eighty percent of your business comes from 20 percent of your customers; 80 percent of a problem comes from 20 percent of the possible reasons; 80 percent of complaints come from 20 percent of your customers; 80 percent of a result comes from 20 percent of your effort; and so forth. In evaluating alternatives, you should focus on the critical 20 percent that drives 80 percent of the outcome. To put it simply: Focus on the top 20 percent—top twenty causes, top twenty customers, or top twenty issues. Focus on the topics and solutions yielding the greatest impact.

Step 4: Analyze Alternatives

Now that you have your list (whether written or in your head) it's time to weigh the alternatives and decide on the best course of action. What you're looking for is fairly simple: the alternative that *best* addresses the need or solves the problem at the least cost and downside risk, and perhaps with the largest upside potential. Getting to that alternative takes a little work.

There is no set process for evaluating alternatives. It varies by the situation, type of decision, time available, and the culture of your organization. Here are some things to consider when evaluating alternatives:

- **Feasibility.** Is the alternative even possible? Does the organization or team have the resources, skills, or "bandwidth" to carry it out?
- **Effectiveness.** Is the alternative likely to be a permanent solution or will it lead to one? Or is it a "band-aid," allowing the real issue or cause to linger?
- **Benefits and costs.** Where possible, define specific benefits and costs of each alternative. While accuracy is desirable, be careful not to spend too much time on this; good estimates are sufficient.
- **Pros and cons.** Once each alternative is analyzed for feasibility, effectiveness, benefits, costs, risks, consequences, and intangibles, it's usually good to list the pros and cons, or advantages and disadvantages,

of each alternative. You've probably done this in your personal life when buying a car or some other big-ticket item. The decision process is similar in management—identifying a good list of pros and cons creates a good rational basis for making the decision.

- **Implications.** As in chemistry and physics, every action has a reaction. If you choose a particular alternative, will some other key result in the business be compromised? Are there consequences? Similarly, are there risks that should be recognized? How risky is each alternative? Is the outcome fairly certain, or is there a downside risk, a substantial likelihood of failure? Or is there a possible upside—a new discovery, a possibility of an outcome more favorable than expected? Part of managing risk is assessing the size and likelihood, particularly of the downside risks, and interpreting the attitude of the organization toward those risks. If you're new to the organization, it's good to get some second opinions on this topic.

- **Intangibles.** Every alternative will have tangible benefits and consequences that are measurable and observable. Others will have intangible consequences to morale, customer perception, organizational stress, and so forth. Good managers factor in the intangibles in their decision-making process. There is no way to learn all of the intangibles in advance; that comes with experience.

As a matter of practice, it usually works well to create tables to identify and evaluate each alternative side by side. Doing an exercise such as this takes time—maybe too much time for ordinary and routine decisions. But for more complex decisions, evaluating each alternative helps to provide a framework for making the decision and communicating it to others. Don't overlook the importance of this step.

Step 5: Select the Best Alternative and Identify Why

There is no formula for selecting the alternative. It's a combination of specific facts, analysis, and intuition or gut feeling. Depending on your environment and your own personal risk tolerance, you may opt for an alternative with a lot of risk, or a smaller, incremental alternative that still leaves wiggle room to do something else if necessary. Just as when you buy a car, you have to rely on facts and judgment and then learn to live with your decision. And you will also learn from your decision as well, getting better at capturing and weighing the relevant facts and intangibles. You'll get faster at decision-making, too, and you'll find yourself needing to use a structured process less often.

Don't stop with just choosing the alternative. It's important to document *why* you chose that alternative. Why document it? Three reasons: (1) people will ask you why you chose it, (2) if an assumption changes, you'll know that it's time to re-evaluate the decision, (3) when you evaluate the decision later on, you'll be able to recall the facts used and the assumptions made, so that it becomes a learning experience for the future.

Step 6: Implement the Decision

And once you decide, are you done? Hardly. Now, as manager, you have to implement the decision. Decisions aren't worth anything unless they are carried out. Seems kind of obvious, but many managers stop short of following through. Depending on the scope and scale of the decision, you may want to build a structured plan (as discussed in Chapter 8) around the decision and consequential actions. If the decision affects your department plan, be sure to adjust the plan accordingly, and communicate the adjustment. Or, if it is of smaller consequence, just make sure you or someone else gets ownership for making it happen.

Step 7: Evaluate the Decision

As Katherine Neville wrote in her novel *The Eight* (Ballantine Books, 1989), "What can be measured can be understood, and what can be understood can be altered." The value of this fabulous quote, and the concept behind it, goes well beyond this piece of the decision-making process; it should be part of your structured planning mentality from start to finish.

The upshot: when you make and implement a decision, you should take great care to make sure results are measured against it. As such, the decision becomes a learning experience, and it will get carried out, with possible ongoing adjustments, in the best possible way. The following processes to monitor decisions are similar to those used to monitor business plans:

- **Checkpoint meetings.** Once a decision is made, and particularly if it is integrated into your department plan, you should schedule checkpoint meetings at various intervals, usually timed evenly out into the future. At these checkpoint meetings, evaluate the decision, make sure the results are right and the assumptions are consistent, and look for possible changes or adjustments, and don't be afraid to make them, if they are warranted—stubborn refusal to alter a bad decision doesn't work.

- **Review the plan and implementation.** The right decision or strategy executed poorly won't work out; neither will the wrong decision executed well. Make sure, in your review and evaluation, that you examine the merits of both the decision *and* the execution independently. Good decisions often look bad because they aren't carried out properly.

- **Set up a "war room" if necessary.** In every business, crisis situations will arise, where some big issue, problem, environmental change, or whatever, will disrupt or be potentially disruptive to the business. When one of these issues comes up, many organizations set up a "war room"— a frequent meeting to review each day's or week's results against the decision or plan.

- **Progress reports.** For key decisions, it is good to produce a progress report generated by you or responsible people on your team. Progress reports keep everyone focused on the outcome and the success of the decision. Again, these are not necessary for minor decisions.

Decision Tools

Can't decide? Can't decide *how* to decide? You're not alone. Management decision-making—particularly for large and complex decisions—can be a real challenge. Often you must wade through scenarios, and scenarios of scenarios, of possible decisions and outcomes. You must develop a rationale for the outcome you select, and be able to communicate that rationale to your superiors, peers, and your employees so everyone understands and supports your decision.

Most major management decisions require a mix of facts, analysis, and intuition. Fortunately, there is a field of management theory and practice built around making good decisions in complex situations known as "management science." A deep tour of management science is obviously well beyond this book, but it helps to be aware of some of the concepts, because they may help you through the decision-making labyrinth. Don't worry—we're not about to embark on a lesson in statistics, either!

Payback/ROI Analysis

Fundamental in any commercial (and for that matter, public or nonprofit) endeavor is the notion of investing to get a return or payback. It probably seems obvious that decisions should be made based on potential payback for the amount invested in a project or course of action. Indeed, this is the case. In fact, this is the first place you should start for most business decisions, the possible exceptions being those that impact purely personal or manager/employee relationship issues. Some of those can be solved or decided with numbers, but not all.

Did we say "numbers"? Numbers are nice, because they are factual (or should be, anyway) and usually represent dollars—the currency and life force of any business or economic activity. But not everything in business (or life) boils down to numbers. Payback can also be represented by intangibles. For that matter, so can the investment. Any parent would subscribe to this, and most businesspeople can, too.

"Payback" is simply the amount returned for the amount invested, and it should be considered over a period of time; a "100 percent payback in one year" is quite different from a 100 percent payback in twenty years. ROI is an acronym for "return on investment," really the same thing as payback. Payback, and especially ROI, are usually represented as percentages of the original investment.

Any business activity or decision should be evaluated in terms of payback. There are many tools to calculate payback (be sure to document your assumptions). There are some subtle mathematical issues we'll ignore right now, such as the time value of money (a dollar received three years from now is worth less than one received today). It's best to understand how your organization wants to measure and look at payback, and build your "business case" accordingly.

What Is a Business Case?

"Business case" is a somewhat jargony expression commonly used in business. It is analogous to a legal case for a trial or judicial decision. What are the facts? What are the unknowns? How will you deal with the unknowns? What is the ROI or payback? What is your recommendation and why? When you make a decision or propose a business action, you should always have your business case ready, at least in thought, if not on paper.

Simulate Me

Although it seems kind of basic, many managers use simulation to model different possible outcomes. It's sometimes called "Monte Carlo" simulation, where, essentially, you "roll the dice" conceptually with your team to try to model real life. If you're developing a new product, your Monte Carlo session may include members from within and outside your team. People can call out possible situations or problems as you go through your assumptions and defend your decision. The following sequence is an example:

1. You introduce the product.
2. Your competitor lowers price.
3. You start an ad campaign.
4. The campaign doesn't work, but data shows your product is still selling to certain groups.

People can keep adding in factors until they run out of possibilities. Or, you can assign these scenarios to numbers and have some kind of random number generator (deck of cards, dice) to call out events. You can test a plan or decision this way and try to break it with bad scenarios. Simulation not only helps to construct and validate decisions, but also prepares you for what might happen afterwards.

Up a Decision Tree

Decision trees are another management decision-making and modeling tool. Decision trees are similar to simulation, except that you lay out events on each branch deliberately, not randomly as you would in a Monte Carlo simulation. Decision trees start with the options facing you in your current decision, then branch all the way through all possible outcomes of each decision. Many trees assign costs, benefits, and intangibles to each branch. When the tree is fully drawn, pinpoint the set of branches with the highest benefit, lowest cost, or best set of intangibles, and follow it. Decision trees provide good structured decision-making, and can help you analyze *and* visualize potential outcomes.

Mindtools
Numerous published and online tools can help you with the analysis and decision-making processes. Most management books and texts cover the topic of decision-making, and there are some very pricey "management science" books that will get you ample detail on the subject. One of the best online tools we've found for managers is "Mindtools" (*www.mindtools.com*). Mindtools is a management career development site offering good, concise, practical information on decision-making tools and strategies.

Presenting the Decision

Once you've made the decision, are you done? Emphatically, no! As manager, and particularly as leader, the next and equally important task is to communicate the decision to those it will affect. In doing this you have two goals: (1) to get everyone on board with what has been decided and what is going to happen; and (2) to build support for your decision, mainly by explaining the decision itself and how you arrived at it. How much of the latter you need to do depends on your environment and the nature of the decision. There is no rule of thumb, but if you find that people don't readily support or carry out your decisions, you should plan to spend more time in this arena.

Building the Business Case

We mentioned the idea of a business case earlier, and it bears repeating. Decisions are supported by reasons, and unless you're a Marine sergeant, your audience will want, and generally has the right, to hear the rationale behind the decisions—maybe not all of the reasons, because time is precious and certain information may not lend itself to disclosure, but at least the top reasons.

To get the support you need, it's a good idea to not only explain the reasons, but also to highlight some of the alternatives. Explaining why certain alternatives were not chosen only helps to strengthen support for your decision. Just as in a business presentation, it also reduces tension with your constituency, for they will recognize that their favorite alternative or idea was considered and dismissed for a good reason. As a manager you need to create support and diffuse arguments at the same time.

Finally, the business case should show numbers, because most everything in business is measured in numbers—or dollars. There may be some situations where numbers are totally irrelevant, but where numbers are involved, you need to show a summary. Again, it shows you've done your homework; it also displays your assumptions, which can also create support and diffuse arguments.

The bottom line for the business case: it should be as "transparent" as possible; that is, it should show and tell everything that is relevant in a clear, crisp way. A business case that possesses good logic, doesn't hide anything, and leaves nothing to confusion will carry the day.

Linking the Plan to the Pitch: "SA3RT"

In our companion book *Knock 'em Dead Business Presentations* (Adams Media, 2002), we offer a logical construct for building information content known as "SA3RT," or "situation, alternatives, recommendation, rationale, requirements, and timetable." If you "fill in the blanks" for each of these components, you will create an *actionable* decision; that is, a supportable decision with requirements, assignments, and a timetable, *which serves simultaneously as a presentation format and a plan.* How convenient! You started with basic analysis and preparation to make a decision, you made a decision, and now you have the communication framework and go-forward plan all ready for presentation. If you learn to think and act in SA3RT format, you'll do better in your management assignment.

Summary

Good decision-making habits and practice are central to becoming an effective manager. If you follow a methodical and logical approach, you'll make better decisions. In fact, a good decision-making framework works well for large, formal, group decisions and equally well as a thought process for smaller, real-time decisions that guide the team and the business. Don't forget to build solid business cases around your decisions, and make sure those decisions and business cases are transparent to those who must follow or are affected by your choices.

10 | There Is No "I" in Team—All about Team Building

Teams work better than groups of individuals. Your team depends on you to be motivating and authoritative, but it also needs you to be a member in addition to a leader.

Go to any company management meeting, association convention, or industry symposium, and team building will be on the agenda. If the organization has money to spend you'll be treated to the opinions of a winning NFL team's head coach. Lacking that there will perhaps be a training video starring—you guessed it—that same famous winning coach.

Not that team captains and head coaches don't have something to say about team building and leadership, but while there are many similarities, there are also important differences between developing and leading a team of professional athletes and a team of professional wage earners.

In a professional sports team, you are dealing with individuals who all . . .

- Have a natural talent for the activity.
- Want to be there.
- Believe there is nothing else they would rather be doing.
- Don't have money worries.
- Are motivated by significant bonuses under written contract.

And perhaps most important and also easily overlooked, is that they all already have an innate sense of personal sacrifice for the common good. They know what it means to win, and that a team effort is required (in most sports, anyway) to get there. And if that isn't enough, there is also the guarantee that if they make a really special effort and pull out all the stops, they'll have the adulation of tens of thousands of adoring fans.

None of this is to take away from the admirable and special talents of professional athletes and their coaches; their advice is usually worthwhile as far as it goes. It's just that *your* job is considerably more challenging.

227

Now, about *Your* Team

Now, let's take a closer look at *your* situation. In running a department, you are dealing with individuals who . . .

- Don't necessarily have a natural talent for the activity.
- May or may not want to be there.
- Mostly have something else they would rather be doing.
- All have money worries.
- Are rarely motivated for long by significant contractual bonuses.

And perhaps most important, they by no means all have an innate sense of personal sacrifice for the common good. And further, they likely perceive that a really special effort will bring nothing but the roaring sound of silence. Yes, compared to you, sports coaches and their team captains have it easy. This is not to say that your job is impossible. Challenging, yes, but well within your capabilities.

A Whole Greater Than the Sum of Its Parts

In essence, team building is *harnessing the power and commitment of individuals to a common goal that exceeds their individual capabilities.* When people bond together with a common purpose, their power for change expands exponentially. The dynamics of a diverse group focused on a common goal generates ideas, insights, energy, commitment, and results that are impossible for a single individual, or group of people not committed to the common good, to generate. A committed group of individuals produces, in a word, synergy.

The resultant upsurge of ideas, insights, and energy comes from the synergy of people with vastly different life experiences, living and working together in common cause. As the manager, you head the house in which these people lead their daily professional lives. As their appointed leader you are empowered to guide and facilitate it toward its best outcome. You hold your position of power and privilege because *your* management believes you will give your people all they need for them to willingly give on behalf of company goals.

While fulfilling your role as parent, teacher, confidant, coach, and cheerleader, you probably realize that you are but one person whose capabilities are finite. Yet the team you build with the sweat of your brow in turn will become a support system for itself and for you, because at its heart, building a team is also like building a strong family where people care about and take responsibility for each other.

Doing Less Means Getting More

Your department will never transform itself into a team from a handful of motivational speeches. Building a team happens over time as you apply all the management techniques we have been discussing in earlier chapters, and will continue to address throughout this book.

You will become a team leader as you slowly realize that the professional growth of all your people is gradually changing your everyday responsibilities. You won't be providing the same degree of hands-on coaching that was once necessary. You will still be helping people grow, but they will now be building on a foundation of essential professional competencies, and growing at a faster rate and with less oversight from you. Learning from each other, they become self-starting and self-motivating, and will gradually require less and less specific direction in meeting your goals. You are looked at as someone they can rely on for support at all times, guidance when they need it, and a safe and level playing field on which to score touchdowns for you and the company (pardon the sports analogy).

Being a team leader is not always about inspiring people to achieve more than they think they are capable of doing, although many management theorists would have you believe so. Almost all the people you hire have a desire to succeed, so that, in turn, their personal life will have a greater chance for success. Therefore, your role as manager and team leader is to inspire them to achieve what they are already quite capable of achieving. You do this by acting fairly and consistently in your words and your actions, by gaining their trust and giving them yours.

Team Building in the Real World

So much has been written about the role of motivation in the development of teams that anyone could be forgiven for believing that cheerleading is all that is required. Whenever you hear this, you nod and think, yes, that would be nice in the best of all possible worlds, but I live in the real world, and my real world is a company with a less than perfect history with its workers.

Very few workers have the privilege of working for Apple, H-P, Nordstroms, or the handful of other exemplary employers of the world. Most companies are flawed at best, if for no other reason than, as people, we are flawed. All too often we work for companies that encourage people to do what hasn't caused problems in the past. Attitudes such as "same old way" and "don't reinvent the wheel" and "don't put too much trust in 'em" shape the business and team climate of most companies.

Companies give lip service to team building, as do employees, yet both see a yawning chasm between the lip service and reality. Most workers don't believe that management knows they exist. If your people are to give their best efforts as individuals and as members of a team, they need to know that you are there for them, in word and in deed. They look for these qualities in a leader:

- **Hard work.** You must be seen as embodying the results of hard work, honesty, and commitment.
- **Belief in them.** Your people must believe that you are there for them and that you believe in their ability to succeed.
- **Empathy.** You must show that you understand their situation and needs, both as individuals and as a team.
- **Action.** They believe your actions more readily than they believe your words.

With these four criteria visibly in place, your staff becomes ready to listen to your teambuilding messages. Your people need to see personal benefit on some level for anything they do on behalf of the company. For example, while they need to develop professionally to do the best they can for the company, their efforts should be rewarded with enhanced professional buoyancy. They will become more desirable as employees at this company or another. They need to believe that what they are doing at your behest for the company, they are also doing for themselves. When people feel they have a personal stake and benefit in helping your goals succeed, they are ready to sacrifice for a common good, knowing the common good also relates to personal good.

To Be a Team Builder You Must Be a Team Member

We talked earlier about the exponential strength that comes from people banding together with a common commitment. While you must be the team builder in your department, you will be more effective if you are also a team member. Within your own department, your particular function as a team member is to facilitate the efforts of the rest of the team. When you do this, your people will see you not only as the boss, but also as a bona-fide member of the team, carrying your share of the burden to help everyone else succeed. You will gain the respect of your people as a valued boss, and their acceptance and camaraderie as one of the team with your own special talents and contributions.

The Bigger Team Picture

You also have a need and responsibility to be a team player with your peers in the management strata of the company. It has been said that you cannot lead until you learn to follow. In following and working for the common cause on the management team, you will learn and hone your management skills from your interactions with other managers. If you apply yourself on this team, you will have the opportunity to see who the real leaders in the company are, and in the process gain the opportunity to form mentor relationships with these important players on the company scene. Then, sooner rather than later, because of your role as a team player and the visibility of your teambuilding efforts back in your own department, you will be seen as a leader by your peers, and someone ready for further promotion.

As you observe the leadership of others in the management ranks, the real players will make themselves known by their words and actions. Their commitment to what is best for the company will color all their thinking, words, and actions. You will notice that they listen well and acknowledge others' contributions, that they offer cooperation and get it in return, and that they seek advice just as often as they offer it. They habitually put the common good above personal interests.

You'll find yourself drawn to these people. You'll want to work with them on projects because their obvious common sense, work ethic, and conviction convince you they will succeed. Your own common sense tells you that throwing in your lot with people like this can only be helpful to your own career. Becoming a genuine team player on the management team is in your own enlightened self-interest, because it will teach you most of what you need to know and the things you need to avoid in building your own team.

Building Blocks for Team Building

The only firm foundation on which you can build a reliable team is open communication, in a safe, supportive atmosphere where your employees feel valued and encouraged to grow. People want to be part of a team due partly to their need to belong and the emotional rewards of camaraderie, and partly to the need to be part of something worthwhile that is bigger than themselves alone. To sign up on your team they need to believe this about you:

- You are honest, optimistic, and confident.
- You understand the business and its strategies, and can break them down into meaningful team tasks.
- You communicate well, and build the path for successful team communication.
- You recognize people for who they are and what they can be.
- You care about providing a safe and supportive environment.
- You recognize their right to a personal life.

Optimism, Honesty, and Confidence

We all like to be around happy, honest, and confident people in our personal lives, and it is the same at work. In the workplace, teams form around charismatic people, because they exude the personality characteristics that we are all drawn to.

We see confidence in others coming from personal expertise and experience with success, and want to be associated with successful people so that we might learn the same experiences and formula. We find success, and the formulas for success, fascinating; we want to be close to it and to learn the secrets for ourselves.

There is nothing people like to see more in their leaders than honesty. We are drawn to honesty because our peace of mind is enhanced when we believe and trust in people. Yet in most of our professional lives, knowing that we are getting the truth is about as rare as getting raises in double-digit percents. When you live in the dark, a man who brings light is your savior.

Just like you, your reports can tell the difference between the truth and obfuscation. When you are honest with your staff, they will see you as a person of integrity, and they will listen to your advice and direction because they know you speak the truth. The truth might not always be palatable, but it will be accepted nevertheless, because ultimately everyone can handle the truth.

And finally, like the common cold, optimism is highly contagious; but unlike a cold, it is something we'd all do well to catch. Accompanied by honesty and confidence, optimism brings out the sunshine in our lives because we see good outcomes for our endeavors. Together, optimism and honesty create an environment where morale is high. Nothing feels better at work than the feeling of success. If people believe in their ability to succeed, they are eager to accept challenges and are ready to get to the work at hand.

Your people want to feel successful, just as they want to feel good about themselves and the work they do. Feeling good in their professional lives carries over to happiness in their personal lives, too. Learning to handle the challenges of work in an optimistic way only helps us apply the same techniques to our personal lives—in both contexts the result is increased optimism.

Creating Meaningful Challenges

As a manager, you may have greater confidence than your staff, if only because you have more experience turning workplace challenges into successes. Among the behaviors that encourage you to believe in your success is the ability to break complex tasks into their logical parts, and organizing those parts into the small steps that lead you to the achievement of your goals. This ability to break down projects and take organized action is the reason good managers don't get overwhelmed when they are presented with complex challenges.

This trait not only defines leadership, but also the ability to successfully build and motivate teams. It draws people to you, because they will recognize your ability to get things done. Management has already recognized and rewarded this to you, and your people will also reward you with their loyalty and energy. Your confidence in work situations, based on your logical approach to challenges, will rub off on your people, too. As they learn to analyze approaches and break insurmountable challenges into the necessary small doable steps, they will develop confidence within themselves. Multiply this by the people in your department and as a team you will become unstoppable.

Your confidence increased over the years as your approach of organized action proved itself again and again. In turn this led you to a better understanding of the need for patience and understanding. You know from your own experience that things can go wrong, but what is most important is to recognize the problem and come back at it again from another angle. In doing so you are exercising patience, persistence, and perspective. Those are all tools that help you face work-life challenges in an honest and forthright way. When you see things in perspective, and break down problems into actionable steps, your patience and persistence will be obvious to all.

Your role as a manager is to face today's realities and turn them into the desired outcomes of tomorrow. Those realities aren't always going to be rosy; you'll know it and so will your staff, so hiding the truth serves no one's purpose. You also know from past experience that you can get wherever you want to go, just so long as you . . .

- Know where you stand today.
- Know where you want to stand tomorrow.
- Know how to break the journey down into logical steps.

These are principles that give you confidence and optimism, which can gradually be developed by all of your people. They are essential underpinnings of team building and leadership. When you embody these principles in your day-to-day management activities, you unleash a storm of energy and effort in your people, because they feel they are standing on solid ground.

Effective Communication

In a way, management, and this whole book, for that matter, is about persuasive communication—the swaying of people to your worldview and harnessing their energies to your vision of the way things should be. Yes, you need to communicate with staff members about how you want a particular job done, and, yes, you have to communicate about performance problems. However, your people want to know what is going on, and they have a need to believe that they are being heard in turn.

Your communication skills must also be applied to gathering and sharing information, so that your group has a real sense of inclusion in the management of the department and in the activities of the company as a whole. Much of the professional endeavor in today's work centers on information, hence the saying "knowledge is power." But by that same token, *sharing* knowledge is *empowerment.*

With all the technology in the workplace there is no excuse for lack of gathering and sharing information with your people. There are telephones, cell phones, faxes, and e-mail; there are in-person meetings and telephone meetings and cyber meetings, and Palm Pilots, and pagers and Blackberrys. The list of communication devices is limitless. Whether you are in the next cubicle or in Mombassa, there is always a tool available to enable you to foster a feeling of inclusion amongst your people.

Wandering Around

Of course when you are in the office there is absolutely no substitute for dropping by someone's office or cubicle. When you informally talk with your people during the course of the day, you are seen to be showing both a professional and a personal interest in them. That goes a long way to their getting to know you as a person, as they do the other team members. As you "manage by wandering around" and get to know people, you should gather information about the following:

- The person's work
- How that work is done
- The group work
- The person's goals
- The person's life

At the same time you should share these things with your employees:

- Useful information that will help the work progress
- Useful information about the work of other departments
- Relevant information about the company
- Achievements of other groups and how they got there
- Confidence, honesty, and optimism
- Pride in the group's ability and potential

You share what you are learning from the group as a whole and seek further insights from the person with whom you are talking. You become the prime information channel for your group. Not a gossip channel, of course, because confidences remain sacrosanct, but the prime source for reliable information that will help your people feel connected to you, their job, the group, and the company as a whole.

A by-product of paying attention to your people is that as you spend time gathering information, you will also be learning the nuts and bolts of jobs you have never done, but which you need to understand to manage effectively. An ever-increasing understanding of what makes people productive in different jobs is important in your grasp of how companies work, and will prepare you for greater responsibilities.

Creating Your Teambuilding Vocabulary

It is easy to complicate things. You see people do it all the time, even though the simplest way is often the most effective. It is the same with communication; keep it clear and keep it simple (without talking down to your audience), and you will avoid misunderstandings. This applies when directing the work activities of your team, and it also applies to the messages you want them to receive about what is important to you and to the company.

In thinking about your job, you have likely envisioned how you want your group to operate and what you want the atmosphere to be like. If you have taken the messages in this book to heart, you will be thinking in terms of "personal achievement," "professional growth," "individual good is tied to the common good," "we work as a team," "I believe in you and your ability to succeed," "we believe in honesty," "we believe in creativity and initiative," "we believe in getting the job done right the first time." Your list of key thoughts might be longer or it might be different, but it probably includes most of these thoughts, or others very much like them.

Having positive, empowering thoughts is one thing, but they are more likely to become reality if everyone else in the department is having them as well. The best way to get everyone to think as you do is to develop a lexicon of phrases that embody, on a consistent basis, your beliefs and desires for the department, and use them consistently. In talking to a staff member, you congratulate him on a particular achievement and perhaps what it means to his professional growth. When the team has worked well together on a project, you reinforce what has happened by talking to them about "what is possible when everyone works for the good of the group," and "how proud it makes you feel to be part of this."

If an individual or the group is having a tough week, or something has gone wrong with a job, you let them know in no uncertain terms that you believe in their ability to succeed. If there is a right way or a wrong way to handle a situation, talk about taking the time to do it right the first time. When your people show creativity and initiative, use the words "creative" and "initiative" in your recognition of their actions to reinforce those qualities.

When you develop a lexicon of key words and phrases that embody the way you want your people to think and feel about their work, and you use them with regularity, these words act as reinforcements to your belief system. Gradually your team members will adopt these phrases for themselves, in discussions with each other, and with other departments.

A BUM's Rush

Your team lexicon can include—and probably should include—informal and humorous phrases and names for things that originate within the group. Behavioral researchers have found that when a group speaks its own language, camaraderie and team spirit grow; team members feel as though they are a part of something, and that "something" is just a little exclusive (recognizing that *too* exclusive is not a good thing). So "business unit managers" becomes "BUMs" and "Microsoft" becomes "Mr. Softee" and "dual channel port controllers" becomes "ducky-puckies." If the team is creative in this way, by all means let it ride and have some fun with it.

A Safe and Fair Place to Work

If you expect the members of your department to come together and think and act as a cohesive unit, you have to provide them a safe and fair place to work. Of course this means that your workplace at least meets OSHA requirements and hopefully exceeds them, but for this discussion, we are really taking these elements of physical safety as a given. When we talk of a safe place to work, we mean an environment where the rights, sensibilities, and beliefs of an individual are treated with respect. When people are treated with respect, they are likely to repay the compliment with honest effort.

A fair place to work is a workplace where employees are judged exclusively by their abilities, contributions, and attitudes. While the more overt manifestations of discrimination are openly addressed in today's workplace, to imagine that the problem of discrimination doesn't exist on more subtle levels would be delusory. Only if you can make a real effort to become sensitive to the needs of people who didn't grow up with your particular worldview and life experiences, can you create a team where all its members feel they have the same opportunity.

The biggest problem we face in helping a diverse group of people coalesce into a team is our own tribalism. Anthropologists have proven that we all have needs to belong to small identifiable groups and that these needs are essentially burned into our genetic codes. We identify ourselves with tribes via skin tone, religious beliefs, age, sex, education, and socioeconomic background. We also choose to identify ourselves with tribes by the way we dress, the way we speak, the cars we drive, and the accessories with which we decorate our lives.

The need for different forms of tribal identity thrives in all of us; it is part of how we define ourselves as unique and special, while at the same time taking succor from like souls who support us with warmth and acceptance. Anthropologists can safely talk about tribes when they address the need for belonging within all of us, but in the workplace we have become more comfortable with the word "teams."

This tribal identity provides raw material to work with. On the plus side, we are social animals, and belonging to groups gives us energy and validity and the willingness to spend the majority of our waking hours at work with a preselected group of strangers. On the negative side, you and everyone else in that group probably hold some inaccurate beliefs about other group members who, on the surface, are not like you. We are all capable of stereotyping others because of superficial external factors when we have little personal knowledge of their group. We have a natural tendency to validate the way we see ourselves by diminishing those with whom we are unfamiliar. We are often suspicious of others' behavior and motivation and have low expectations of their capability and work ethic.

We are all different from each other. Some of those differences are as a result of birth and upbringing; other differences come as a result of personal taste or preference. Recognizing that we are all different, and cherishing those differences, is what can make team building so much fun for all concerned, and so profitable for the company. But we have to overcome the natural and cultural tendencies that can disrupt teams.

Recognizing the Commonalties

As we move through both our personal and business life, there are certain axioms of human nature that define our expectations and our abilities to work well as a team. They provide the "raw material" for you as a manager to work with. Here are a few:

- **We all want to be treated with respect.** We all want to be recognized, appreciated, and rewarded fairly for our efforts.
- **We all want to belong to a successful and elite group.** We all want to feel special, and we all want to make a difference with our presence and efforts.
- **A group of people with different worldviews and life experience who are thrown together may be a little wary of each other.** As manager, you need to recognize this and do what you can to break down barriers and offset preconceived notions.
- **All strive to advance their professional future.** Your job is to recognize and accommodate differences in the details where you can, and to treat each person in a way that will maximize her productivity and ensure an equal shot at success.

Diversity

You may already have a widely diverse work force; it is also possible that you or your predecessors have favored your own sex, ethnic, or religious groupings to one degree or another. Understand that when the makeup of your group reflects the rich potpourri that is American society, it will be able to apply a deeper understanding of the market's needs and offer the benefits of creativity that significant cultural diversity engenders. This does not mean that you should be thinking in terms of quotas, because you should always hire the best person available for any job. It does mean that you have to be more aware of your own natural biases against people who are unfamiliar to you as a group. It also means you should work to mitigate any biases your team may have against such diversity. If you can create a department that reflects the makeup of our society, your team will recognize and be energized by your obvious efforts to present opportunity for all. You'll be seen to be walking the walk, not just mumbling the talk.

We're All Human

Managing people like yourself is the easiest proposition; you have a lifetime of experience on which to draw when it comes to understanding what folks like you are saying by how they say it. Unfortunately, this isn't such a cakewalk when you have to work with people unlike you. Whether it be differences in culture, environment, heritage, or even geographic roots, people are all different. They approach situations and problems differently. They have different needs and motives. The better you can appraise these differences and accommodate them, the better you will do as a manager.

Good communication is the first step. Talk, ask questions, and listen. Find out what makes them tick. Understand their past situation and experiences, and how these shape whom they are today. Try to find common ground between them and yourself, and the other team members. Related to communication is observation; take time to observe and make mental notes of people's behaviors. Make sure their behaviors are consistent with their words. Whether consistent or not, behaviors can be more powerful than words. You are building a relationship with your team, and you are helping them build relationships with each other. Just as in personal or marital relationships, it takes work, patience, observation, and communication. Just as you invest the time and make the effort to communicate well, you should inspire each team member to do the same.

Put the Needs of Your Group First

Make the effort to get to know each of your people. A cup of coffee together and lunch once in awhile go a long way to creating, understanding, and establishing rapport. The lunch can be a sandwich or a burger; the commitment of time and the interest it denotes is what's important. Not only will you get useful answers, but valuable rapport will be established as well.

Following is a list of suggestions to help you get to know each of your people. They are not intended as the substance of a single conversation. That would be too much like an interrogation. Do the following with each of your people over a few weeks, and share details about yourself in exchange:

- Get to know each other as people.
- Get an understanding of how that person experiences the world.
- Get an understanding of how that person's experiences shape her needs, motives, and behaviors today.
- Know what makes the person uncomfortable.
- Understand how to get the person's best performance.

It starts with what many may perceive as small talk; that is, little door-opening questions about the person, her background, and interests. Better than calling it small talk is to refer to these questions as icebreakers; that is, they open the way to more in-depth conversation and may reveal some important traits and characteristics in and of themselves. Here are some topics you can use as icebreakers:

- **Biographical information.** Where are you from? How long have you been living here? How many times have you moved in your life? Do you have a family? Tell me about them. How did you meet your spouse?
- **Interests.** What are your personal interests outside of work? What are your hobbies? Do you watch or participate in any sports? What shows do you watch on TV? How much, and what, do you read? What movies have you seen lately?
- **Goals and ambitions.** What are your goals in life? For yourself? For your family? What are your career goals? Where do you see yourself, both personally and career-wise, in the next few years?
- **Work style.** What is your work style? How are you most productive? What kinds of things do you like to see in a manager? Who are the best and worst managers you have ever worked for, and what made the experiences stand out? What is the best way for me, as your manager, to share advice? What is the best way for me to give direction? What is the best way to work with you if things get off track? Do you like to work with a team or prefer to work as an individual? Why?

These and other questions like them, give you the tools to provide direction in a way the employee has already told you is most palatable to him or her.

With questions like these you are asking your people to share with you who they are and what they require to perform to your levels of expectation and satisfaction. Don't forget that—as with most productive communication—this is a two-way street. When you get into these personal areas it is essential that you share some of your life experiences, background, and goals, too. And don't forget you will not only find out what helps you deal with your employee, but also what helps your employees work well with each other.

When you facilitate maximum productivity of your people by satisfying their individual needs, you are doing the essential work of a manager. As a manager building team spirit, you exemplify someone who cares about each member as a unique human being, a recognition that goes a long way in a world where most workers don't feel their management knows they exist.

Translating Teamwork to Performance

Simply understanding the individual needs of your team members is not enough; you need to put that understanding to good use. You need to "connect the dots" with your team to make sure they cooperate with you and with each other. This takes special skill, much of which you learn by doing and observing through your experience. It is hard to teach this in a book, but here are some pointers.

Winning Cooperation While Having Fun

Winning the cooperation of your reports is another strand in that complex web of requirements that, woven together, are the heart of your responsibilities as a manager. You need the cooperation of your people striving together toward designated goals if you are to make a success of your job. Without their cooperation, every day will be an uphill climb.

Cooperation comes about when people want to work together toward a common goal. The mechanics of management we discuss throughout this book all work together to encourage cooperation, and the more you apply these lessons, the easier it will be to elicit the cooperation of your people toward your chosen goals. You need the cooperation of everyone in your department. A handful of true believers is better than nothing, but less than desirable. Some of your people will understand the message immediately because they have an innate understanding of how to get things done in life, because of how they grew up or because of other work experiences. Others in your department will need to learn that cooperation makes possible a sense of belonging, which is important to all people. Others, still, will need to learn cooperation and have it drawn out of them, by yourself and the group as a whole.

The best thing about building a sense of cooperation in your people is that it makes work *more fun.* When people cooperate they have more frequent positive interactions with their coworkers, the days pass more quickly, and they have a greater sense of individual achievement and of being an important part of the greater whole.

How do you get your team to have more fun? Well, taking them to play laser tag or paintball every Friday afternoon might help, but this might wear out quickly and be perceived as irrelevant and time consuming in short order. Better is to create an environment of team spirit and camaraderie within the confines of work. Open communication is a start, and creating an environment where people can be friendly with one another helps. Taking breaks together or eating lunch together starts applying the glue that binds team spirit. Create a break area or lunch area. Play a lunchtime card game. Have a daily discussion of last night's TV shows, sports events, or yesterday's current events. A word of caution: Sports activities like softball, golf, soccer, or bowling can be good bonding activities, but be careful because some people can't or don't want to participate in certain sports, and may feel left out. Different groups will be interested in different things, and the more all inclusive your teambuilding activities are, the better.

Finally, it helps to create some good-natured competition within the group. A contest to see whose desk is the neatest (or messiest) at the end of each day for a week can be fun. Charge a dollar to the last person to show up at the weekly staff meeting, and pocket the funds for an end-of-year luncheon. But be wary not to make these contests *too* competitive—how may widgets John makes versus Mary—because quality can suffer and feelings can get hurt.

Create a Mutually Felt Sense of Direction

For any two people to cooperate they need an initial sense of direction, they have to know where they are headed, and they have to know why heading in a particular direction is in their enlightened self-interest. It goes beyond receiving a paycheck and getting to keep their jobs. Your reports need to understand that their individual efforts will have a greater impact and they will gain more recognition from the more visible strides a team can make together.

As a manager, you're always under pressure to promise and deliver more. Making promises is easy; delivering on them can be an entirely different matter.

The planning process we described in Chapter 8 must now be put into action with your team. You need to stir your team into cooperative action, and nothing is more important here than everybody having a clear understanding of what the team must accomplish.

Whenever there is need for concerted effort in your department . . .

- The goal needs to be specific and measurable.
- The goal to be accomplished needs to be understood by everyone.
- Everyone needs to be clear on the importance of the role they play in achieving that goal.
- Everyone needs to agree on and commit to achieving the goal.

When people agree on a goal and commit to its achievement they are, ipso facto, committing to cooperation. How long that commitment will remain depends entirely on the degree of mutual respect that exists between you and the members of your department.

R-E-S-P-E-C-T

Respect is a two-way street—*the most effective way to get it is to give it.* If you have been doing your job as a manager, leader, coach, and mentor, the giving of your respect should be no more than a vote of confidence in yourself. This is where you say to yourself: "If I have trained my people to the best of my abilities, if I have tried to replicate myself in each of these reports, it is my responsibility to show them the respect I would expect to have in their position." Your respect is your vote of confidence in their ability to do the job.

This is leading by example. When you show professional respect in your dealings with others, they will in turn, show it to you and to each other. It is really the golden rule applied—doing unto others that which you would have done unto yourself. When cooperation exists, personality becomes less of a dominating factor in interpersonal conflict. Conflict won't disappear, but it is far more likely to be focused in a professional manner on the issues than the personalities involved.

As your people learn to work together as a team, they will also learn from each other, and learn together as a result of working as a unit. They will learn what doesn't work and why, and develop improved approaches. They will anticipate what's coming, and work proactively to solve problems and improve performance without your immediate direction. This is one of the first visible examples you will see of the team beginning to manage itself.

Now, while you will want to give your people the space (read respect) to do their jobs and experience self-management, you don't want to be ignorant of the advances made. Rather you want to stay abreast of how group projects are going, and at the same time capture knowledge the group has developed from their efforts. When you capture the knowledge for yourself you are learning with your people, and it also puts you in a position to pass on the knowledge to others as time and circumstances offer the opportunity. Holding regular group progress or project status/review meetings will allow you to stay on top of things. They will allow you to keep things on track, and provide the opportunity to catch your people doing things right and offer public recognition.

Don't Forget to Look Up

We are talking about engendering a cooperative spirit within your department as an important facet of team building. However, that spirit of cooperation can be damaged when the higher ups suddenly decide they want to get involved; this can be disruptive unless you manage the process from the beginning. The best way to do this is *to involve that superior from the beginning.* Practically speaking, this is no more than you managing upwards, getting your superiors involved with team projects in a way that will ensure their constructive support.

You can avoid having a boss bring your activities to a grinding halt by involving him or her in important projects from the beginning, both by seeking your boss's advice as part of your ongoing communication, and by asking for her involvement. That involvement can consist of being a sounding board for you, or contributing special skills that could be of use to your team. It is better to seek advice than have it offered when you don't want it, and it is better if you can manage a superior's involvement in your department's affairs to maximize the chances of your success.

Sharing "Best" Practices

Because time management and organization are the underpinnings of any successful endeavor, you will probably evolve the plan-do-check-act cycle (see Chapter 8) into the daily functions of every team member. Having people follow, more or less, the same processes in their work lives will serve to bring them together and increase communication, cooperation, and, ultimately, productivity.

Another tactic you can employ is getting employees to share "best" practices. When someone finds a better way to do something, make sure you foster the opportunity to expose others to that practice. Not only will it get your group to think and act as a team, but the best practice becomes more widely known, and it comes from a credible source (a team member, not you!). Finally, it presents a growth opportunity for the best practice creator to practice her leadership skills and get visibility—from upper management, not just your team. Sharing best practices is a true win-win-win proposition, so make sure you, as a good leader/team builder, create the forum to make it happen.

Getting Them *Really* Involved

People who create tend to support, and they also tend to work together. Bring your people together in a group setting to plan strategies for ongoing projects, and to involve them in setting the direction of the department's activities. When this happens your team members will believe they have both input and control over where and how they invest their energies. With this feeling of ownership of the department's affairs, your people will work together toward goals on which they had input and to which they have already committed. When they commit as a team—instead of *you* committing them—things go better.

You can lead these meetings yourself, outlining the agenda, bringing everyone up to speed on current activities, then seeking input from key individuals on specific issues and opening up the discussion for everyone to have input. You can also coach your staff to run these same meetings, too; doing so will build skills and enable activities to stay on track when you aren't present. Understanding meeting protocol is important for cooperation within your department, and it will also speak well of your coaching and management skills when your people are active in interdepartmental affairs. As time goes by and the individual members of your department coalesce into a single unit, these group meetings can also begin to replace the individual coaching sessions you run.

When you include department members in the decision analysis and action plans for departmental affairs, it enables everyone to gain a closer understanding of how their activities tie into the group's agenda, and how they make a contribution to the goals of the company. This gives each individual a real connection to the greater whole, and a sense of belonging and ownership for the success of the group. You are involving your people in the decision-making process by empowering them to make decisions for the good of the group and the company as a whole. The sense of empowerment that comes from this is an infectious morale booster for everyone.

The Leader Is Servant and Cheerleader to the Team

When you show the team that you have faith in their judgment to make the right choices, and in their ability to subsequently implement those choices, you are honoring them as team players. You are there to guide them with the right questions to ensure that conclusions are reached with all available information; as you do this you are moving away from management by dictate (do this because I said so) to management by consensus, and ultimately self-management.

When you can manage by consensus you know that you have taken a giant step forward toward creating a self-managed and cooperative department, where everyone is committed to the common good. By becoming a facilitator to your employees' activities, you enable your people to pull together as a team. In a management context, facilitating means doing whatever is necessary to free up others from frustrations and roadblocks, so that they can focus on production of the end work product. You lead your team by setting direction and giving focus. You support your team by doing what needs to be done so they can focus on getting the job done. You help out when they get stuck, and you cheer them on as the team's most ardent supporter.

As team facilitator, you may take on some mundane but brutally necessary tasks. Such a task can be ensuring a steady supply of material or other resources, software, hardware, administrative support. Or automating tracking procedures or quality control initiatives. Or outsourcing a time-consuming part of the process or bringing in temporary help to pick up the slack. Such tasks can also include the little things like making sure the heat and air conditioning are functioning properly, that water and coffee are in ready supply, that the bathrooms are always clean, or that the lights work. All these minutiae are important productivity tools that shouldn't be dismissed. Over eighty years ago, early in the twentieth-century industrial era, studies were done on productivity in manufacturing plants. The task was to determine what level of light would encourage the greatest productivity. They changed the level of light and productivity went up; they changed it again with the same result. No matter what the light level, the result was the same: productivity rose. The inescapable conclusion was that because the workers felt that management was trying to make their work environment better, they responded with greater effort.

The message is that any effort you make on behalf of your people is noticed. Even something as small as making a fuss about an annoying hum from the fluorescent lights demonstrates to your people that you care, and at the same time removes an irritant that allows them greater focus on real productivity.

Being seen as willing to take these small actions doesn't hurt either. The boss who is seen making the coffee once in awhile or cleaning up in the kitchen rises in status with his troops. This encourages everyone else to take care of the team by taking care of the little things as a matter of professional pride.

Your job is to provide whatever you can that gives your people a clear and uninterrupted view of their goal on the horizon. Having been in the trenches yourself, it shouldn't be hard to fathom dozens of actions that demonstrate you are there to free up your people to do their jobs to the very best of their abilities. If you aren't sure, listen to the banter in the department. When you hear whining and see rolling of eyes about "it's just the way things are around here," you've probably identified an irritant that can be easily solved and make you an (albeit temporary) hero to your troops.

When you act as a facilitator, removing the minor irritants is almost as important as the big roadblocks to productivity. Plus the relative ease with which a manager can solve the small irritations adds up to almost constant reinforcement that you are really there for your people. When you demonstrate your esteem by your willingness to do battle for your troops when necessary, they will win the war for you in return.

Foster Relationships

Firm friendships take time, and don't always rise from an instant rapport. It has been observed that the most enduring relationships are those forged over time by people forced to endure ups and downs together. These relationships emerge with people you know and who know you, and together you share a history and slice of life's experience. The good and bad times we experience together at work offer exactly the environment in which long-term supportive relationships can easily develop, with your help.

Not all work is fun. In fact, given the choice, most of us would rather be somewhere else, engaged in other activities. You should always encourage your staff in word and deed. If someone is screwing up, focus on helping that person figure out what went wrong and why, then showing him or her the right way to do it, rather than harping on the mistake that has been made.

Things will go wrong even in your department, and when a committed individual or your team does get off track, they can get demotivated and lose faith in themselves. This is when you need to step up to the plate and tell them: "It's okay. Everyone who makes an effort sometimes makes mistakes. Those mistakes are merely a sign that we are doing something." Explain that the only people who don't make mistakes are the ones who do nothing, and move on to what it will take to resolve the issue. "All we need to do is identify everything we have done to bring us to this point. The things we did right we'll do more of, and the things we did wrong we'll change." The more you can take ownership for the group's problems the more you have the right to take ownership of their successes, too.

How Close Is Too Close?

As you build relationships, however, be careful not to get too chummy with your team. Your first responsibility as manager is to get things done toward the interests of the business. When a relationship gets too close, it can be hard to make those tough but necessary decisions not likely to be favorable to your closest buddy. Therefore, we stress the word "relationship" and may use the word "friendship," but make sure as you go along that the friendship doesn't get in the way of business.

In talking about leadership and team building (two sides of the same coin), we have talked about "persuasive communication" as a tool for swaying people to your point of view, and "sphere of personal influence" as a concept for creating alliances. It is worth revisiting these areas as we wrap up this chapter on building team spirit.

There still lingers a mythology about the aloofness of management and the power that it bespeaks. Posing as an aloof captain of industry won't do anything except get you cut out of the communication chain. A measure of distance between manager and worker has historically been prescribed because there can be obvious difficulties when personal relationships enter into the affairs of business. However, there is a difference between being friendly and being friends with someone. When you are friendly rather than aloof, your sphere of influence widens and people are drawn to you. From a teambuilding (and political) perspective you cannot have too wide a sphere of personal influence, because the greater the number of professional contacts you have, the greater the number of people you can sway to your cause. This obviously includes the people in your department, and many from outside it, too.

It's All about Attitude

Your outgoing attitude and willingness to pitch in can make you allies from the loading dock to the boardroom, and everywhere in between. Over time all these people will have an opportunity to smooth the way for you and your causes. There will come a day when an ally on the loading dock will make sure your urgent shipment gets the priority you require, and there will come a day when the chairman's secretary will get you the ear of the big kahuna, even on a busy day. You make these allies by your professional competence, optimism, honesty, and willingness to smile and exchange a friendly word or lend a hand in simple but meaningful ways. Holding a door for the uniformed guy with an armful of packages doesn't diminish your management stature; it marks you as a considerate human being. By cooperating with people whenever you can, you are widening your personal influence by drawing people to you.

When you strive to cooperate with people and ease their way, they are happy to reciprocate and will see you as a leader of strength and character. The well-being of your team is a constant priority; you, as a team leader, never shelve the concerns and problems of your people, but rather you stop, listen, and learn. Then you set about solving problems for your employees. As a leader you facilitate their well-being so that they in turn can concentrate on productive work. When you are connected to the affairs of your people you are connected to the activities of your department. You are in the loop and not in the dark.

When you are connected to the affairs and activities of your group you are in a better position to facilitate their well-being, and thereby maximize productivity. The building blocks are easy to assemble:

- You lead by your infectious example of competence, confidence, optimism, and honesty.
- You build cooperation between team members by making it a way of life for yourself.
- You create and use a teambuilding lexicon.
- You create a safe haven for your workers where they are respected for their professionalism and contributions, not their sex, race, or golfing prowess.

- You provide the opportunities for inclusion in the planning, decision-making, and execution of departmental affairs, which adds meaning to your people's work.
- You provide the opportunities for challenge and professional growth that keep people motivated and committed to your leadership.
- You empower your people when you demonstrate your faith in them by letting them do the job for which you have trained them.

Summary

Building a team is an example of enlightened self-interest. By putting others' well-being before your own, you, as a manager, motivate your people to repay the compliment with their best efforts for each other—and for you.

11 | Building Your Managerial Brand

As you become recognized as a reputable leader, always work to enhance your professional stature into a complete package with a "brand." It will pay dividends for years to come.

We start this chapter with an anecdote from our own personal experience. It's one of the best examples we can offer to illustrate what "managerial brand" means and how important it is to build your managerial brand throughout your career.

During the writing of this book, Jennifer, the wife of coauthor Peter Sander, found out that the California division of the New York publishing company she worked for was shutting down. Doors closed completely in three months, and twenty-five people were out of a job—including herself! She had held an "individual contributor" management position with no direct reports but otherwise had all the responsibilities of a full-blown manager. Was this a blow? Yes. Is she worried? Not really. Why? Because she has established a solid reputation and network of contacts in her industry and the local business community at large. She is an industry professional. In fact she has even written books herself—almost twenty-five titles to date, including titles for aspiring writers on getting published. She spoke at Mark Victor Hansen's "Book Marketing University" in front of 1,700 publishing professionals and aspirants. She has held numerous workshops, conducted publishing panels, appeared on local TV and radio several times to talk about publishing. She has also appeared frequently on national radio. Jennifer has achieved the second-to-highest level of accreditation in the local chapter of Toastmaster's International, the professional speaking organization. She is on the Board of Directors of the Sacramento Philharmonic Orchestra. Her successes as a publishing professional and author have been written up in the local daily newspaper and the regional business magazine. Does she have a "managerial brand" in the publishing industry? You bet. Does she have one in the local business community? Probably so. Is she well-positioned to get another job and advance in the publishing industry (or others for that matter)? We'll let you answer that one.

In case you're still groping for that answer, know that within the first three hours after the company's announcement, Jennifer's phone rang several times. One call was from a former president of the now-discontinued publisher asking her what she thought about starting another company in the same niche, and what she thought of a number-two role as vice president and editorial director of what would be a multimillion-dollar publishing business.

Can this be the way things turn out for you? Yes! It appears that you, too, are driven to take the extra steps necessary to rise above the heads of your peers; otherwise you wouldn't be reading the last chapter of a management book. That drive also marks you as making every effort to stack the odds in favor of reaching your goals and aspirations. Once you stack the odds in your favor, then you harness your energy and stoke your commitment until you achieve what you set out to accomplish. It has probably been this way for you as far back as you can remember. Your goals might have changed over the years, perhaps from a new bike to more adult dreams. "If I get that bike I'll never want for anything else," or "If she'll go out with me my life will be perfect," or "If I get into Acme Welding school my life will be set," or "Working as a lawyer with Reamed, Covertrax and Split, I'll never have to worry again."

But soon after reaching each of those goals, you noticed that you wanted other things in life, and the goal that once promised a perfect existence left you feeling slightly empty. If you are a goal-oriented person, your life might never seem completely fulfilling for long. It might seem that no matter what you achieve, life's opportunities always offer another goal to strive for. You aren't alone; all goal-driven people experience certain restlessness after achieving a sought-after goal. In some ways that is the nature of people who strive. They are motivated and energized by straining for the heights, and once they have scaled them, they are soon looking around for the next mountain range to conquer.

For some reason, otherwise rational people can arrive in the ranks of management and really believe that it is now okay to relax. This couldn't be farther from the truth. In our earlier example, did Jennifer relax? Hardly. Although she chose not to engage in a management position with direct reports, don't take this as "relaxing." She preferred to focus energy instead on building her brand in her current job through achieving industry recognition and leadership, not taking higher-level positions inside the organization.

The higher you climb in your professional life, the more money you make and the more you are able to surround yourself and your loved ones with the trappings of success. At the same time, the higher you climb the more rarefied the air, the fewer the jobs, the greater the competition, the slipperier the slope, and the longer and harder the fall from grace. You strive to achieve responsibility, but along with the golf clubs, martinis, and luxury cars come a downside. You still aren't immune from termination when things go wrong; in fact, you are more vulnerable in some ways because of your elevated position. Remember the world of sports: The coach gets his walking papers long before the team does. Sometimes it is better to be the best player than to be the coach, and if you're the coach, it's better to be widely recognized for your accomplishments than to be promoted to the highest position in the front office.

Reaching management status is no different from your other life goals. It is not an end in and of itself; it is just another means to an end—that you live a rich and fulfilling life. Becoming a manager may be part of it (for the rewards it can bring) but it is only a play in your overall game plan for life.

What Is a Managerial Brand?

Whether you are in the process of building a fast-track career, or are happy staying with the specialty you're currently in, it always helps to build your managerial brand. You will command more respect, do special and important things, and get more opportunities to advance—both in your organization and in your profession. Aside from the occasional busyness and stress that building your managerial brand sometimes entails, it is almost always a good thing. You can always say no to any opportunities that come your way, but by getting noticed you have options you would not have had if your track record and persona were more "generic."

Building a managerial brand means developing a persona, a managerial style, a set of attributes, and a lifestyle that permanently sets you up for success. Brand managers talk about brand recognition and a brand message or "promise," a characteristic everybody learns to look for in that brand. In management, the brand promise is a level of experience, expertise, and consistent leadership behavior known to get good results. Your name becomes synonymous, both inside and outside the company, with that success.

Why Develop a Managerial Brand?

You will get the recognition you need and deserve which in turn helps to accomplish more with relatively less on-the-job effort. And yes, in times of downsizing or industry shifts such as Jennifer got caught in, you are infinitely more marketable to others, both within and outside of your industry. Believe us, *it feels good* when people seek you out, particularly in contrast to the alternatives.

Like most other things, there is an investment required (time and effort, mainly) that eventually pays off (money, prestige, sense of accomplishment). As you enter and develop your management career, you should continuously contemplate the wide range of options in which to make your investment. While this is not a book on career management, this last chapter addresses some important personal management issues that will affect your life in management and your managerial brand, which include . . .

- Advancing in your job and professional community.
- Acting with politically enlightened self-interest.
- Preparing for storm clouds that will inevitably appear.
- Achieving balance between your professional and personal life.

Build Your Professional Platform

Just as a famous, well-known name on a box of detergent distinguishes it on the grocery shelf, so does a similar aura of brand recognition for your professional skills and accomplishments. Your brand serves not only to build your credibility and stature for greater growth and responsibility in your organization, but to make your management life easier, because you earn the trust of others around you. Want to be a Knock 'em Dead manager? Build a brand and a platform.

But how do you get from here to there? Brand building for products and services is an expensive, complex, and often risky proposition. Are we talking about putting billboards alongside the route the CEO takes to work? Do you have to drop leaflets on people's desks and sponsor contests? Hardly. Even if you did have time for that, it isn't the right way to go. So what *does* work, anyway? Naturally it varies somewhat by the nature of the organization and individuals involved, the industry, and your position and skill sets.

First, Do Your Job Well

Obviously, the first step is to perform well on the job. Brand is all about reputation, and the cornerstone of reputation is performance and results. So, job number one is to focus on your responsibilities and deliver results. It takes a lot to do this, and don't underestimate its importance. Good performance, delivered consistently, with a good attitude and workplace demeanor, go a long way.

Just as any product marketer would do, you should periodically check the quality of your "product" as a manager. Talk to superiors, peers, and your subordinates. Do some cake tests to make sure things are going well, and that you are delivering what is expected in everyone's minds. Take corrective actions as necessary, and invoke your own plan-do-check-act cycle if certain measures are off target.

And just as any product marketer would do, check the *perceived* quality of your product. Regardless of how good you know your results are, make sure you understand how others perceive you and your results. Even if your numbers are okay, if people are wary of you and perhaps even mistrust your results, you have a problem.

The moral of the story: You as manager are producing a "product," a "service" called "management" to your organization. Check with your "customers" continuously to make sure your "market" is getting (1) what it *needs* and (2) what you *think* they are getting.

Building a quality management "service" and testing it within your organization takes you most of the way. Let's just say that without a quality service, or without a service that is perceived as good quality, it's nearly impossible to establish your managerial brand no matter what else you do. Good performance and results are necessary—*but not usually sufficient*—to build a managerial brand.

As a new manager, you have to learn a whole slew of new people and management skills. But you also have to (especially in this day and age) thoroughly learn the subject matter and processes you manage, and go beyond that to become an expert on the business and industry, and even beyond that, to *contribute* to the business and industry.

Keep Your Skills Up

There are managers who thrive over the long haul using nothing but the skills of management and none of the skills needed for the processes they manage. But these types of managers are becoming few and far between as we move into the next decade. Increasingly the successful manager also has a working knowledge of the processes they manage. Some of these functions you will have learned along the path to management, others you can learn on the job, which gives you an additional reason to show real interest and respect for the roles of the people you manage. Without these hands-on skills you have greater exposure in times of downsizing, and less marketability for internal promotions or for job opportunities with other companies. Whether a job opening is internal or external, you can expect any job interview to examine your understanding of the work processes you manage.

Every day at work you are privy to workplace changes as they are conceived, planned, and implemented. Pay attention to them and how they affect the roles of different job titles. Be especially alert to how these changes affect the skills necessary to be successful in those jobs. Even if you are not responsible for a particular work area today, the future may hold an opportunity that puts you in that position. Landing any job will require an awareness of the functions, the roles they play, and the skills necessary to succeed in these jobs. This knowledge will be invaluable in the interview process, and, once you're in the job, will help you interview potential employees to join your new team. As you climb the management ladder, you are also learning (or at least developing a working knowledge of) the skills of all of those people who report to you. The more you learn about the responsibilities and challenges of all the different functions, the wider your frame of reference and the higher you can climb.

Ongoing professional education plays an important role in your future as well. The Bureau of Labor Statistics has predicted a significant increase (upwards of 20 percent by the end of the decade) in management jobs that require at least a bachelor's degree, and that's just the entry-level requirement. But even with a degree under your belt you can't relax. Thanks to technology and the resultant globalization of work, the work world continues to change at a dizzying pace. You need to keep up with what's happening in your industry. We have addressed the importance of joining professional associations and networking in your industry as a way of increasing your professional competency. You also need to be sensitive to the educational paths other successful managers in your profession are pursuing and consider similar endeavors for your own professional well-being and ongoing employability.

If you are not acquiring new workplace skills every year, then you are not growing; and if you are not growing, then you are stagnating—and you know where that leads. Without the skills seen to be in demand, your future employability will suffer to an equal degree. Many companies encourage ongoing education for their staff, picking up part or all of the costs.

Aerospace giant Boeing was an early large-scale supporter of ongoing education despite worries that people would increase their skills and then leave. About 50 percent of Boeing employees are involved in some kind of further education, and the result has been beneficial from both employer and employee viewpoints. The employer discovered that not only did these people become more productive and valuable employees, they, in fact, did not leave the company. From the employees' point of view the benefit was obvious; they became more valuable to the company, their jobs became more secure, and their professional horizons widened.

You should look into workplace skills that might be worth acquiring and see how your company will support your educational efforts. If your company won't support you, one of your long-term goals might be to find a position with an employer who does.

Reach Out and Touch Your Profession

Beyond education and technical-skill development, there are a whole host of external opportunities on which to build a professional platform. Within your profession there will usually be a host of professional organizations, some "broad brushed" around your field and some very specific. If you're a marketer, there's the American Marketing Association (AMA), and if you're a direct marketer, there's the Direct Marketing Association (DMA). There are societies for every engineering field; The American Society of Mechanical Engineers (ASME) is just one. The "alphabet soup" goes on for miles, covering almost everything.

So how do you engage with these organizations? The first and most obvious way is by joining. Often your company will pay; if it doesn't, make the investment yourself. At minimum, you'll get a newsletter informing you of who's who and what's what in the profession. And you'll find out about more opportunities.

Most of these organizations hold annual meetings and conventions, and most meet more frequently. Attending the meetings will help you—especially in the early phases of your career—learn more about your profession and how other professionals work in it. You'll learn not only about new technologies and how they're applied, but also about management techniques and trends. And you'll get a chance to network—that is, meet other professionals, including higher managers—in your field. That list of contacts always helps. Not that you're going to share critical competitive data with these folks, mind you, but you may share some of your experiences, sources, and resources that help you get your job done. And someday, that network will come in handy when you want to grow or change.

Networking helps to create your brand as you become known outside your organization. You may use the network to bring in something (or someone) to deliver improved or breakthrough results for your organization. But beyond—way beyond—the networking opportunity lies a still greater opportunity to build your brand.

As a professional and a manager, you should always look for opportunities to "give back" to your profession, to make some "above and beyond" contribution that will give you (and often, your company) some recognition. Do you have a new way of doing something? Do you have a sharable success story? Maybe you have expertise to teach others in your profession? Make sure to get an opportunity to present this experience or breakthrough to one of these organizations. How? Give a speech or present a paper at a meeting or conference. Or write an article for the organization's journal, or some other publication related to the field. Or try a local newspaper or news magazine, or maybe the local business journal. The list is endless.

What does this accomplish? It is a two-edged benefit. First, you get recognition for outstanding thought and leadership external to your company. At minimum, this paves the way for you to write more articles, present more papers, maybe even write a book on the subject. But beyond that—and the part that most people overlook—you get recognition and credibility *inside* your organization. "Did you know that Jeff presented a paper at the last ASME meeting on his new system for managing the papermaking process?" is the buzz heard in the hallways.

And maybe you can go the distance and get a patent or other intellectual property protection for your innovation. No manager has ever suffered for having a U.S. patent hanging on the wall. The discussion of intellectual property protection is beyond our scope, but never let it escape your consideration.

Got Stage Fright?

If you asked most managers what is the greatest barrier to building brands within their profession, they would probably say (1) "I don't have anything to talk about" and (2) "I'm afraid to get up in front of all of those people." We can't help too much with the first one, because it is profession specific. Just think "outside the box," try things, work hard, and it will come to you. But for the second issue, we have a lot to say, and we said it in *Knock 'em Dead Business Presentations* (Adams Media, 2002). We would add that joining a professional speaking organization such as Toastmasters International (*www.toastmasters.org*) will help you to not only sharpen your speaking and meeting skills in a nonthreatening environment, but also greatly assist you in building your network within the local business community. Knock 'em Dead managers should all be Toastmasters members. It's fun, and you'll get a chance to go out for lunch every Wednesday.

Build Bridges

Bitter people sometimes mutter that, "it's not what you know but who you know." They are half right. Being good at your job is only half the battle. Having a wide sphere of personal influence is the other half of the battle; this means knowing lots of people and knowing the *right* people.

First and last, you need to be known as a decent human being, a hardworking professional, and a trustworthy person. Then there is the wise advice you've heard from everyone: Treat others as you would like to be treated yourself. Positive, hardworking professionals have lots of contacts because their values and character make them energizing to be around. Be friendly with everyone. It starts with your peers and the people in your department and with being a reliable colleague, but it shouldn't end there. The more people you get to know in your organization and others, the wider your sphere of influence. Here are some suggestions:

- **Get to know people at all levels of the organization by name.** The more people who have a good word to say about you the better, and even low-level functionaries sometimes have influence in surprising places.
- **Wander around and interact with people as you go.** Use this as an opportunity to respond to phone messages and e-mails in person.
- **Get involved.** If your company has extramural activities such as softball or the like, join and get to know people you would never otherwise have met in your daily professional life.
- **Volunteer for committees, work related and personal.** Committee participation, and especially leadership, will help build your managerial brand. But don't ever let these activities pull you away from your primary responsibilities.
- **Volunteer to work on or lead the annual company meeting.** You don't have to be onstage to make an impact, and you'll get to meet lots of people in the process, not just at the event itself. You will also be seen as a "go to" person, someone who makes and helps unusual things happen.

As you get involved in the larger activities of your company, you will get to meet and know all the important players. As this happens, you will gradually get a feeling for the inner workings of the company and the projects that are seen to have special relevance. Over time this makes it possible to become involved in the real *inner circle* of the company. Additionally, because you made the effort to get to know people at all levels; you will have a better picture of how things actually get done in a company. This knowledge will make you a more effective manager, and you will be seen as a person in the know, and one who knows how to get things done.

Storm Clouds Invariably Follow Sunny Weather

Over the years, you may have seen individual coworkers laid off and whole departments wiped out or incorporated into another. Now in the hallowed ranks of management, you are no more immune than you were before. The only difference is that the higher you climb on the rungs of the corporate ladder, the fewer the opportunities and the greater the competition. You have to take sensible precautions to protect your job and your employability, but you should also be alert to coming storm clouds on the horizon and be ready to pursue options.

Would you notice the signals if your professional "weather" front was taking a turn for the worse? In almost thirty years of career management work, coauthor Martin has lost count of the times that seasoned executives have cried on his shoulder about "not seeing it coming." Developing contingency plans and defenses against job and career upheaval are an important part of life as a manager. As stressed earlier, your managerial brand is an important part of this defense system.

As you continue through your work life, you will learn to notice the signs and signals of change. You will learn to anticipate and deal proactively, making change a lot easier and, hopefully, less painful. Here are a few signs to look for and actions you should take:

- When there are rumors about layoffs and the company denies them, don't discount the scuttlebutt. Companies in trouble or those that are restructuring will not tell you the real story, for fear of losing productive employees and further hurting profitability. They will strive to control the event and information flow.
- If your boss shows increased concern about your department, and is asking for more reports, more evaluations, and more promises, keep your weather eye open. Build extra time, staff, and money into your requirements to lessen the chances of failing due to missing deadlines and lack of productivity.

- Always document everything! Use memos, reports, e-mails, and notes to put the activities of your department in context. This is especially important when corporate changes beyond your control affect your department's ability to perform.
- Be aware if your usually good performance reviews suddenly take a downturn and you genuinely don't know the reason. Don't take this lying down. Ask for an explanation and make sure you know what your personnel file contains; you have a right to access these records and should do so. You also have the right to place your own records and statements in your official personnel file.
- Look at the company's performance and expected performance through the eyes of the financial community. If the stock (for a publicly traded company) falters, be wary. Read analyst reports and trade press scuttle-butt. (A good source is Yahoo!Finance at *http://finance.yahoo.com,* but other financial periodicals and Web sites do a good job, too.) Look for stringent cost-cutting measures if you work for a smaller company.
- Analyze the signals you have noted in the past that led to individuals or whole groups being let go, and don't believe that "it can't happen to me."

It is one thing to be aware of potential problems on your professional horizon; it is quite another to be in a position to protect your economic and professional well-being. This requires three actions on your part:

1. **Stay active in your professional community.** Your active membership in professional associations connects you to the brightest and the best in your professional community. This is a major reason why you should take an active part in it. Networking opportunities are quickly exhausted without an extended professional network, which your involvement in the professional community provides. When you are a known entity you will have access to people you could never otherwise hope to know, and they all work for companies who could be looking for someone just like you.
2. **Update your resume.** If it is just a compilation of your work history you probably need to rewrite it from scratch to reflect your growth to your present position and focus on your next logical step. Your resume is an important tool in effective career management because it is the single most important instrument in opening the doors to your future.
3. **Manage your personal finances as you do your business.** Too many of us live up to our income and not up to our dreams. Saving for

retirement may seem a long way off, but the odds are that sometime in your professional life you will be unemployed for a period of time. God forbid, but it may happen that this period could extend to months or more. The higher you climb, the longer it takes to find a job, so you need to be prepared financially. Start saving a little every month—20 percent of your income would be great, but if you can't do that, 10 percent, 5 percent, or anything at all is better than nothing. When you get a raise, you don't have to buy a new car, new house, new boat, or whatever; you could put that raise into a savings vehicle of some kind. It is money you have never had so you won't miss it.

Like so many things in life, dealing with career contingencies is a matter of preparation. Let's explore in a little more detail some of the strategies and tactics, for keeping yourself employable—and making yourself *more* employable.

Managing Your Employability

There are four immutable facts about job hunting you should have firmly imprinted on your mind:

1. There are far fewer jobs for generals than there are for soldiers.
2. You have higher perceived value as a potential employee when you are employed.
3. You have more leverage in salary and benefit negotiation with a new employer when you are employed.
4. Once you reach forty, your age and earnings both begin to work against you.

Clearly this indicates that the older you get and the higher the corporate ladder you climb, the more you need to take whatever precautions necessary to manage your career intelligently. In the best of all possible worlds, you would have a database that gives you an instant picture of all the employers in your chosen geography who hire people like you. Such a database would include descriptions of suitable positions those companies have filled before. This would put you in control of your career management, rather than reacting frantically to unforeseen external events. Because you have developed "in demand" skills and professional connections through active membership in professional associations, you provide yourself with some very desirable options:

- You can network the inner circles at all the companies in your region because you are connected to the professionals in your industry.
- You can monitor the employment marketplace on an ongoing basis, and stay aware of who is looking for whom and the skills required. This will ensure you don't miss a dream opportunity by having myopic vision restricted to your existing job.
- When storm clouds appear on your professional horizon, you are in a position to take confidential and considered action to protect your career from employment interruptions before the ax falls.

You might think setting up a database is possible only in a perfect world, and just a few years ago you would have been right. However, with the maturation of the Internet, you now have a tool available that makes this all possible. You can implement your strategy in stages over the coming few months, and if you have a family, family members can help get things implemented even more quickly. Even if you have to do it yourself, you can get set up over a weekend and create a healthy up-to-date database in just a couple of hours a month.

Step 1: Create an E-mail Identity

Your first step is to set up a confidential e-mail address, which allows you to communicate (when necessary) with corporations in a professional manner without having your privacy invaded at home or revealing your business e-mail address. Much of the time you will simply be collecting information, but at some point you will be sending electronic resumes and engaging in two-way communications.

While you probably already have a home e-mail account, we recommend not using it for your career management. Things inevitably get lost and deleted before you see them. We also recommend you do not use your business e-mail address because, though the chances are relatively small, you don't want an HR person or anyone else within the company to know your private business. If your current ISP doesn't allow you to create free alternate e-mail addresses, you can either pay the $10 to $20 a month for a separate account (possibly tax deductible as a job hunting expense) or pick up a free e-mail account at *www.hotmail.com* or one of the other free sites. If you go the free route, the tradeoff is that you will have to accept a certain amount of onscreen advertising, which is probably something you can live with because you won't be using the account on a daily basis. In the set-up process you will have occasional options to avoid some advertising, so opt out whenever you can.

Choose the name for your new account carefully. With e-mail communications, your e-mail name and subject line act like newspaper headlines. So you should select a name that describes what you do: *ITexec@hotmail.com, financialsales@earthlink.net, HRmanager@aol.com,* etc.

Step 2: Perfect Your Resume

If you're like most people, your resume is probably a recitation of all the jobs you have held over the years, and in reality, looks more like a patchwork quilt than a resume. It is worth updating your resume to reflect the path you took to reach your present status. Make sure you highlight specific positions, skills, and achievements. The ideal resume focuses on a specific target job, pulling from the past only that which is relevant to the targeted position. Even if you don't have a clear focus on your next job right now, creating a resume that reflects your inexorable climb into management will still stand you in better stead than your current resume. You can always enhance and target the resume with an effective cover letter. *Resumes That Knock 'em Dead* by Martin Yate (Adams Media, 2001) will help you create a powerful resume for both print and electronic distribution.

Step 3: Know Who's Hiring

Companies that hire accountants today and hired them last year, will, most likely, hire them next year as well. The same hiring principle applies to your professional designation. Knowing which companies hire people like you and having an idea of their typical requirements will allow you to tap into what is mysteriously referred to as the "hidden job market." Most people labor under a sad misapprehension that if they do not see a company's help-wanted advertisement or online job posting, the company isn't looking, when in reality all it means is that you aren't looking in the right place. Remember, ads cost money and don't always attract the right people.

Effective career management requires developing and maintaining a job-hunting "map." This is a comprehensive picture, developed over a period of time, that shows all the employers in a target geography who hire people like you. Your database should include both print ads from the newspapers and professional magazines, and online job postings. It is unwise to rely simply on one or the other because companies use a combination of both. Here's how you do it:

1. **Create a print-ad bank.** Spend a month collecting position advertisements from your Sunday newspaper, *Wall Street Journal*, professional association magazine, or newsletter, etc. Clip all the ads that seem interesting to you, and paste them into a three-ring binder. Every week clip and paste new ads; then at the end of the month make a master list of all the job titles these opportunities appeared under. If you have a nonworking spouse or responsible teenager in the house (it can happen), here's where you can begin to delegate some of your career management responsibilities. Most nonworking spouses would be only too happy to lend a hand to valuable work that helps a family survive and prosper. Explain to the family member what you are doing and why you are doing it. For the kids, it's another way for them to earn their allowance and at the same time learn a valuable life lesson about career management before they enter the work force.

If you get volunteers, give them the master list and have them scour and clip the ads under the headings from your master list. If you keep old newspapers, or have a family member who does, scan those papers, too. Not that those positions are still open, or that you would apply for them even if they were, but they are rich with ads from companies that hire people like you, and you need to know about them. The odds are a company that has hired people in your field in the past is likely to hire them in the future.

2. **Complete a parallel process for the online job banks.** Not all job banks are useful to all people, so, again, it could take a month to sort out the ones you want to monitor. If you don't know where to begin you should check out *Knock 'em Dead 2004* (Adams Media, 2004). This companion volume in career management is a comprehensive work on job hunting and interviewing. Naturally it includes useful chapters for online job hunting and a comprehensive database of job sites. You will probably want to visit the major employment portals such as Monster, Hotjobs, and Career Builder. And you will also want to check out association sites, local sites, and places like Employer Direct (an association of blue chip companies with a common portal for online recruitment activities, that allows them to bypass job portals). Obviously you will also visit the job banks at Web sites for your professional

associations. As you are going through this process, keep a watchful eye out for the requirements that are in demand. If you have what the market is looking for, so much the better. If, however, you are seeing requests for skills that you don't have, it's a clear signal that further education can only help your career growth and ongoing employability.

Make Job Sites Work for You

When you visit job sites you will usually have the opportunity to post your resume or to load a brief profile of yourself. The options vary from site to site and range from the painless to the excruciating. Reading *Resumes That Knock 'em Dead* by Martin Yate (Adams Media, 2002) will help minimize the frustration.

You have two options with the employment portals:

1. You can visit on a regular basis and search for job titles from the master list you are developing. This, however, requires that you be proactive in order to get results.
2. You can post a sanitized online version of your resume to a job bank's resume database. By sanitized we mean that you remove all identifying information from it, like your name, address, telephone number, home e-mail, and name of your current employer. In the Internet age, recruiters are quite used to seeing a resume that replaces traditional contact information with, for example, "Finance Executive" for the name, and *"FinExecf@hotmail.com"* for an address. They are also comfortable reading that your current employer is a "midsized commercial bank in the Midwest." If you post your resume, the site will then reward you by sending alerts to your career management e-mail address whenever a matching job is posted by one of its clients.

Once you are registered in this way with a number of sites you will get inundated with e-mails about job opportunities. Not all of them will match your needs. If a site sends you too many inappropriate job openings (the most likely scenario), you can further define your needs definition; if you receive too few listings you can try broadening your definition. If neither of these adjustments works, it might mean that these particular sites won't be useful to you.

Most job sites survive by selling help-wanted advertising to employers. They do this by selling the number of resumes they have registered, and how fresh they are. This means that every three to six months most sites wipe out the older resumes. They don't entirely disappear but go into an archive that can still be searched by employers and headhunters, but won't be looked at as frequently. For greatest visibility you will need to make a note of when each site you use cleans out the old resumes, and then post yours again. It will take you awhile to get this process down, but once you do, you have another task that can be delegated to a family member. Whether it's simply visiting the sites and harvesting the matching jobs from the e-mail alerts you receive, or re-posting your sanitized resume whenever renewal time rolls around, your family member can handle it for you.

> ### Don't Forget to Click on "Job Opportunities"
> It seems kind of obvious, but many job searchers neglect one of the most obvious ways to connect with an employer, particularly an employer they would like to target as a place to work. Nearly every Web site in the commercial and public sector has a jobs page, with current—and usually available—openings. Part of your definition of what you'd like to do should include who you'd like to work for—and all other players in that industry. Make a list of company or public agency sites and check their "opportunities" pages frequently. Although this involves a lot of searching and repetitive work, there's a better chance of finding a match (1) to your interests and (2) to a job that is truly available and not swamped with applicants. You will get a feel for what jobs are in demand even if your "dream" job doesn't show up. Also keep in mind that companies might shy away from the cost of an ad, but can place postings on their sites virtually for free, so this is one more you can research for postings.

Archiving Your Job Opportunities

We have already addressed archiving the suitable print help-wanted advertisements you find in a simple three-ring binder. Just about any e-mail program will offer you the same ability in an electronic format.

Sort Out the Possibilities

By the time you achieve the ranks of management, your experience has probably reached the point where you can do many different jobs. You'll notice this as you read the newspaper ads and surf the job sites in the early stages of setting up your career-management database. You can usually list more than one potential job title on a site, for e-mail notification of available openings. You can sort the incoming job posting into different potential areas of your professional expertise, creating a new folder for each category. This categorization can also be applied if there are certain dream companies you are tracking. If, for example, you have a goal of one day working for Microsoft, you would create a folder for Microsoft and then sub folders for the different categories of jobs for which you might be qualified at that company. In this instance you or your volunteer family member would visit the target company Web site on a regular basis (individual company sites don't always have e-mail alerts). Over a period of a few months the collection of different job postings you amass will begin to give you an interesting view of just what it is that pushes the buttons of your target company.

This same technique can apply when your goal is to one day move to a particular city somewhere else in the country. Here you would set up folder for, say, Savannah, and then within it create the appropriate sub folders. When you are targeting a particular geography you will, of course, make a point of identifying and regularly visiting all the local job banks specific to that area, and the chapter site of your profession association in that area.

The Payoff

Maintaining such a database gives big payoffs over time. The Bureau of Labor Statistics tells us we can expect to change jobs approximately every three to five years. Three to five years on a resume demonstrates acceptable professional stability; however, you can't always control the length of time you stay with a company. Also, if you want real choice on your next opportunity, you should start implementing a job hunt a year prior to an expected move.

With a career-management database, you will always have your finger on the job market. You will be aware of the choice jobs as they come along, probably making your next career move in a considered and unhurried fashion. If, on the other hand, you see those storm clouds on the horizon, you won't have to stand there frozen with fear and indecision wondering if you are going to get struck by lightning. Instead, you will have the option to take the appropriate actions to enrich your knowledge of what's out there.

Career Transitions: A Final Thought

It goes without saying that when the time does come for you to hand in your resignation as the next step in your inexorable ascent, don't burn your bridges.

The job market today is very fluid, and you may find yourself working with some of today's colleagues down the road.

You got into management because you took control of your career and made the extra effort to reach your elevated goal. Applying the same effort and integrity to the larger picture of your overall career management is only a matter of common sense in these volatile times. Doing this part right is part of maintaining—and deploying—your management brand.

Achieving Life Balance

Big changes happen when you move into management and feel the weight of its responsibilities on your shoulders, because the step is a watermark transition point in your life. And as if the work challenges weren't enough, the pressure washes over into your personal life.

It is likely you will overextend yourself at work, at least initially, and you will happily accept this as part of the honor of achieving management rank. You thrive on being a visible and important player in an enterprise larger than your life, but you must be careful about the areas in which you extend yourself as you settle into your new roles. Putting in the extra hours to coach your team into an irresistible force, as we have been addressing throughout this book, is ultimately productive use of your time. Putting that same energy into doing everyone's jobs for them is self-defeating, You are being paid to guide, nurture, coach, and manage the process, not to do it all yourself. Your brand becomes more that of coach and less of player.

You will tend to relegate your family and personal life to the back burner, and accept this, too, as part of the honor of your rank, allowing you the enhanced lifestyle that it comes with it. The management culture of your company may well encourage this mindset. Yet no matter the conflicting pressure and responsibilities you now hold, you must learn to keep things in perspective. If you watch the news carefully over the years, you may sometimes notice that the corporations that make the most stringent demands on their mid-level executives, like high-tech or financial services firms, are often the most successful, and can be the most lucrative for the employee in the long run.

Leading a personally fulfilling life demands that you maintain balance in all your life's activities. Little in adult life is entirely right or wrong; everything we do has both the payoffs and the tradeoffs we inevitably make to get them.

Sacrificing all for your corporate career won't ever compensate for missing your children grow up or seeing your marriage fall apart.

Even in the early days of your management career you must make time for the things that are important to you: family, friends, and the activities and interests that put the juice in your life and make it worth living. We all have different values and interests, which change as our life needs and interests evolve through the years. Yet underneath it all we all seem to share some similar immutable needs: family, friends, and financial prosperity.

Summary

Building your professional stature and success requires building a professional brand and building a lifestyle and set of career habits to support it. All of this appears above and beyond the sets of skills and competencies outlined in the rest of this book, but really it all fits together. Truly reaching your goals and aspirations—and enjoying the ride—requires transcending your management skills and competencies and building yourself out into a completely branded, "whole" business manager. Remember, it's not just the product that sells; it's the package.

Index

A

Accountability, 72
Achievement need, 15
Action plans, 142–45
Authority
   delegating, 71–72, 189
   maintaining, 132
   motivating without, 21
   as motivation, 15
   position power and, 4–5, 51, 52

B

Balancing
   management, 9
   new job, 54–55
   personal/professional life,
     269–70
Best practices, 244–45
Big picture
   defined, 27
   details and, 17, 27
   knowing, 11, 22, 24
   leadership and, 173, 180
   management model and, 27
Bosses. *See* Higher managers
Brand. *See* Managerial brand
Building process, 55, 68
Business
   environment, understanding, 29
   speed of, 6
Business case, 223, 225
Business models, 8, 26

C

Cake test metaphor, 63, 64
Calendars, 58–59
Career development, 13, 15
   archiving opportunities, 262–63,
     267–68
   creating e-mail identity, 263–64

developing resume, 261, 264
finding opportunities, 264–66
job fluidity and, 268–69
job loss preparation and,
   251–53, 260–62
managing employability, 262–67
online resources, 265–67
reference resources, 264, 265–67
See also Managerial brand;
   Starting management jobs
CEO/CFO/CMO/COO/CIO, 18–19,
   51
Challenges, 7
   confronting directly, 177, 181
   creating meaningful, 233–34
   by management level, 51–52
   team building and, 233–34
Change
   anticipating, 13
   communicating, 11
   driving, as motivation, 15
   managing, 13
Chief officers, 18–19
Climate, organization, 35–36
Coaching, 104–30
   buddy assignments, 117, 122–23
   catching 'right action' and, 121
   communication skills, 119–20
   company expectations, 104–5
   delegating and. *See* Delegation
   employee response to, 113–14
   environment for, 110
   evaluating, 117–18
   experience sharing and, 120–21
   Golden Rule and, 111
   knowledge sharing and, 119
   learning from mistakes, 111–13
   mentoring vs., 128
   methods/tools, 117–23, 124–25,
     126–27

neglecting, 106–8, 109
plan, 115–17
requirements, 108–13
for results, 113–15
setting example, 110
staff quality range and, 125–27
steps, 117–23
tailoring approaches, 105,
   113–15, 126–27
telling/showing/involving and,
   118–19
time management, 123–24
training vs. developing and, 106
trust/truth and, 111
See also Development; Team
   building; Training
Commitment, 15, 211
Communication
   clarity, 70–71
   coaching skills, 119–20
   connecting and, 55, 61–63
   coordinating, 171–72
   delegating and, 70–71, 72–73
   duties, 43, 44
   hands-on, 8, 11
   informality, 8
   presentations, 225–26, 258
   protocols, 72–73, 191
   skills, 16, 17, 19
   styles, 43
   team building and, 234–35, 239
Communicator role, 26, 27, 41, 43
Complexity, 6
Conceptual skills, 11, 12
Confidence
   leadership and, 168, 178
   team building and, 232, 233–34,
    236
Connecting, 55, 61–63
   cake test and, 63, 64

formally/informally, 61
with physical tours, 61–62
with staff, 62, 239–41, 247–49
See also Relationships
Consistency, 179, 193
Constituents, 26, 27–28, 49–51
Contingency plans, 208
Controlling
    defined, 47
    duties, 47, 48
    management model and, 26, 27
CPH (cost per hire), 78
Crises, 177–78, 181
Culture, organization, 35
Customers
    employees as, 26, 49–50
    external, 27, 49
    higher managers as, 26, 50–51
    internal, 27–28, 49
    keeping happy, 49–51
    management model and, 26,
        27–28
    peer managers as, 26, 50

D

Data, aptitude for, 17
Decision-making, 214–26
    analyzing alternatives, 219–20
    business cases, 223, 225
    decision trees for, 224
    defining situation/problem,
        215–16
    developing alternatives, 217–19
    80/20 rule and, 219
    evaluating, 221–22
    identifying knowledge
        gaps/constraints, 216–17
    implementing, 221
    Monte Carlo simulation, 223–24
    overview, 214, 226
    Pareto analysis for, 219
    payback/ROI analysis for, 223

presenting decision, 225–26
role, 26, 27, 41, 42
selecting alternatives, 220–21
simulation models, 223–24
steps, summary, 215
tools, 219, 222–26
Delegation, 182–90
    art/science of, 183–85, 187
    assigning roles/tasks, 69–70,
        175–76, 180, 187
    authority, 71–72, 189
    of candidate interviews, 98–99
    communicating and, 70–71,
        72–73
    complete, tasks, 184
    development and, 184, 185–86,
        192–93
    essence of, 182–83
    follow-up protocols, 72–73
    identifying tasks for, 183–85,
        187
    leadership and, 176, 181
    managing, 187–90
    in new job, 70–73
    partial, tasks, 184–85
    process, 187–90
    responsibilities unfit for, 184–85
    responsibility/accountability
        and, 72
    task clarity and, 70
    tracking mechanisms, 191
    training successors and, 23, 24
    See also Leadership (leading)
Deliverables, 189–90
Details, staying above, 173, 180
Development
    defined, 106
    delegating and, 184, 185–86,
        192–93
    growth, training and, 105–6
    individual, plans, 210
    making people better, 23, 24

methods/tools, 117–23, 124–25
overview, 104, 130
See also Coaching; Team
    building; Training
Disciplinary action, 147–53
    actions warranting, 154
    employee signatures for, 153
    fairness, 150
    letters of intent, 151–52
    progressive, 147–49
    relaying seriousness of, 149–50
    verbal warnings, 147–49
    written warnings, 150–53
    See also Termination
Diversity, 238–39

E

Economic influences, 32
80/20 Rule, 99, 219
E-mail
    personal address, 263–64
    setting up, 60
Employees. *See* Staff
Employment at will, 155
Empowerment, 23, 189
Enthusiasm, 173, 180
Entrepreneurism, 6
Environment
    effect of, 36
    for leadership, 174–75, 180
    See also External environment;
        Internal environment
Evaluating, 55, 63–68
    coaching, 117–18
    decisions, 221–22
    employees. *See* Performance
        appraisals
    formal/informal organization, 65
    peers/stakeholders, 65
    staff, 64, 66
    SWOT analysis for, 66–68, 204
    See also Performance appraisals

Expectations
    clear, 176, 180, 189–90
    reasonable, 191
External environment
    direct influences, 29, 30–31
    financial, 40–41
    focus on, 8, 11, 29–30
    indirect influences, 29–30, 31–33
    visual model, 26–28

F

Facilitation
    advantage of, 192
    defined, 192
    of team building, 246–47
Fair workplaces, 237–38
Files, 59–60
Financial management
    data aptitude and, 17
    duties, 8, 26–27, 40–41
Financial rewards, 15
First-line management, 20, 51–52
Flexibility, 56
Following, leadership and, 171, 246–47
Formal organization, 65
Four Ps, of marketing, 38
Functions, of management, 9, 44–48
    management model and, 26–28
    roles/scope vs., 41
    summary of, 48
    See also specific functions;
        Roles; Scope, of management

G

Goal orientation, 143–45
Goals
    defined, 196, 198
    quantity of, 197–98
    team building and, 242–43
    See also Structured (strategic)
        planning

Golden moments, 53–54
    defined, 54
    optimizing, 57
Golden Rule(s)
    of coaching, 111
    of leadership, 170–72
    resigning staff and, 163
    respect and, 243–44
    of team building, 238

H

Higher managers
    management model and, 26
    satisfying needs of, 50–51
    team building with, 231, 244
Hiring, 102. *See also* Recruiting;
    Recruiting sources; Staffing
Historical perspective, 4–5
Hoshin planning, 197–98
Human resources (HR) department, 46, 88

I

Informal organization, 65
Initiative, 16, 17
Innovation, 22
Internal environment
    financial, 40–41
    focus on, 11, 212
    influences of, 33–36
    visual model, 26–28
Interpersonal skills, 10–11, 12
Interviews, 96–102
    delegating, 98–99
    first, 99–100
    objectives, 95
    planning/structuring, 94–95, 96–97
    second, 100–101
    telephone, 97–99
    third, 101–2

J, K

Job descriptions, 82–84
Job shadowing, 117
Knock 'em Dead managers, 21–24
Knowledge requirement, 6–7

L

Leadership (leading), 16, 17, 167–94
    big picture and, 173, 180
    characteristics, 46–47, 167–68
    coaching, delegating and, 184, 192–93
    confidence and, 168, 178
    confronting problems and, 177, 181
    consistency, 179, 193
    coordinating, 171–72
    crises and, 177–78, 181
    defined, 16, 46–47, 167–68
    elements, 46–47, 48, 169–70, 172–79, 180–81, 191–93
    enlightened self-interest for, 169–70
    enthusiasm and, 173, 180
    environment for, 174–75, 180
    by example, 192
    expectations and, 176, 180, 191
    facilitation and, 192, 246–47
    flexibility and, 56
    following and, 171, 246–47
    golden rules of, 170–72
    greatest example of, 182
    learning, 169
    with light hand, 192
    looking ahead and, 173–74, 180
    management and, 26, 27, 167–68
    managers vs. leaders, 47–48
    negotiation vs., 57
    order, routine and, 172, 180
    overview, 167, 194
    removing barriers and, 174, 180

responsibility and, 173, 180

starting new job and, 56–57

style, 178–79, 181, 191–93

success-oriented, 168

team building and, 246–47

time frame for, 193–94

winning attitude for, 168

See also Delegation; Managerial brand

Letters of intent, 151–52

Levels, of management, 18–21

challenges by, 51–52

first-line, 20, 51–52

mid-level, 19–20

project/product/program, 20–21, 52

top-level, 18–19

Leverage, 9

Long-range planning, 208–10. *See also* Structured (strategic) planning

M

Management

breadth of, 4, 7, 17

careers, 13, 15

defined, 3–4, 5, 8–9

evolution of, 5–8, 24

good vs. bad, 3, 8

history, 4–5

leadership and, 167–68

skills/traits, 10–13, 15–18, 21–24

trends, 5–8, 24

as 24/7 job, 16

visual model, 26–28

Management style, 21

Managerial brand, 251–70

active participation and, 259–60

advantages of, 251–54

defined, 253

example, 251–52

job loss preparation and, 251–53, 260–62

making speeches and, 258

managing employability and, 262–67

networking and, 87–88, 163, 257–60

overview, 252–53, 270

performance and, 254–55

professional platform for, 254–60

skill development for, 255–57

See also Career development

Manager(s)

becoming, reasons for, 14–15

everyone as, 14

Knock 'em Dead, 21–24

leaders vs., 47–48

Managing by wandering around (MBWA), 37–38, 39, 61, 63, 64, 234–35

Marketing

of accomplishments, 43

duties, 26–27, 37–39, 40

four Ps, 38

share of customer and, 39

strategic, 38

tactical, 38–39

Maturity cycles, 66

MBWA. *See* Managing by wandering around (MBWA)

Meeting protocols, 72–73

Mentors

coaches vs., 128

defined, 65, 128

finding, 65–66, 128–30

Micromanage, 27

Mid-level management, 19–20, 51–52

Mindshare, 39

Mindtools, 224

Mission statements, 34–35

Models

business, 8, 26

decision tools, 224–25

management, 26–28

Modus operandi (MO), 33, 172

Monte Carlo simulation, 223–24

Motivation

achievement as, 15

authority as, 15

for being manager, 14–15

of employees, 23

power as, 16

status as, 14–15

without authority, 21

N, O

Negotiation, 57

Networking, 87–88, 163, 257–60

Network managers, 7

Objectives

defined, 197, 198

See also Structured (strategic) planning

Observation

evaluation and, 63–64

leadership and, 173–74

looking ahead, 173–74

One-person bands. *See* Project/product/program managers

Operations

duties, 26–27, 39–40

MBWA and, 39

Opportunities, identifying, 68–70

Optimism, 232–33, 234, 235–36

Order, establishing, 172, 180

Organization structure

influence of, 34

informal vs. formal, 65

maturity cycles and, 66

Organizing

calendars for, 58–59

defined, 45

duties of, 45, 48

e-mail/voice mail, 60

files, 59–60

management model and, 26, 27

starting new job and, 55, 57–60
structured planning, 203–4
Outsourcing, 39–40
Overpromising, 146
Ownership influences, 32

P

Pareto analysis, 219
Payback/ROI analysis, 223
PDAs, 59
PDCA (plan-do-check-act) cycle, 207
Peers
    as constituents, 26, 50
    evaluating, 65
    management model and, 26
    team building with, 231
People-manager role, 26, 27, 41, 42
People skills, 10–11, 12
Performance
    managerial brand and, 254–55
    rewards, 7
    standards, expectations, 133–34
Performance appraisals, 121–46
    action plans, 142–45
    discipline and. *See* Disciplinary
       action; Termination
    evaluation process, 137–41
    goal vs. task orientation and,
       143–45
    length, 141–42
    meetings for. *See* Performance
       review meetings
    no surprises in, 133
    as ongoing process, 132–33
    overpromising in, 146
    overview, 131–32
    preparing employees for, 133,
      136, 141–42
    progress reviews, 145–46
    ratings, 138–39
    standards, expectations and,
      133–34

topics, 139–41
    value of, 132
Performance review meetings, 134–37
    frequency, 135
    objectivity in, 136–37
    one-on-one, 135–36
    as ongoing process, 132–33
    preparation, 136
Personal relationships, 248–49
Philosophy influence, 34–35
Planning
    defined, 45
    duties of, 45, 48
    evaluating need for, 69
    leadership and, 173–74, 180
    looking ahead, 173–74, 180
    management model and, 26, 27
    pervasiveness of, 45
    starting new job and, 55, 68, 69
    See also Structured (strategic)
      planning
Policy influence, 34
Politics
    defined, 36
    government, influences, 31
    internal, 7, 36
Position analysis, 80–82
Power
    as motivation, 16, 17
    of position, 4–5, 51, 52
Presentations, 225–26, 258
Pressure
    increasing, 6
    tolerance for, 16, 17
Priorities
    A, B, C categories, 124
    time management and, 123–24
Proactive management, 23, 24
Problems. *See* Challenges
Professional contacts, 87–88, 163,
    257–60. *See* Managerial brand
Progressive discipline, 147–49

Progress reviews, 145–46. *See also*
    Performance appraisals
Project/product/program managers,
    20–21, 52
Promotions, training for, 23, 24
Protocols, establishing, 72, 191

R

Recruiting, 79–102
    basic requirements, 95
    hiring costs and, 78
    interviews, 94–95, 96–102
    job descriptions for, 82–84
    making hires and, 102
    needs, listing/prioritizing, 83–85
    ongoing nature of, 79
    overview, 77, 103
    position analysis for, 80–82
    screening and, 94–95
    skills for, 78
    visualizing perfect employee,
      81–82
    See also Staffing
Recruiting sources, 85–94
    headhunters, 90–91
    help-wanted ads, 89
    HR department, 88
    internal employees, 85–86
    job fairs, 91–92
    networking, 86–88
    online, 92–94
    professional contact leads, 87–88
    referrals, 86
    temporary agencies, 89–90
Reference resources, 151
    career development, 264, 265–67
    decision tools, 224
    hiring, 98
    Internet e-mail, 60
    online resumes, 92–94
    personal study, 117
    presentations, 225–26, 258

task tracking, 191
termination, 151
Relationships
building managerial brand, 259–60
networking and, 87–88, 163,
257–60
with other managers, 231, 244
personal, 248–49
with team, 239–41, 247–49
See also Connecting
Resigning employees, 163
Resources, influence of, 36
Respect, 243–44
Responsibility, 72, 173, 180
Results
coaching for, 113–15
goal vs. task orientation and,
143–45
Resume(s)
developing your, 261, 264
online, 94
Reviews. *See* Performance
appraisals; Performance review
meetings
Rewards, 7, 15
ROI analysis, 223
Roles, 41–44
functions/scope vs., 41
management model and, 26–28
summary of, 44
visual model, 26–28
See also specific roles;
Functions, of management;
Scope, of management
Routine, establishing, 172, 180
Rules, influence of, 34

S

SA3RT decision tool, 225–26
Scenario plans, 208
Scope, of management
defined, 36

duties summary, 40
elements, 26–27, 36, 37–41
functions/roles vs., 41
management model and, 26–28
See also Financial management;
Marketing; Operations
Shackleton, Sir Ernest, 182
Share of customer, 39
Skill development. *See* Development
Skills/traits (management), 10–13,
15–18
Knock 'em Dead managers, 21–24
managerial brand and, 255–57
summaries, 12, 17, 24
See also specific skills/traits
SMARTER planning acronym,
202–3
Social influences, 32–33
Socialized power motivation, 16, 17
Social skills, 16, 17
Span of control, 6
Speed, of business, 6
Staff
common needs, 238
connecting with, 62, 239–41,
247–49
as customers, 26, 49–50
delegating to. *See* Delegation;
Leadership (leading)
development. *See* Coaching;
Development; Team building;
Training
diversity, 238–39
evaluating, 64, 66, 112–13, 116
maturity cycle, 66
quality range, 125–27
resigning, 163
terminating. *See* Termination
Staffing
cost per hire (CPH), 78
defined, 46
duties, 46, 48

management model and, 26, 27
quality importance, 77
See also Recruiting; Recruiting
sources
Stakeholders, 27, 65
Standards, 133–34
Starting management jobs, 53–73
balanced approach, 54–55
building and, 55, 68
connecting and, 55, 61–63
delegating and. *See* Delegation
evaluating and, 55, 63–68
fear of, 53
flexibility and, 56
golden moments, 53–54, 57
identifying opportunities and,
68–70
leadership and, 56–57
observation and, 63–64
organizing and, 55, 57–60
overview, 53, 73
steps, 55
Status motivation, 14–15
Stewardship
defined, 28
of organization, 25, 28–29
Strategies
defined, 196–97, 198
quantity of, 198–99
See also Structured (strategic)
planning
Streamlining, 6
Strength/weakness evaluation. *See*
SWOT analysis
Stress, ix, 177–78
Structured (strategic) planning
bad, causes, 210–12
components, hierarchy, 197
contingency plans, 208
for department, 204–7
departments, 212
documenting, 205–6

failing at, 195, 212
fleshing out plan structure, 205
goals and, 196, 198–99
Hoshin planning and, 197–98
individual development, 210
insufficient skills for, 210–11
internal focus and, 212
lacking commitment to, 211
long-range, 208–10
mechanics of, 199
meetings, 203–4
objectives and, 197, 198
offsite meetings, 204
organizing, 203–4
overview, 195–96, 212–13
participation in, 204–5
PDCA cycle, 207
poor information/assumptions
   in, 211
requirements, 200–202
reviewing plan, 206–7
scenario plans, 208
short-term focus and, 211
simplicity of, 197–99
SMARTER acronym, 202–3
for specific problems, 207–10
SWOT analysis for, 204
tactics and, 196, 197, 198, 199
terms defined, 196–97, 198
validating plan, 206
validation problems, 212
Success
   creating environment for, 23, 24
   leadership for, 168
   mutual support for, 170–72
Superiors. *See* Higher managers
Supply chain, 30–31
SWOT analysis, 66–68, 204

T

Tactics
   defined, 196, 197, 198

flexibility of, 199
quantity of, 199
See also Structured (strategic)
   planning
Task orientation, 143
Team. *See* Staff
Team building, 227–50
   attitude, 230–31, 249–50
   best practices sharing and,
      244–45
   building blocks, 231–34
   common needs, 238
   communication and, 234–35,
      239
   confidence and, 232, 233–34,
      236
   developing relationships and,
      239–41, 247–49
   diversity and, 238–39
   by example, 230–31, 249–50
   facilitating, 246–47
   fairness and, 237–38
   fun, cooperation and, 241–42
   involving members and, 245–46
   jargon for, 236
   leadership, 246–47
   MBWA and, 234–35
   mutual goals and, 242–43
   optimism and, 232–33, 234,
      235–36
   with other managers, 231, 244
   overview, 227–29, 250
   performance and, 241–43
   reality of, 229–31
   respect and, 243–44
   sports vs. business, 227
   synergy of, 228
   tribal identity and, 237–38
   value of, 227–29
   vocabulary, 235–36
   workplace environment and,
      237–38

Teamwork
   as management basis, 9
   performance and, 241–43
Technical skills, 10, 12
Technology impact, 33
Termination, 154–62
   carrying out, 158–61
   checklist, 159
   day, 160–61
   employee history and, 157
   employment at will and, 155
   healing team after, 162
   legality of, 151, 155–56
   meeting, 159, 160–61
   problem clarification and, 157
   reasons for, 154–55
   steps, 154–58
   unbiased approach to, 156–57
   in writing, 159
Thinking outside the box, 22, 24
Time management, 123–24
Top-level management, 18–19, 51
Tracking mechanisms, 191
Training
   defined, 106
   formal, 117
   growth, development and, 105–6
   successors, 23, 24
   value of, 46
   See also Coaching;
      Development; Team building
Traits. *See* Skills/traits required
Trends, 5–8
Trust, 23, 111, 229
Truth, 111, 233–34

V, W

Value
   adding, 22, 24, 25
   statements, 34–35
Voice mail, 60
Warnings. *See* Disciplinary action

Knock 'em Dead Business Presentations

Martin Yate & Peter Sander

For more than a decade, *Knock 'em Dead* has been the first, middle, and last word for job seekers on navigating a competitive, and often cutthroat, job market. However, *Knock 'em Dead* knows it's not just about getting the job—it's about managing a career. The ability to present authoritatively is critical—and often required—to succeed in the career arena. In today's business environment, a "presentation" is not limited to a speech at the annual meeting—trade shows, product launches, media inquiries, phone calls, interviews, and even performance appraisals are all considered business presentations.

Trade paperback, $12.95
ISBN: 1-58062-760-9
272 pages, 8" x 9 ¼"

Knock 'em Dead Business Presentations includes information on:

- Researching your presentation
- Finding the "magic bullets" that will capture your audience's attention
- Effectively using visual aids to make a point
- Crucial preparation points that shouldn't be ignored
- Audience involvement techniques
- Combatting speech anxiety
- Making the most of nontraditional speaking venues
- Using presentations to build professional recognition

Knock 'em Dead Business Presentations gives you the tools you need to make a dynamic impression.